CO-OPERATION, LEARNING AND CO-OPERATIVE VALUES

The rapidity of change in education has intensified in recent years. With the emergence of 'co-operative schools' and a new framework focusing heavily on co-operation, a direct challenge to ways of thinking about education at both school and university level has developed.

Co-operation, Learning and Co-operative Values addresses the urgent need to describe, analyse and assess the growth of co-operative education. The relationship between co-operation and education is a complex process and this book critically reflects on the tensions and obstacles facing this movement. It brings together the contributions of academics and practitioners from a range of backgrounds and explores topics including:

- theories and histories of co-operative values and principles
- critical views of the practice of co-operative education
- case studies of processes in action from both schools and higher education
- co-operative education in a wider context.

This book provides an essential introduction to a new and expanding area of research with chapters by many leading commentators in education. It will be of interest to researchers and educators interested in education and social policy.

Tom Woodin is Senior Lecturer in Education at the Institute of Education, University of London.

CO-OPERATION, LEARNING AND CO-OPERATIVE VALUES

Contemporary issues in education

Edited by Tom Woodin

LONDON AND NEW YORK

First published 2015
by Routledge
2 Park Square, Milton Park, Abingdon, Oxon OX14 4RN

and by Routledge
711 Third Avenue, New York, NY 10017

Routledge is an imprint of the Taylor & Francis Group, an informa business

© 2015 Tom Woodin

The right of the editor to be identified as the author of the editorial material, and of the authors for their individual chapters, has been asserted in accordance with sections 77 and 78 of the Copyright, Designs and Patents Act 1988.

All rights reserved. No part of this book may be reprinted or reproduced or utilised in any form or by any electronic, mechanical, or other means, now known or hereafter invented, including photocopying and recording, or in any information storage or retrieval system, without permission in writing from the publishers.

Trademark notice: Product or corporate names may be trademarks or registered trademarks, and are used only for identification and explanation without intent to infringe.

British Library Cataloguing in Publication Data
A catalogue record for this book is available from the British Library

Library of Congress Cataloging in Publication Data
A catalog record for this title has been requested

ISBN: 978-0-415-72523-1 (hbk)
ISBN: 978-0-415-72524-8 (pbk)
ISBN: 978-1-315-77801-3 (ebk)

Typeset in Bembo
by RefineCatch Limited, Bungay, Suffolk

Printed and bound in Great Britain by
TJ International Ltd, Padstow, Cornwall

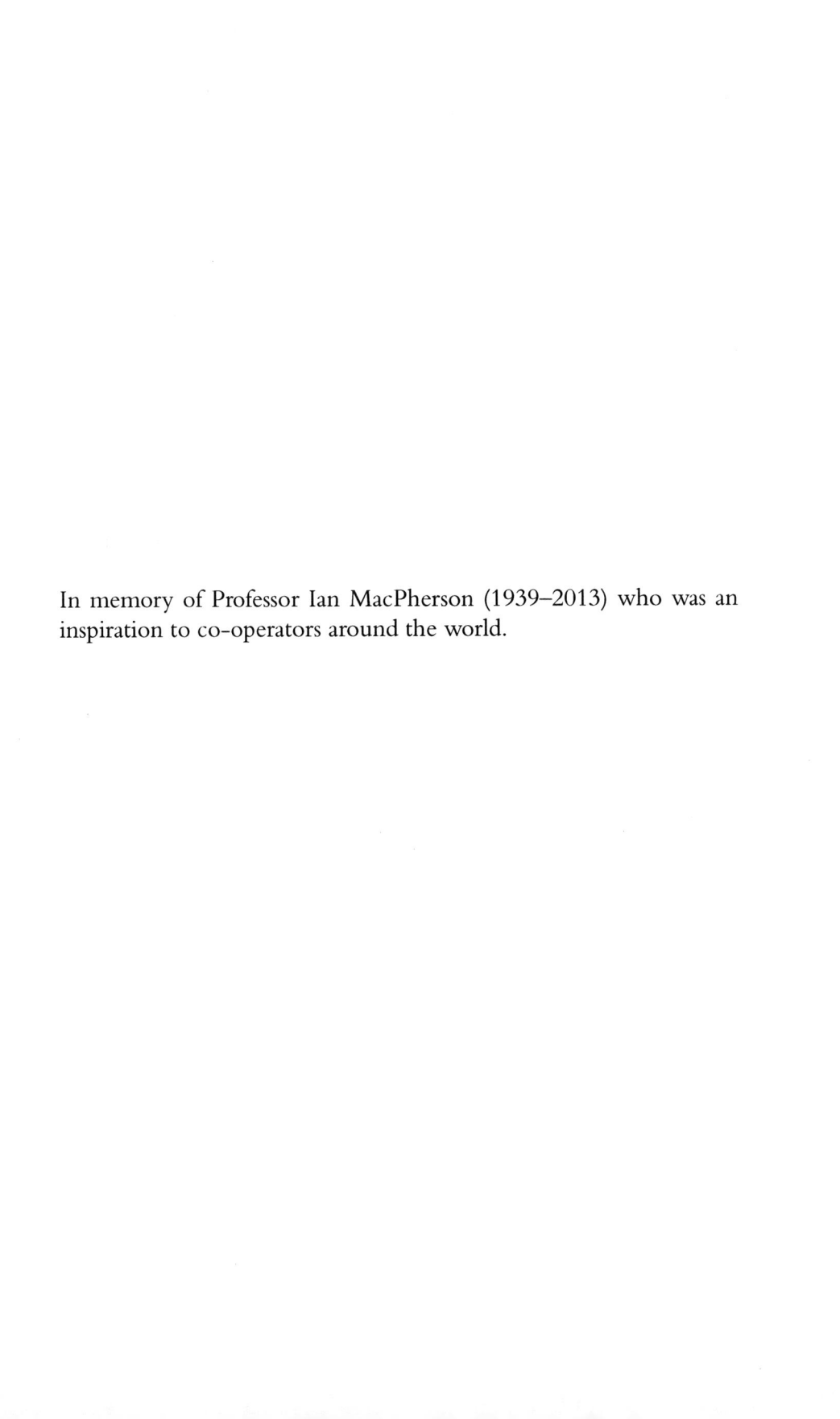

In memory of Professor Ian MacPherson (1939–2013) who was an inspiration to co-operators around the world.

Contents

Figures and tables — *ix*
Contributors — *xi*
Acknowledgements — *xv*

1 An introduction to co-operative education in the past and present — 1
  Tom Woodin

PART I
Frameworks for co-operative education — 15

2 Why co-operative schools should oppose competition and what they might do instead — 17
  Michael Fielding

3 No school can go it alone: the necessity of partnership and co-operation — 31
  Richard Pring

4 Co-operativism as an alternative: choice, assimilation and challenge — 42
  Philip A. Woods

PART II
Co-operative schools — 55

5 Co-operatives, democracy and education: a critical reflection — 57
  Gail Davidge, Keri Facer and John Schostak

viii Contents

6 Contrived collegiality? Investigating the efficacy of
co-operative teacher development 74
Sarah Jones

7 Co-operative democracy in practice – a learner's perspective 87
Ashley Simpson

8 The impact of co-operative skills and approaches on young
people's development and attainment: an ASDAN perspective 99
Dave Brockington

9 Co-operative schools: putting values into practice 112
Tom Woodin

PART III
Co-operative education in co-operatives and higher education 129

10 The co-operative university? Transforming higher education 131
Stephen Yeo

11 Policy, principles and practice: co-operative studies
in higher education 147
Diarmuid McDonnell and Elizabeth Macknight

12 A turning point? Mapping co-operative education in the UK 161
Linda Shaw

13 Mainstreaming some lacunae: developing co-operative studies
as an interdisciplinary, international field of enquiry 177
Ian MacPherson

Co-operation and competition – a commentary 195
Tim Brighouse

Conclusion 201
Tom Woodin

Appendix: Statement of co-operative identity 204
Index 206

Figures and tables

Figures

2.1	'Co-operation and emulation, not competition'	20
4.1	Strategic identities	46
4.2	Boundary orientations	47
13.1	Co-operative stewardship	189
13.2	Stages of co-operative development	190

Tables

6.1	Co-operation and collegiality	77
11.1	Conceptualizing the development of co-operative education	155

Contributors

Tim Brighouse was the chief education officer for Oxfordshire 1978-1988; professor of education and director of the Centre for Successful Schools at Keele University 1989–1993; chief education officer for Birmingham 1993-2002; visiting professor at the Institute of Education in 2002 and Commissioner for London Schools 2002-2007. His publications include, *What Makes a Good School?* (Network Education Press 1991); *How to Improve your School* (with David Woods) (Routledge 1999); *What Makes a Good School Now?* (with David Woods) (Continuum 2008); and *The A to Z of School Improvement* (Bloomsbury 2013).

Dave Brockington is a co-founder and development and strategy adviser for ASDAN, the Award Scheme Development and Accreditation Network Educational Charity. He served on the Labour government's National Advisory Group for Personal, Social and Health Education (PSHE), the Bernard Crick Citizenship Assessment Subgroup, and contributed to the Tomlinson Working Group on 14–19 Reform and the Nuffield Review of 14–19 Education and Training in England and Wales. His publications include *In and Out of School. An Account of the Bristol Raising of the School Leaving Age (RoBLA) project* (Routledge 1978) and *Tales out of School: Consumers' Views of British Education* (Routledge 1983) as co-author. He was previously the head of the Accredited Training Centre at the University of the West of England and also taught philosophy at Bristol Polytechnic.

Gail Davidge is a psychology graduate currently researching the new and emerging sector of co-operative schools at the Manchester Metropolitan University as part of her PhD research, a funded Education and Social Research Institute scholarship. She is in the process of undertaking an in-depth ethnographic study that considers the subjective impacts of co-operative practices in education on the sense of wellbeing and agency of teachers, parents and children. Her publications include *Every Different Child Matters: Understanding the Construction of Children's Stories of Difference and Normalcy in the Twenty-First Century* (MMU Psychology Dissertations 2011).

Keri Facer is Professor of Educational and Social Futures at the University of Bristol, Graduate School of Education. She works on rethinking the relationship between formal educational institutions and wider society in relation to environmental, social and technological disruption. From 2002-2008 Keri was Research Director at Futurelab developing new approaches to education. From 2007-2009 she led the Beyond Current Horizons strategic foresight programme for the Department for Children, Schools and Families. Her most recent publication is *Learning Futures: Education, Technology and Social Change* (Routledge 2011), written while Professor of Education at Manchester Metropolitan University from 2008-2012. She is now an AHRC leadership fellow for the Connected Communities Programme, researching and imagining the future of the university.

Michael Fielding taught for 19 years in some of the UK's pioneer radical comprehensive schools and for a similar period and with identical commitments at the universities of Cambridge, Sussex and the Institute of Education where he is currently Emeritus Professor of Education. Widely published in the fields of student voice, educational leadership and radical education, Michael has been a life-long member of the co-operative movement. His widely acclaimed book, co-authored with Peter Moss, *Radical Education and the Common School – a Democratic Alternative* (Routledge 2011) seeks to reclaim education as a democratic project and a community responsibility and school as a public space of encounter for all citizens.

Sarah Jones has been Vice Principal of Lipson Co-operative Academy since 2003. She works with local HEIs to deliver a Master's programme and is currently undertaking a professional doctorate in education with Plymouth University while working full time at Lipson. She has also trained with the National College for Teaching and Leadership to deliver programmes on middle and senior leadership in schools. Her interests lie in research evaluating the impact of co-operative learning in schools and the styles of leadership required to lead co-operative schools. Her work centres on leading professional development of teachers and leaders at all levels, and working within the Schools Co-operative Society to share good practice. She has a number of publications, for example, in the *Journal of Co-operative Studies*.

Diarmuid McDonnell received his BBS in Information Systems (Honours) in 2010 from Cork Institute of Technology. He was the associate in the Knowledge Transfer Partnership project between the University of Aberdeen and the Co-operative Education Trust Scotland. He now works as a consultant on a number of projects: developing student co-operatives and embedding teaching and learning about co-operatives in Scottish universities. He was co-author or editor on five publications including *Democratic Enterprise: Ethical Business for the 21st Century* (CETS 2012) and *The Co-operative Model in Practice: International Perspectives* (CETS 2012) and completed an MSc in applied social research at the University of Stirling.

Elizabeth Macknight is an Australian academic who lectures in European History at the University of Aberdeen. Prior to moving to Scotland in 2007, she taught at the University of Melbourne where she completed her PhD. Her principal research publications are in the field of modern French history. In 2005, she was commissioned to write a history of Melbourne University Credit Union, which inspired her to develop collaborative research in co-operative studies. She was the lead academic for the Knowledge Transfer Partnership between the University of Aberdeen and the Co-operative Education Trust Scotland completed in June 2012. Her publications include *Democratic Enterprise: Ethical Business for the 21st Century* (CETS 2012) and *Co-operative Entrepreneurship: Co-operate for Growth* (CETS 2012).

Ian MacPherson was director of the Co-operative Institute for Peace and Social Inclusion, professor emeritus of history and a former department chair, dean of humanities and director of the British Columbia Institute for Co-operative Studies at the University of Victoria. He wrote, edited and co-edited 20 books as well as some 150 articles. Most of his work was concerned with the Canadian and international co-operative movements and with co-operative studies as a distinct field of enquiry. An elected co-operative official for over 40 years, he received several awards from the provincial, national, and international co-operative movement. He chaired the process and wrote the documents whereby the International Co-operative Alliance developed an Identity Statement for the Twenty-First Century at its Manchester Congress, 1995.

Richard Pring was Director of the University of Oxford Department of Education, 1989-2003, and Lead Director of the Nuffield Review of 14–19 Education and Training for England and Wales 2003-2009. His most recent book is *The Life and Death of Secondary Education for All* (Routledge 2012).

John Schostak is professor of education at Manchester Metropolitan University. He has been involved in directing some 70 funded projects focusing variously on schools, health, community, policing and information technologies. He has published 11 books on education and on research methodology. His most recent book, co-authored with Jill Schostak, and published by Routledge, is *Writing Research Critically. Developing the Power to Make a Difference*, 2012.

Linda Shaw is Vice Principal at the Co-operative College in Manchester, responsible for research and international programmes. Prior to joining the College,

Linda worked at the University of Manchester, the Open University in the UK and for an NGO working on women's labour issues internationally. Her current research interests include co-operative education in the UK and internationally and the history of co-operative development in Africa. She has published widely in a number of academic books and journals which included co-editing *The Hidden Alternative* (Manchester University Press 2011) and a recent review of co-operative education in the UK.

Ashley Simpson is an associate consultant for the Co-operative College and a co-founder of Reddish Vale Co-operative Trust School, England's first co-operative trust school. He is currently studying at the University of Manchester.

Tom Woodin is a senior lecturer at the Institute of Education, University of London. He has researched co-operatives from historical and contemporary perspectives, including a historical review of *Community and Mutual Ownership* for the Joseph Rowntree Foundation (2010). He researches the history of education, culture and social class. His publications include *Secondary Education and the School Leaving Age: Coming of Age?* (Palgrave Macmillan 2013, jointly with Gary McCulloch and Steven Cowan) and is completing *Working Class Writing in the Twentieth Century* (Manchester University Press 2015). In 2012 he was the visiting professor in the history of education at the University of Sassari. He co-edits the *History of Education* journal.

Philip Woods holds a chair in educational policy, democracy and leadership at the University of Hertfordshire. His work focuses principally on questions of democracy, educational policy and governance, leadership, alternative education and entrepreneurialism. He is Vice Chair of the British Educational Leadership Management and Administration Society (BELMAS) and Fellow of the RSA, as well as an expert adviser to the European Policy Network on School Leadership and an active member of the US-based New DEEL (Democratic Ethical Educational Leadership) network. His books include *Democratic Leadership in Education* (Sage 2005) and *Transforming Education Policy: Shaping a Democratic Future* (Policy Press 2011).

Stephen Yeo is a social historian who has devoted much of his life to the study of co-operation and co-operative movements. He worked at the University of Sussex from 1966-1989 and went on to be the Principal of Ruskin College, Oxford. More recently he has worked with the LSE Centre for Civil Society, CfBT, the Co-operative College and a range of other organisations. He has written widely about British social history and its contemporary significance as well as the role of co-operation in modern society. His publications include *Religion and Voluntary Organisations in Crisis* (Croom Helm, 1976) and *New Views of Co-operation* (Routledge 1988).

Acknowledgements

Most of the papers began life at a conference jointly organised with Anthony Webster, Alyson Brown, Keri Facer, Linda Shaw, John Schostak, David Stewart, Rachael Vorberg-Rugh, John Walton and John Wilson. Some of the research was funded with a small grant from the Society for Educational Studies. There is a growing network of people developing and researching co-operative education who contributed indirectly through ideas and critical dialogue, including Mervyn Wilson and staff at the Co-operative College; participants at the Institute of Education seminars on co-operation as well as other conferences and meetings; and perhaps most of all, the schools and educational organisations which have accommodated researchers and begun to research themselves. Natasha Ellis-Knight, Philip Mudd and Jane Madeley at Routledge have all nurtured this book. Finally, special thanks go to Susan, Ella and Eva who provided support and humour throughout the editing.

1

An introduction to co-operative education in the past and present

Tom Woodin

At a time of tumultuous social and economic change, co-operation is offering a vision and a strategy for transforming education. The emergence of co-operative education represents a potential alternative to the prevailing focus upon competition, choice and a narrow definition of standards. Understanding the role of co-operation provides unique insights into contemporary educational and social change. It helps us to resist the tendency to view the current situation in education as a Manichean struggle between two opposing camps because it engages with, while also challenging, the new educational order.

As a concept, co-operative education is under active construction and encompasses a broad church of practices. Co-operative values and principles have been applied to an array of educational institutions. Most notably, 'co-operative schools' have exerted a leading influence and have driven a wedge of co-operative values into the grain of education policy. The emergence of new types of schools such as trusts, academies and free schools have brought in external partners to contribute to and give direction to schools.[1] In the process, unexpected opportunities for shaping a more democratic and community-based education system, one which responds to the needs of all, have emerged. The numbers of schools involved, and the alacrity with which some of them have adopted co-operative values, has taken many by surprise. From the first co-operative trust in 2008, by January 2014 there were over 700 co-operative schools, primarily trusts and academies, in England. Their success has made the whole notion of co-operation more attractive to a wide range of educationists and learners. Co-operative models for the organisation of further and higher education are starting to receive attention as are new forms of partnership and curriculum development which reflect the real economic and social presence of co-operatives nationally and internationally. In the past, early years education and childcare were frequently organised along co-operative lines and new co-operatives have also emerged in this area (Co-operative Childcare

2013). This is clearly an agenda which speaks to modern times and could potentially lead to a major change in the ways that education is organised over the next century.

Education and co-operation have strong affinities, as social forces and as institutional formations. In using the values and principles of the international co-operative movement, educators have fashioned new institutional formations and pedagogical processes. The Statement of Co-operative Identity (see appendix) was written at a time of renewal in the mid-1990s, a process led by Ian MacPherson, a contributor to this volume and to whom it is dedicated following his untimely death. In summary, co-operatives subscribe to the values of self-help, self-responsibility, equality, equity, democracy, solidarity as well as ethical values of honesty, openness, social responsibility and caring for others. The key principles focus upon democratic member participation and control, autonomy and independence, care for the community and co-operation among co-operatives. The other principle is, crucially, education and training, although all of them are relevant to the concerns of this volume.

Co-operative and mutual enterprises have been seen as offering a solution to a variety of contemporary problems in public services, social inclusion and economic development (compare Woodin et al 2010; Julian 2013). Co-operation has been used to describe the mode of human development in a general historical sense as well as specific forms of togetherness and social interaction (Kropotkin 1987; Axelrod 1990; Sennett 2013; Sloan Wilson 2007). Although co-operative organisation existed in Roman times, from the late eighteenth century, distinctive co-operative organisations were formed by working people to meet their common needs as part of a process of changing society. Co-operation served both as a technical business mechanism as well as a force for social transformation through democratic fellowship. Today, co-operatives can be found in many sectors including agriculture, food, environment and education. Consumer, worker, producer and educational co-operatives have proliferated. Having germinated, co-operative and mutual enterprises thrive where they embed values and principles. They tend to cluster in geographical areas – an inherently invasive practice which manifests the principle of 'co-operation among co-operatives'. It is for this reason that co-operative strongholds and clusters can be located around the world, including Mondragón in Spain, Trentino in Italy, Davis in California, USA and the network of Desjardins credit unions in French Canada (Briscoe and Ward 2005; Restakis 2010; Williams 2007; Bajo and Roelants 2011). While the largest 300 co-operatives have an economic power equivalent to the Canadian economy, it has been estimated by the UN that co-operatives have supported at least half the world's population and this fact helped to justify designating 2012 as the International Year of Co-operatives.

Despite the innovative nature of recent developments, it is possible to identify a number of antecedent ideas and practices internationally. In Spain, where the state was historically unable to provide the resources for universal education, co-operative education became particularly important in areas with strong regional identities such as Andalusia, Catalonia and the Basque Country where the Mondragón co-operative complex has also established a co-operative university (Delgado 2013; Matthews 2013). In France, modern co-operative educational networks develop co-operative research and learning, especially in primary schools, with the blessing of the state (for example, ICEM 2013; OCCE 2013). Their origins lay partly with the influential pedagogue Célestin Freinet (1896–1966), whose educational ideas and practices were saturated in co-operative values and organisation. Freinet went on to have a widespread impact across France, Italy, Germany and Brazil although he proved less popular in Britain (Freinet 1990; Beattie 2002). In addition, Poland boasts over a century of co-operative activity in schools. Within co-operative movements themselves, education has played an essential role in nurturing new skills, identities and the capacity to work together. Co-operative colleges exist in Europe, North America, Asia and Africa where they service the broader educational needs of co-operatives (Shaw 2011). A number of research centres are also in existence which have been established to develop knowledge and understanding of co-operatives, for example, the European Research Institute on Co-operative and Social Enterprise (EURICSE) based at Trento University, the Co-operatives Research Unit at the Open University, the Centre for Co-operative and Community Based Economy at the University of Victoria and the Centre for the Study of Co-operatives at the University of Saskatchewan. In universities internationally, student unions have developed co-operative structures in order to offer services and a democratic voice to their student members (Wise and Erbmann 2009).

'Co-operative learning' is a further area championed by the International Association for the Study of Co-operation in Education (IASCE) that was formed in the 1970s. Emerging from the related fields of education and social psychology, co-operative learning has been presented as an effective and participatory educational approach. Researchers came together from Australia, the Netherlands, Canada, the Philippines, Mexico, England, the United States and Israel and developed ideas that were incorporated into the work of such advocates as Spencer Kagan (1994) and Robert Slavin (1995). Kagan's *Co-operative Learning* argues for the interlocking principles based upon the acronym PIES: positive interdependence, individual accountability, equal participation and simultaneous interaction. Co-operative learning is commonly seen as a specific and effective pedagogical technique but has also been used to effect wider educational and democratic change beyond the classroom walls (see Gillies and Ashman 2003, Joliffe 2007, IASCE 2013).

Another incarnation of co-operative education is the mini-co-operative enterprises that have been established in schools, referred to as Young Co-operatives (2013). These small and sometimes temporary businesses are created by and for pupils in order to introduce a participatory and democratic business model based upon services, school supplies, fairtrade, musical performances and other pursuits. Moreover, curriculum projects have attempted to redress the historical exclusion of co-operation within schools and educational institutions, a process that has been charted in a number of countries, such as Finland and the USA (Hill 2000; Kalmi 2007). Finally, co-operative education can refer to collaborative forms of work-based education common in North America and elsewhere. Today, it is possible to identify the potential confluence of multiple streams of activity which are opening up new educational possibilities within policy frameworks which both limit and enable co-operative action. Surviving amid these social forces, while transforming them through the extension of a co-operation, is a demanding but necessary agenda that reveals much about the current context of education and learning.

Co-operation and neoliberalism

Paradoxically, the expansion of co-operative education appears to be predicated upon the erosion of assumptions built into the post-war public system of education. Co-operatives have added complexity to debates on the relative roles of the public and the private. The close engagement by co-operatives with trends which, in the eyes of critics, were moving in the 'wrong' direction has led to some criticism and confusion – was this simply 'privatisation by the nice guys' as the Anti-Academies Alliance claimed (Woodin and Fielding 2013)? Rather than providing a united front in opposition to current policies, co-operative schools appear to have broken ranks in pursuing a co-operative alternative (Benn 2012: 169).

In Britain, and more particularly in England, strong continuities in education policy have been evident since the 1988 Education Reform Act. An uneasy coexistence has developed in education between themes of centralization and conservatism on the one hand, and autonomy and diversity on the other. Each step in this process has cleared the ground for successive governments and secretaries of state to step further along a common path. On a wider canvas, changes in welfare, ownership and control have reconstituted the state, reducing direct service provision in favour of a more regulatory and co-ordinating role. Local education authorities have been consistently undermined, being viewed as inefficient and unresponsive. A direct political appeal to parents has been achieved partly through the mechanism of 'choice' within a diversifying educational 'marketplace'. Greater autonomy for schools has been complemented with a tighter political control of curriculum and pedagogy which has been exerted through the national curriculum and Ofsted inspection regime. The prevalence of a neoliberal discourse has attached education to the presumed requirements of the economy, partly achieved by the introduction of 'private' partnerships and business methods. During the New Labour years, from 1997–2010, education policy took these assumptions on board and focused upon a narrow pragmatism, reducing the breadth of education to 'what works' (Chitty 2009; Ball 2013). In higher education, the speedy introduction and raising of fees now means that students are more and more viewed as consumers of educational services.

From 2010, the Coalition Government accelerated these trends which, ironically, resulted in considerable change. Michael Gove, the Secretary of State for Education, zealously extended a franchise model of 'chains' of schools, a major modification to the educational landscape. From 2012, Ofsted inspections were ratcheted up in such a way that failing schools could more easily be named and shamed and subsequently forced down a sponsored academy route. The fear, or hope, has certainly been expressed that, if enough schools can be brought together, for-profit players will enter state education (Stanfield 2012; Laird and Wilson 2012; Glatter 2012).

These educational reforms are embroiled in a number of momentous societal changes. Economic and educational inequalities have become more marked in recent years with harmful educational results (Wilkinson and Pickett 2010). A growing democratic deficit has led to lower levels of political participation and awareness across society. In certain respects, education has even contributed to this crisis, for instance, the governance arrangements for academy schools carry great risks for overexpansion and fraud. Prominent questions, in need of a broad public debate, have become urgent: 'who owns education?' and 'what is education for?' (Fielding and Moss 2011; Pring 2012).

However, we must resist the temptation to represent these changes as an unstoppable avalanche moving in a singular direction – such a belief implicitly subscribes to an end of history ideology and an over-socialised view of human activity. Every historical trend necessarily gives rise to countervailing forces and opportunities. Co-operative education represents one such development, an unintended consequence of 'opening up' education to external forces. In doing so, the co-operative movement has proven to be adept at representing itself in relation to both private and public spheres, as a private initiative contributing to the renewal of public education. For instance, rather than simply increasing the levels of 'responsibilisation' that teachers and schools face, the co-operative assertion of self-responsibility aspires to refashion education along more democratic and community based lines.

The co-operative educational trajectory through these changes has been relatively quick (Woodin 2012; Facer et al 2012). In 2002, the Co-operative Group embarked on the sponsorship of what became ten specialist business and enterprise colleges in which co-operative values and principles were applied and adapted. A simultaneous curriculum project, led by the Co-operative College with funding from the Co-operative Group, created curriculum resources and interventions in a number of subjects, including business, history, English and ICT which incorporated the ethics and experience of the co-operative movement (SCS 2013). These living examples of co-operative education helped to stimulate the idea that much more might be possible. There were calls, not least from schools themselves, to embed and sustain what had been achieved. In Stoke, Leeds and Manchester, the Co-operative Group subsequently sponsored three academies. Following on the heels of new legislation, particularly the 2006 Education and Inspections Act, co-operative models have been created for trusts and, subsequently, converter academies and free schools. The Department for Education and its predecessor bodies have ratified legal structures based upon co-operative values and principles and the direct representation of core stakeholder groups – pupils, teachers, parents, community and alumni who meet in a forum that feeds directly into the governance structure. In place of the officially favoured hierarchical chains which pay homage to profit motivated business, co-operative models, implicitly and explicitly, focus upon participation, community and values-based education.

There is no single idea of a co-operative school given that co-operative values and principles allow for flexible interpretation. The very notion of a 'co-operative school' is a hybrid which has grafted co-operative ideas onto mainstream institutions. Although such schools may not be strictly co-operatives in a legal sense, they base themselves on co-operative values and principles and use these to develop governance, pedagogy, curriculum and ethos. Co-operatives UK (2012) certainly considers these schools to be one of the fastest growing examples of co-operatives.

Practical action is stimulating new educational visions. The growing network has created the Schools Co-operative Society which acts as a lobbying body, social movement network and a provider of services. Regional associations have been established in order that schools can work together on a wider basis. The movement has developed a 'Co-operative Identity Mark' which encourages schools to strengthen their practice of co-operation. An agreement has been signed with educational trade unions (TUC 2013). The House of Commons Education Committee (2013) on School Partnerships and Education, which welcomed a greater role for co-operation, as well as Meg Munn's 10 Minute Rule Bill in Parliament, that aimed to allow schools, including nursery schools, to register under industrial and provident society legislation, both indicate the potential for positive co-operative models of education and learning (Co-operative Party 2013). Such steps contribute to building confidence in the ability of co-operation to refashion the world and ideas have spread to proposals for higher, further and early years education. Although setbacks continue to afflict co-operatives, such confidence is a key theme of a resurgent global movement which is also learning from its history.

Co-operation and history

The history of the co-operative movement, and its varied educational initiatives, provides a valuable source for understanding challenges faced today. Interconnections between education and co-operation can be traced through times of dramatic social, economic and political change. For long stretches of history, both co-operative and educational institutions supported the economic, social and cultural well-being of great numbers of people, much of which went on beneath the surface of public debates.

From the inception of the co-operative movement, sights have been set high as everyday organisation melded into dreams of social transformation (Gurney 1994; Yeo 1998, 2010). In 1844, the aspiration of the Rochdale Pioneers, widely seen as the first successful co-operative, to 're-arrange the powers of production, distribution, education and government', testified to a self-assurance that society could be remade along co-operative lines. The notion of a 'new moral world', deriving from Robert Owen and the Owenites, to replace the old immoral one, tainted with the 'dismal science' of political economy, remained rooted within the later history of co-operation. As democratically constituted bodies, co-operatives could only advance as far and as fast as their members would allow them and this depended upon education. Indeed, the rapid expansion of co-operatives in the nineteenth century took place on the back of the loyalty, support and commitment that was shown by members in supporting their societies as they moved into production, banking, insurance, agriculture and other businesses. Their very existence depended upon a learnt associational identity (Woodin 2011) as well as advanced technical and managerial training to fuel the growing demands of an expanding business (Vernon 2011).

In the twentieth century, educational work broadened into wider activities. As the paper membership of consumer co-operatives grew to around eight million by 1939, educational and social activities were developed to funnel the loyalty, interests and aspirations of members for the benefit of the individual, their co-operatives and society in general. These included classes on subjects such as industrial history, citizenship and co-operation together with children's groups like the Woodcraft Folk which pursued participative outdoor activity. Cultural provision, choirs, drama and bands were organised in addition to commercial and professional performances and even full-scale pageants. Sporting clubs and events were also popular. The various guilds organised educational work, notably the Co-operative Women's Guild that campaigned on behalf of working class women. The International Co-operator's Day provided a celebration of the worldwide movement. At the heart of societies, members attended meetings and participated in elections.

Historically, co-operative education has been shot through with the twin emphasis upon building 'co-operative character' as well as contributing to civic and educational life. Co-operators have been well-attuned to the fact that learning and education are themselves never simply individual acts of improvement and knowledge acquisition but represent the growth of collective awareness and social action. By building up libraries and reading rooms, for example, co-operatives developed educational forms which were extended across the country (Rose 2001). For a short period, a co-operative school was even established in Wallsend following the 1870 Elementary Education Act (Todd 2013). In the late nineteenth and early twentieth centuries, co-operatives became important in the development of adult education, university extension and the Workers' Educational Association which argued for a 'broad highway' in learning in order to raise the working class together. One of the leading educationists of the twentieth century, R.H. Tawney, was in the thick of these events. He openly recognised the value of the co-operative movement in pioneering new educational forms although he expected the state to develop them more fully (Tawney 1912). Externally, co-operators served on school boards, until they were abolished by the 1902 Education Act, and on a range of public bodies, for example, as councillors and magistrates (Vernon 2013).

The journey between the highpoint of co-operation in the late nineteenth and early twentieth century and the post-war period of decline, particularly acute from the 1960s, has been a tortuous and difficult path for co-operative and mutual enterprises and, as recent events testify, it may not yet be over (Walton 2009; Co-operative Group 2014a; Co-operative Group 2014b). On its own, co-operation was unable to resist the pincer movement of encroaching state provision in public services and fierce commercial competition in the business context. Co-operatives were represented as ineffective businesses based upon historically declining constituencies – a claim repeated in the wake of the precipitous losses to the Co-operative Group in 2013. Moreover, ensuring the existence of co-operative structures within dominant conceptions of common ownership in the post-1945 period, proved to be testing for co-operators as statist definitions of social progress became pervasive. Co-operatives were increasingly marginalised and this led to a loss of vision – the isolation of co-operatives went hand in hand with a gradual closing down of what co-operators thought possible in education (Woodin et al 2010).

But co-operative ideas have persisted. Mutual models for public services had been discussed in the early years of the Labour Party as well as with the expansion of a post-war welfare society. Writing in *The Observer* in 1917, Sidney Webb had noted that Clause IV of the Labour Party which called for 'common ownership of the means of production, distribution and exchange' was not a prescriptive declaration but offered substantial leeway for debate:

> ... it leaves open to choose from time to time whatever forms of common ownership from the co-operative store to the nationalised railway, and whatever forms of popular administration and control of industry, from national guilds to ministries of employment and municipal management, may, in particular cases commend themselves.
>
> *(Webb 1917)*

These ideas are currently being revisited. Co-operative ideals which continued as a marginal force for many years have begun to re-enter public debates. In the UK, from the 1990s, a decade which witnessed not only the demutualisation of building societies but also the drafting of the Statement of Co-operative Identity, co-operative practices developed a presence across civil society. In particular, co-operative education is now beginning to clear a space in which mutual ideas can actively circulate. By offering a model of working from the here and now, from within existing policy contexts, co-operative schools are building a dialogue with traditions of community and comprehensive education (Woodin and Fielding 2013) and retrieving an idea of the 'commons' (Ostrom 2010).

In the past, co-operative educators faced a number of dilemmas which remain pertinent today. Innovative educational activity and organisations were forged. By engaging with emerging developments in welfare, education and social service, co-operators aimed to ensure that public resources were appropriately distributed and employed. This ran the danger that the distinctive nature of co-operation would be lost as it was swept up into broader social changes. The subordinate position of co-operators within the labour movement did little to assuage this fear. Nonetheless, some co-operators saw the state as a higher form of co-operation and willingly supported municipal and state ownership, which had the effect of simultaneously extending and containing the impact of co-operation. In terms of education, one reaction was to sustain a co-operative educational identity and concentrate upon specifically co-operative subjects but this could result in isolation from the main educational currents. Negotiating such tensions became an inherent part of the co-operative project. Today, it is likely that co-operative education will face similar issues in enhancing autonomy and democratic control within state structures. For example, the dilemma between accentuating the uniqueness of co-operative education and blurring the boundaries with wider educational currents is widely felt. In pursuing both strategies simultaneously, the distance that educators are able to travel down the co-operative road, amid powerful neoliberal forces, remains to be seen.

Furthermore, premature expectations should be tempered by the reality that all examples of progressive change have been subject not only to external opposition but also internal contradictions and tensions. Co-operative education has struggled to build a coherent identity. In higher and further education, co-operation is more of a proposal than an actually existing practice. We must be alert to the fact that co-operative education may prove to be a short lived phenomena given the resistance of educational systems to previous attempts at reform (Tyack and Cuban 1995). The co-operative advance in primary and secondary education has created a situation in which changes in names and structures have preceded cultural shifts in pedagogy, ethos and relations within and between schools themselves. The most significant successes have often confirmed pre-existing collaborative practices. While some schools have been proactive in seeking out co-operative status as a means of educational development, others have changed very little. The long-term educational impact of co-operative values and principles is unknown. At one point, co-operators believed that foundation hospitals might be a means of constructing a co-operative health service although these claims have subsequently abated given the limited changes and structures that emerged. The direction of education policy, as well as deepening social and economic inequalities, hardly offer an auspicious starting point for co-operative and democratic education. The resulting tensions between the promise and the reality, and between the dream and the actual life of co-operative education, underpin the essays in this book. The papers contained here began life at a conference on Mainstreaming Co-operation, held in 2012 at Manchester and Rochdale, which focused on the ways in which co-operation is being adopted in multiple social contexts (Webster et al, forthcoming 2015).

Themes

The contributions to this book present a number of perspectives upon co-operation in schools and higher education. Three essays in the first section develop different frameworks in relation to co-operation and schooling. Michael Fielding robustly asserts the need to pursue co-operative action as a means of achieving truly democratic fellowship in schools. He analyses the post-war experience of Alex Bloom's St George-in-the-East school in East London as a model worthy of emulation.

Richard Pring takes a wide view of co-operation by highlighting the forms of collaboration which have emerged in the English education system over recent decades. He suggests that the democratically elected school boards of the late nineteenth century might offer a way forward today. Philip Woods then explores the conceptual understandings of an educational alternative based upon choice, assimilation and challenge. Strategic identities and orientations are delineated in considering the future for co-operative schools.

The following section scrutinises the role and significance of co-operative schools in more detail. Gail Davidge, John Schostak and Keri Facer employ concepts of equality with freedom in order to comprehend developments in capitalism and education. Within co-operative schools, they uncover quite mixed experiences and propose an agenda for future action and research. This is followed by three case studies of people working in or with co-operative schools which are indicative of a dialogue between academics and practitioners in the area. Sarah Jones, from the Lipson Co-operative Academy, reflects on her experience of co-operative continuing professional development as an experimental powerhouse of new ideas on co-operative learning within the school. She points to the contradictions and conflicts which necessarily arise in any creative process of change. From the perspective of an ex-pupil, Ashley Simpson recounts the democratic developments in England's first co-operative trust school as well as the limitations that were placed on pupil participation. Simpson's subsequent experience in working with co-operative schools and enterprises informs his observations on the theme of democracy. Following this, Dave Brockington assesses the role of the curriculum development agency, ASDAN, in developing co-operative qualifications. These initiatives have been successful in terms of pupil results and Brockington investigates the principles underlying this achievement. The section is closed with Tom Woodin's paper on co-operative values in schools, and their role in fostering membership, identities and networks. These nascent developments provide evidence of creative educational thinking and action as well as elements of confusion and re-working of existing practices.

The final section moves into wider contexts of co-operation and education, primarily in the world of higher education. Stephen Yeo opens with an essay that traverses past and present in considering the potential for the co-operative university. Co-operative values and principles enable us to rethink not only specific elements of universities but also the 'higher education system' as a whole. Diarmuid McDonnell and Elizabeth Macknight pursue a case study of incorporating co-operation into the higher education curriculum working on a knowledge transfer project with the Co-operative Education Trust Scotland (CETS). They investigate both the intellectual and practical issues in addressing the absence of co-operation in the curriculum of universities. Next, Linda Shaw reports upon her survey of co-operative education and training in the UK which covered further and higher education as well as training providers. She offers a complex picture of great diversity while describing the challenges of building sustained action. Finally, Ian MacPherson outlines a new agenda for co-operative studies based upon his encyclopaedic knowledge of the international co-operative move[...] operative studies is intimately connected to broader historical an[d...] changes and MacPherson faces up to the potential advances and dangers [in the] future. Ian was working on his chapter when he died and it has been shortened a little and lightly edited. It is appropriate that this contribution was a historically grounded but forward looking chapter. MacPherson was a huge figure on the international stage of co-operation yet remained rooted in his Canadian experience. His scholarship brings into focus many international case studies that help to generate new insights and perspectives.

In the concluding section, Tim Brighouse comments upon the contributions as a whole and argues that the forces of co-operation and competition need to be re-balanced. Finally, the conclusion contemplates a number of options and contradictions facing co-operative education. Taken together, the book evaluates a growing field of research and practice which is likely to expand in the coming period.

Note

1 Trusts remain within the local authority framework and establish charitable trusts to involve external partners and support the work of one or more schools. They can also take ownership of land and resources. Academies are publicly funded 'independent' schools with autonomy from the local authority and often with sponsors who provide a guiding vision. Some academies have formed chains of schools with an overall chief executive. Free schools are types of academy but may be newly established schools with the impetus coming from various groups such as teachers, parents, charities and businesses.

References

Axelrod, R. M. (1990) *The Evolution of Co-operation*, Harmondsworth: Penguin.
Bajo, C. S. and Roelants, B. (2011) *Capital and the Debt Trap. Learning from Co-operatives in the Global Crisis*, Basingstoke: Palgrave Macmillan.
Ball, S. J. (2013) *The Education Debate*, Bristol: Policy Press.
Beattie, N. (2002) *The Freinet Movements of France, Italy and Germany, 1920–2000: Versions of Educational Progressivism*, Lampeter: Edwin Mellen.
Benn, M. (2012) *School Wars. The Battle for Britain's Education*, London: Verso.
Briscoe, R. and Ward, M. (2005) *Helping Ourselves. Success Stories in Co-operative Business and Social Enterprise*, Cork: Oak Tree Press.
Chitty, C. (2009) *Education Policy in Britain*, Basingstoke: Palgrave Macmillan.
Co-operative Childcare (2013) http://www.thecooperativechildcare.coop/ (accessed 14 June 2013).
Co-operative Group (2014a) *Report of the Independent Governance Review* (Myners Report), Manchester: Co-operative Group.
——(2014b) *Failings in Management and Governance. Report of the Independent Review into the Events Leading to the Co-operative Bank's Capital Shortfall* (Kelly Review), Manchester: Co-operative Group.
Co-operative Party (2013) Co-operative schools bill brief, March. http://party.coop/files/2013/04/Co_operative_School_Bill_Brief.pdf?1030c5 (accessed 29 March 2013).
Co-operatives UK (2012) *The UK Co-operative Economy 2012. Alternatives to Austerity*, Manchester: Co-operatives UK.

Delgado, A. (2013) 'Co-operatives, democracy and education: the Basque ikastolas in the 1960s and 1970s', *Forum*, 55/2: 309–321.
Facer, K., Thorpe, J. and Shaw, L. (2012) 'Co-operative education and schools: an old idea for new times?' *Power and Education*, 4: 327–341.
Fielding, M. and Moss, P. (2011) *Radical Education and the Common School. A Democratic Alternative*, London: Routledge.
Freinet, C. (1990) *Co-operative Learning and Social Change. Selected Writings of Célestin Freinet*, Toronto: OISE Publishing.
Gillies, R. M. and Ashman, R. F. (eds) (2003) *Co-operative Learning: The Social and Intellectual Outcomes of Learning in Groups*, London: RoutledgeFalmer.
Glatter, R. (2012) 'Are we heading for full profit making schools?' *The Guardian* 28 March 2012, http://www.theguardian.com/commentisfree/2012/mar/28/full-profit-making-schools (accessed 25 June 2012).
Gurney, P. (1996) *Co-operative Culture and the Politics of Consumption in England 1870–1930*, Manchester: Manchester University Press.
Hill, R. (2000) 'The case of the missing organizations: co-operatives and the textbooks', *The Journal of Economic Education*, 31: 281–95.
House of Commons Education Committee (2013) *School Partnerships and Co-operation*, London: Stationery Office.
IASCE (2013) http://www.iasce.net/ (accessed 14 June 2013).
ICEM (L'Institut Coopératif de l'École Moderne) (2013) http://www.icem-pedagogie-freinet.org/presentation-association-icem (accessed 1 June 2013).
Joliffe, W. (2007) *Co-operative Learning in the Classroom. Putting it into Practice*, London: Paul Chapman.
Julian, C. (2013) *Making it Mutual. The Ownership Revolution that Britain Needs*, Lincoln: ResPublica.
Kagan, S. (1994) *Co-operative Learning*, San Clemente: Kagan.
Kalmi, P. (2007) 'The disappearance of co-operatives from economics textbooks', *Cambridge Journal of Economics*, 31: 625–47.
Kropotkin, P. (1987) *Mutual Aid. A Factor of Evolution*, London: Freedom Press.
Laird, A. and Wilson, J. (J. Groves ed.) (2012) *Social Enterprise Schools. A Profit-Sharing Model for the State-Funded School System*, London: Policy Exchange.
L'OCCE (Office Central de la Coopération à l'Ecole) (2013) http://www.occe.coop/federation/ (accessed 1 June 2013).
Matthews, D. (2013) 'Inside a co-operative university', *Times Higher Education*, 29 August, http://www.timeshighereducation.co.uk/features/inside-a-cooperative-university/2006776.fullarticle (accessed 23 September 2013).
Ostrom, E. (2010) *Governing the Commons. The Evolution of Institutions for Collective Action*, Cambridge: Cambridge University Press.
Pring, R. (2012) *The Life and Death of Secondary Education for All*, London: Routledge.
Restakis, J (2010) *Humanizing the Economy: Co-operatives in the Age of Capital*, Gabriola Island: New Society.
Rose, J. (2001) *The Intellectual Life of the British Working Classes*, Yale: Yale University Press.
SCS (Schools Co-operative Society) (2013) Curriculum materials and support. http://www.co-operativeschools.coop/message/curriculum_materials_and_support (accessed 23 September 2013).
Sennett, R. (2013) *Together. The Rituals, Pleasures and Politics of Co-operation*, London: Penguin.
Shaw, L. (2011) 'International perspectives on co-operative education', in Webster, A., Brown, A., Stewart, D., Walton, J.K. and Shaw, L., *The Hidden Alternative. Co-operative Values, Past, Present and Future*, Manchester: Manchester University Press.
Slavin, R. (1995) 2nd ed. *Co-operative Learning. Theory, Research and Practice*, Boston: Allyn and Bacon.
Sloan Wilson, D. (2007) *Evolution for Everyone. How Darwin's Theory Can Change the Way We Think About Our Lives*, New York: Bantam Dell.

Stanfield, J. B. (2012) *The Profit Motive in Education: Continuing the Revolution*, London: Institute of Economic Affairs.

Tawney, R. H. (1912) *Education and Social Progress*, Manchester: Co-operative Union.

Todd, N. (2013) 'The Wallsend Owenites', *Forum*, 55/2: 279–291.

TUC (2013) Schools Co-operative Society, Co-operative College and the Education Unions, *National Agreement and Statement of Joint Principles*, London: TUC.

Tyack, D. and Cuban, L. (1995) *Tinkering Towards Utopia. A Century of Public School Reform*, Cambridge, MA: Harvard University Press.

Vernon, K. (2011) 'Values and vocation: educating the co-operative workforce, 1918–1939', in Webster, A., Brown, A., Stewart, D., Walton, J.K. and Shaw, L. (eds), *The Hidden Alternative: Co-operative Values, Past, Present and Future*, Manchester: Manchester University Press, 37–58.

Vernon, K. (2013) 'Co-operative education and the state, c, 1895–1935', *Forum*, 55/2, 293–307.

Walton, J. (2009) 'The post-war decline of the British retail co-operative movement: nature, causes and consequences', in Black, L. and Robertson, N. (eds), *Consumerism and the Co-operative Movement in Modern British History. Taking Stock*, Manchester: Manchester University Press.

Webb, S. (1917) 'Clause IV' in Coates, K. (1995) *Clause IV Common Ownership and the Labour Party*, Nottingham: Spokesman Books.

Webster, A., Shaw, L. and Vorbergh-Rugh, R. (eds) (forthcoming 2015) *Mainstreaming Co-operation: An Alternative for the 21st Century?* Manchester: Manchester University Press.

Wilkinson, R. and Pickett, K (2010) *The Spirit Level: Why Equality is Better for Everyone*, London: Penguin.

Williams, R.C. (2007) *The Co-operative Movement. Globalization from Below*, Aldershot: Ashgate.

Wise, G. and Erbmann, R. (2009) *Co-operatives on Campus. A Mutual Approach for Student Unions*, London: Co-operative Party and NUS.

Woodin, T. (2011) 'Co-operative education in the nineteenth and early twentieth centuries: context, identity and learning' in Webster, A., Brown, A., Stewart, D., Walton, J.K. and Shaw, L. (eds), *The Hidden Alternative: Co-operative Values, Past, Present and Future*, Manchester: Manchester University Press, 78–95.

——(2012) 'Co-operative schools: building communities in the twenty first century', *Forum*, 54/2: 327–339.

Woodin, T., Crook, D. and Carpentier, V. (2010) *Community and Mutual Ownership – a Historical Review*, York: Joseph Rowntree Foundation.

Woodin, T. and Fielding, M. (2013) 'Co-operative education for a new age?' *Forum*, 55/2: 179–184.

Yeo, S. (1988) *New Views of Co-operation*, London: Routledge.

——(2010) 'Education for association: re-membering for a new moral world', in Derrick, J. et al. *Remaking Adult Learning*, London: Institute of Education, 128–146.

Young Co-operatives (2013) http://www.youngco-operatives.coop/ (accessed 14 June 2013).

PART I
Frameworks for co-operative education

2
Why co-operative schools should oppose competition and what they might do instead

Michael Fielding

We live in times when, in most countries across the world, the dominant assumption is that competition is a good thing. Not only do most of our current economic systems assume and seek to extend the development of 'healthy competition', it is presumed to be one of the most important aspects of our basic human nature and thus both desirable and, in any case, inevitable. Even where mutual models exemplified by the co-operative movement are acknowledged as important, they are essentially seen as a minority phenomenon. The norm remains competition: co-operation is only regarded as legitimate if it contributes towards competitive ends. It is, in other words, an interesting variant within a competitive, market-dominated system, but not a serious challenger to that system, still less a viable alternative to it.

The same is broadly true of education at a systemic level across the world and especially in England. Competition between schools is seen as essential in the drive to improve standards and inculcate values that support the development of innovation, creativity and entrepreneurial energy that neoliberal democracies celebrate and twenty-first century economies are said to require. Competition also has a major internal role to play in shaping how schools work as organizations; how teaching and learning are conceived, enacted and rewarded; and how individual development is described and encouraged.

The argument of this chapter is that this view of human flourishing is deeply, and destructively mistaken. It is a travesty of who we are and who we might become. Far from it being affirming and life-enhancing, a competitive, neoliberal model is a negation of much that is of worth in human society and distorting and corrosive of more generously inclined views of how we might live joyfully and creatively together. Frequently dishonest and dissembling in its discourse, it is oppressive and enervating in its presumptions and diminishing and demeaning in its view of human possibility. In sum, it is a betrayal. It should thus be both exposed and opposed with all the vigour and resolve we can muster and a quite different set of aspirations offered in its stead.

The co-operative schools movement has a particularly important part to play here. It is not only well positioned to take a leading role in the articulation of a quite different narrative, its power to convince lies largely in the daily exemplification of a quite different practical alternative to the corrosive mendacity and myopic misery of competitive performance with which we are now so depressingly familiar.

One important strand of a co-operative alternative will undoubtedly be to reconnect to some of its more radical traditions, in particular, those that reject competition within education and seek to develop a range of positive, practical alternatives that have similar powers to motivate and inspire young and old alike. This chapter is one preliminary contribution to the active re-affirmation, renewal and future development of a praxis that both refuses and refutes the demeaning and diminishing presumptions and practices of contemporary capitalism. It begins by briefly setting out the historical and philosophical case against competition in education and in its stead argues for the legitimacy and power of emulation. It then illustrates and explores the desirability and practicability of emulation rather than competition in schools through a case study of one of the most radical democratic schools England has ever seen. In renewing our commitment to the school as 'a consciously democratic community' the concluding section draws the chapter to a close by urging the new co-operative education movement to develop a form of 'democratic experimentalism' which encourages and evaluates the kind of radical practices described here and thereby helps us to imagine and create a better future now.

'Co-operation and emulation, not competition'

Evolution, history and education

The end of the nineteenth and beginning of the twentieth centuries witnessed a particularly fierce debate about the nature and importance of competition as a dynamic force for progress within the evolution of the human species and, more particularly, within advanced societies and civilizations. Against the social Darwinism of Herbert Spencer who argued for 'the survival of the fittest' (Spencer 1864: 444), writers like Peter Kropotkin (Kropotkin 1939/1902) demonstrated the pivotal importance of mutual aid in evolution and in the development of civilized society. Within economic and wider social fields writers like J.B. Clark were arguing that, 'If nothing suppresses competition, progress will continue forever' (Clark 1907: 374). In stark contrast, scholars like I.W. Howerth insisted that

> All competition is essentially selfish. That is its condemnation. No matter how much competition is "regulated" by forbidding the practice of objectionable methods the selfishness of it remains. The eternal and insuperable objection to competition from the ethical standpoint is the state of mind involved.
>
> *(Howerth 1912: 415)*

The socialist Robert Blatchford mocked, 'Imagine it! The ideal of human brotherhood to be built on a foundation of egotism and self-interest!' (Blatchford 1898: 5). Particularly pertinent to this chapter, Walter Crane, the artist, illustrator of children's books and socialist friend of William Morris, inscribed in his Garland for May Day 1895 'Co-operation and emulation, not competition,' a distinction I shall return to in a moment.

The same sorts of polarization were reflected within the field of education. Whilst the dominant norm insisted on the importance of competition within education and schooling, there were nonetheless, significant alternative voices, amongst the most prominent being the painter and social reformer, John Ruskin, who insisted that, 'Of schools in all places, and for all ages, the healthy working will depend on the total exclusion of the stimulus of competition in any form or disguise' (Jolly 1894: 131).

Debates about the nature and desirability of competition within schools has ebbed and flowed since that time, more often than not in tandem with wider social and political movements. Certainly, within the twentieth century progressive tradition of education, and within the comprehensive school movement, it has always had a significant presence, occasionally surfacing during the 1970s and 1980s, in the underlying intellectual disciplines like philosophy of education (see, for example, Dearden 1972; Fielding 1976; Kleinig 1980).

Standard philosophical accounts exemplified by Robert Dearden argued that competition was a zero-sum activity – i.e. it inevitably had winners and losers – and then went on to spell out a number of other core features such as the importance of rules governing the behaviour of those involved. The key overarching philosophical point Dearden made was that agreeing on the necessary and sufficient conditions for something to count as competition did not involve making judgements about whether or not it was a good or a bad thing. His view was that those value judgements came afterwards and were not part of an analytic account of what was actually meant by competition. Against Dearden I argued that if we look at the history of the concept of competition, the disputes that have raged over hundreds of years include very different accounts of the moral and political nature of competition which are internal to its meaning, not a partisan afterthought. Competition is, in other words, a contested concept. Whether or not it was a good or a bad thing – whether, for example it was a necessarily selfish activity – was for many writers part of what it meant, not an ethical and political judgement which could be added on afterwards.

Competition or emulation? A philosophical interrogation

What then are some of the key arguments that retain a particular relevance to the co-operative schools' movement today? There are a number of preliminary points that tend to recur in attempts to clear the ground. Two of the most important are, firstly, the place of rules governing the process that help mark out the distinction between competition and conflict. Secondly, and as a consequence of this rule-governed criterion, it is often emphasized that, not only is there no necessary incompatibility between co-operation and competition, the two are both logically and psychologically interdependent. People can and do co-operate competitively and compete co-operatively.

Certainly, there will be many, perhaps most, schools within the co-operative movement who hold to this view and see nothing wrong with competition, providing it is conditioned watchfully and appropriately by the wider set of core co-operative values. There will, however, be other schools, almost certainly a small minority, that are heirs to a more radical tradition that insists on a fundamental incompatibility between competition and the development of a way of living and learning together which transforms society into something quite different to the more ameliorative or humane forms of capitalism championed by mainstream co-operation.

One way of helping us to find our own positions and to understand the overlaps and interrelations between the two traditions is to pick up on Walter Crane's distinction between competition and emulation and see how it works out as both a principled argument and a practical proposal. In Figure 2.1 I summarize, albeit in a significantly partisan way, some of the core distinctions and then say a little by way of illustration and advocacy.

For me, one of the key objections to competition is that it is essentially exclusive. It is a zero-sum activity: there have to be winners and losers. Whilst there may be arguments for this way of conducting our affairs in certain spheres of human life, I am not convinced by them and certainly see no significant place for them within co-operative schools. The traditional paraphernalia of marks and prizes and the burgeoning multiplicity of their contemporary equivalents which now invade so many aspects of our highly materialistic, increasingly celebrity culture encourage dispositions we should deplore and orientations that undermine, rather than enhance, our understanding of the world in which we live. In contrast, emulation is inclusive: it honours and celebrates the engagement and contribution of all, not just those

Competition	Emulation
Exclusive – winners/losers (zero-sum)	Inclusive – all can take part
Deflects attention away from standards	Focus on skills/excellence is the point
Encourages cheating	No point in cheating
Taking part less important than winning	Joy of taking part (with others)
Fear often underpins resolve	Love (of others/the activity) the main driver
Socio-political model based on greed, self-interest + perpetuation of privilege/inequality	Socio-political model based on freedom, equality + democratic fellowship

FIGURE 2.1 'Co-operation and emulation, not competition'

who are judged to perform particularly well in all significant respects or who, by whatever means, ensure that others do less well than they might.

My second objection to competition confronts what is often considered to be one of its core virtues, namely, its capacity to lift performance to even higher levels of achievement. The argument that the extrinsic motivation of wanting to beat your opponents/fellow participants drives up standards is, at best, contingent and, at worst, simply false. Competition *may* lead you to attend more successfully to the intrinsic virtues, skills and capacities that lead to greater insight or accomplishment, but it may also lead you to focus on beating others, regardless of the skill or artistry of your own performance. By contrast, emulation focuses unswervingly on the distinctive qualities and virtues of the activity and the stimulus of others leading you to perform, explore or engage more successfully within your chosen field of endeavour. In the context of emulation, motivation is intrinsic to the activity itself and is enhanced by the stimulus of fellow participants as companions in the same quest. What remain centrally important are the goods that are internal to the activity itself. With competition this is too often and too easily sidelined: excellence is a secondary aspiration, at best a happy consequence of the activity or enquiry in which the main point is to win. With emulation, excellence, sought after and exemplified by your own activity and the achievements of others, is the point.

My third companion argument is not only that the link between competition and excellence is contingent. It is also that the vices closely associated with competition are given, if not a legitimacy, then certainly an energizing and seductive freedom within the psychological and interpersonal make-up of competitive activity. The most obvious one that springs to mind is cheating, a phenomenon currently wreaking havoc at all levels in the English education system. By contrast, in the context of emulation cheating makes no sense. If the point is to deepen understanding, or to, say, exercise a skill more fluently and more imaginatively then cheating has no existential or instrumental legitimacy.

If some of the more prominent vices of competition have no significant place within the context of emulation, it can legitimately be argued that there is, nonetheless, some shared ground that accommodates the virtues and satisfactions of joint endeavour. I suspect this is probably, to some extent and occasionally, true. There is, after all, in at least some circumstances, a shared sense of commonality in competitive as well as emulative activity. However, there are, nonetheless, important differences. It is these that give substance to my fourth point, which is that, in competitive situations, taking part is significantly less important than winning. In emulation, however, the stimulus of others who aspire to deeper levels of insight or who exemplify the beauty and courage of excellence is constitutive of the purposes and well as the processes of the activity itself. The sociality of human endeavour has a less instrumental feel to it. Differences are companionable and productive rather than antagonistic or destructive of others' intentions and aspirations. Within a competitive framework, taking part must always be subservient to winning; in an emulative context, taking part is a necessary and uplifting part of more satisfying and intrinsically worthwhile achievement.

My fifth point extends and develops the narrative of fellowship that threads its way through emulative forms of human engagement. It has to do with the often quite different motivational energies that animate significant aspects of competition on the one hand and emulation on the other. In competitive contexts, fear is never far away from the drives that so often direct its attention and its manner of response. Both systemically and at an individual level, fear drives competitive action and response in quite different ways to its emulative counterpart. Whilst not always destructive of valued ends and processes, too often fear brings out the worst in human beings. Take, for example, Nel Noddings' recent observations on current approaches to schooling in the USA where

> At the present time, we are plagued by cheating at every level in our schools. . . . (S)tudents cheat in classroom tests and the tests on which college admission is decided, plagiarize essays – sometimes buying them on the internet – and sometimes hire other people to take their tests. Teachers and administrators, fearing the loss of jobs and financial support for their schools, falsify test results and misrepresent final scores.
>
> *(Noddings 2012: 779)*

One could quite easily add parallel examples from a contemporary English scene in which increasingly reductionist forms of market led accountability are driven by what the late, great Marxist philosopher, Gerry Cohen, characterized as 'typically some mixture of greed and fear' (Cohen 1994: 9).

Within emulative frameworks there will, of course, be anxiety, doubt and varying degrees of soul searching. But the human context will be different. Whilst no less demanding, it is more likely to articulate its ambitions in a manner and an orientation that is affirmative rather than destructive, inclusive rather than divisive, mutual rather than atomistic, welcoming of dialogue and difference rather than arrogantly presumptive and curtailing in its belligerent preferences for the disgusting and deceitful discourse of delivery.

My sixth and final point in this short exploration of the conceptual and pragmatic interrelations between competition and emulation follows closely on the heels of my last reflections. Competition and emulation tend to emerge from and contribute to quite different socio-political models of human flourishing, one valorizing the driving forces of greed, self-interest and fear in a society characterized by significant levels of inequality and privilege; the other animating a society based on freedom equality and democratic fellowship. The contrast is, of course, too stark and articulated in ways that are overtly value-laden and partisan. I hope, nonetheless, to have made a preliminary case for the legitimacy of the competition/emulation distinction and to have indicated why a co-operative school should consider privileging the one over the other. I begin to explore how it might do that, how its daily practices might enable us to live and learn differently in ways that leave no place whatsoever for competition, through a very brief account of the work of the radical pioneering headteacher, Alex Bloom.

Rationalities of resistance

On 1 October, 1945 Alex Bloom opened St George-in-the-East, a new secondary modern school[1] in old buildings in Cable Street, Stepney, a very poor, tough, multi-racial area in the East End of London, littered with bomb craters and the devastations of war. It was to be, in his own words, 'A consciously democratic community ... without regimentation, without corporal punishment, without competition' (Bloom 1948: 121). Within three years the school hosted numerous international visitors, including Dr Gertrude Panzer, a concentration camp escapee and one of the key figures in the educational reconstruction of post-war Germany, who remarked to Sir Robert Birley – later headmaster of Eton and 1949 Reith Lecturer – 'If I could have in Berlin three schools like St George-in-the-East, Stepney, I could revolutionize the education of this city' (Birley 1978: 63). In September 1955, a month short of its tenth anniversary, Bloom died at the school. His passing was marked by an obituary in *The Times* (Anon 1955c) and a front-page article in the London *Evening News* (Anon 1955b). The mass circulation *Daily Mirror* ran a double-page spread with vivid pictures of distraught adults and children mourning his passing (Anon 1955a), an event which prompted Roy Nash, education correspondent of another national daily, the *News Chronicle*, to remark, 'It was an incredible thing to happen, absolutely unique in State education history. In my time I've reported funerals of prominent people, but I've never seen such genuine grief as on that day in the East End' (Berg 1971: 37).

'Compete or co-operate?'

Why should Alex Bloom have seen the eradication of competition as an essential part of 'a consciously democratic community'? A long-standing opponent of what he sometimes called the 'fetish' of competition (Bloom 1941:132), there are two key sources that articulate why he saw it as so destructive, not only of education broadly conceived, but of education as a key agent in the furtherance of democracy.

In perhaps his best known article entitled 'Compete or Co-operate?' (Bloom 1949) that appeared in the progressive educational journal *New Era*, Bloom locates the particularities of arguments for and against competition within the more fundamental commitment to living harmoniously and creatively within a democratic community. This communal locus of both his argument and the lived experience of the school is hugely important. Space does not allow me to pursue it in detail now (see Fielding 2014 and Fielding and Moss 2011 for further reflections): suffice to say here that my sense is that Bloom's experience as a soldier in the First World War and as a London headteacher in World War Two have a significant part to play in his insistence on the reciprocal and necessary relationship between the freedoms of exploration and self-expression and the demands and enabling contexts of a democratic community. Bloom's opposition to competition rests significantly on his view that the kind of harmony that arises from providing and developing a communal context within which the reciprocal responsibilities to oneself and others is lived out on a day-to-day basis, is undermined by competition.

Four points come through particularly strongly. Firstly, we do not need the incentives of competition as a route to knowledge and understanding. Secondly, its imposition often distorts or inhibits curiosity and attentiveness to the object of study. Thirdly, it introduces strife where none is needed. Fourthly, it also exposes the inconsistencies and hypocrisies adults so balefully exhibit in their rhetorical flourishes about attending to the needs of others.

On the first point, Bloom asks, 'What does competition, at home or in schools, extract from children that in right surroundings, they are not ready – and anxious – to give voluntarily?' (Bloom 1949: 170–171). On the second, he approvingly cites Ernest Raymond's insistence that 'the supreme bliss of creation is not won until it is disinterested creation ... and we learn to make the thing for its own sake' (Ibid: 171). Thirdly, he suggests that, 'To rouse the competitive spirit may make easier the teacher's life, but in setting a false pace to action and a specious emphasis on strife, it must make more complex the child's living' (Ibid). Lastly, on the contradictions entailed in so many of our favoured homilies Bloom observes,

> In one breath you say, 'The first one to finish a piece of work will go home early', or 'See if the girls can beat the boys', and in the next breath you talk eloquently about helping lame dogs over stiles or working together for the common good. How can children reconcile the opposing concepts of competing *against* and co-operating *with*? Do you help your brother over one stile and push him away at the next?
>
> *(Ibid)*

As he wrote in a later companion piece, 'Since means control ends, no right ends can be gained by means that are themselves suspect' (Bloom 1952: 141).

'Competition in schools'

A second important source in understanding Bloom's views on competition is his response to a lead article (Anon 1951a) and companion account of the work at St George-in-the-East that appeared in the *Times Educational Supplement* on 27 July 1951 (Anon 1951b). Interestingly, the lead article acknowledges what it calls the 'ludicrous' excesses of competition that have a distressingly familiar ring to us today:

> There has been a tendency to fall back on competition as the only incentive for doing anything well, giving a ludicrous order to school life: marks for every lesson, constant tests and examinations and revisions of class order, prizes for the cleanest hands, 'ladders' for spelling, marks for table manners, and sashes for deportment.
>
> *(Anon 1951a)*

Equally interesting is the fact that the article, 'St George-in-the-East: Modern School in Action' (Anon 1951b), to which the leader responds, only has a small passage on the rejection of competition:

> Competition is out. No individual prizes for work, conduct or sport distract the constant aim of doing a thing for its own sake, trying to beat, not other people's standards but one's own, producing one's best not to shine above the rest but with the maturer pleasure of co-operative achievement.
>
> *(Ibid)*

However, the values and standpoints that underpin that anti-competitive, pro-co-operative stance infuse the whole article and it is these core beliefs and commitments that animated Bloom's long letter of response in the subsequent week's edition of the paper.

Having acknowledged the leader's 'gracious tribute to us as a "school of quality"' he goes on to remind readers of the broader context of social and educational failure that the new tripartite system of schooling inevitably imposed on the vast majority of children who walked through the gates of the school.

> Let me assure you, first, that our purpose in removing the normal incentives to effort is not to hide from the child his weaknesses. So many children enter the secondary modern school trailing dark clouds of failure. These mists and the inhibiting effect of the fear of failure have to be dispelled. The positive compulsions of streaming, marks, prizes, competition and the negative compulsion of imposed punishment – the teacher's 'artful aids' – these cannot help to restore the child's self-esteem. By removing them we enable and encourage him to adventure, and if he fails he fails with impunity … and with a smile, but with every social inducement to improve his skills.
>
> *(Bloom 1951)*

In terms now familiar to us, Bloom ends by insisting that

> Collaboration with and competition against are mutually exclusive concepts. Competition and rivalry impede the free flow of friendly communication and stunt the growth of group consciousness and co-operation. We have therefore discarded them.
>
> *(Ibid)*

Bridging practices: realizing co-operative alternatives

In denying both the legitimacy and the practice of competition as a motivational device and as a social and interpersonal norm Bloom inevitably came up against, not only the dominant socialization and professional expectations of teachers inside and outside the school, he also had to respond creatively and positively to similar expectations and established habits of the students who attended St George's.

Much of his response, inevitably and properly, drew on the development of a highly sophisticated set of structures, practices and cultures that rested on the co-operative and communal foundations of his educational beliefs. Before sketching out some of the most prominent features of this aspect of St George's I look, briefly, at two archetypical competitive practices – sports fixtures and prize-giving – to give readers a feel for how the school made the transition from the traditional competitive norms of the time to the development of co-operative alternatives.

Competition, sport and the search for alternatives

There were at least two remarkable features of the sports fixtures at St George's. In line with the pioneering nature of the school, sports matches with other schools were arranged by one of the student committees that were such an important feature of the radical democratic approach to education that Bloom encouraged. As he explains in one of the last of his remarkable articles written two years before his premature death, 'The Sports' Committees (one for the girls and one for the boys) organize playground games, arrange outside matches and look after sports equipment' (Bloom 1953: 174).

Secondly, as the *Times Educational Supplement* article revealed, since there were 'No individual prizes for work, conduct or sport (to) distract the constant aim of doing a thing for its own sake' (Anon 1951b), this inevitably meant that St George's participation in local sporting activities with other schools had to be appropriately modified. Thus,

> Cricket fixtures are played with other schools, with the request that the results shall not be included in the area league
>
> *(Ibid)*

and, in Bloom's own words, the school

> joined the local athletic association in order to have facilities for play, but on the accepted understanding that our fixtures are not included in the league tables for the various shields. Thus, in common parlance, all our matches – and our matches alone – are called 'friendly' matches. Need more be added?
>
> *(Bloom 1951)*

As one would expect, many children found this anti-competitive/pro-co-operative counter-cultural orientation quite difficult to cope with. Indeed, as Bloom acknowledges in his first article for *New Era*, 'Conditioned as the child has been for many years of competitive experience, he finds this new concept hard to grasp at first' (Bloom 1948: 121). However, he goes on to add 'as he proceeds through the school, he is seen to accept and appreciate the school ethos' (Ibid).

Likewise with regard to sports. Interviewed by the *Times Educational Supplement*, Bloom agreed that 'This comes hard to the children at first,' but goes on to say that 'By the third year [Year 9 in current parlance] they have grasped the idea and don't worry about it.... It so happens that they have won most of their matches this term' (Anon 1951b).

From prize-giving to communal celebration

My second example of St Georges' move away from the hegemony of competition towards a lived co-operative alternative concerns Bloom's transformation of the school's annual prize-giving event. Before describing perhaps the most famous example of Bloom's radical approach, it is worth recalling two contextual factors that make his development of a co-operative alternative even more remarkable. Firstly, the considerable post-war austerity that was illustrated vividly in educational terms by *The Times* of 27 May 1947 which carried a report of the Annual Conference of the National Association of Head Teachers. Here Alex Bloom seconded a unanimously carried resolution which drew 'the Government's attention to the acute shortage of books and of educational equipment in the schools and calling for the release of paper and other materials so that the deficiency may be overcome,' the situation being so dire that 'some London schools were reduced to writing on slates' (Anon 1947). Secondly, despite these privations, the LCC (London County Council) allocated a small sum of money to each maintained school so that an annual prize-giving could be held.

Given Bloom's views on competition, it comes as no surprise to learn that the St George's version of prize-giving was a significantly different event to those that obtained in most schools. There was still an annual 'prize' at an annual prize-giving, but it was a communal prize that the school awarded to itself as a result of appropriate discussion in the School Council (i.e. School Meeting) attended by all students and staff. One of the most celebrated occasions entailed the presence of an illustrious visitor to present the 'prize'. As reported in the *East London Advertiser* of 23 July, 1954, the prize was 'A large pile of books to be used by the whole school' (Anon 1954: 14), presented by none other than the founder of Summerhill School, A.S. Neill, who 'said he didn't believe in individual prizes, rather a communal prize. "Nobody does anything important for a prize. I absolutely agree this method of dividing up the prize between a community is an excellent one"'(Ibid).

The key companion point here is not just the refusal to accede to individualistic rituals of success that so often deny the variety, complexity and idiosyncrasy of human achievement or the solidary, interpersonal texture of so much that enables us to achieve what is worthwhile. It is also that the school developed a range of democratic structures, cultures and contexts for co-operative and exploratory learning that nurtured spaces, both planned and opportunistic, within which the surprise of occasional insight and the long hard road of wisdom were named and honoured in a variety of ways and circumstances. As James Hemming, one of the school governors, later to become president of the British Humanist Association, remarked in a letter to the *Times Educational Supplement* in the debate on competition, 'What is fundamentally stimulating to the child is not competition as such but the experience of achievement in a socially recognized form' (Hemming 1951).

Thus, on the one hand, there were strong, daily, relational continuities between staff and students and between students themselves – for example, through stable form groups, whole-school thematic curriculum enquiry, and regular residential camps. These developed a richness of shared experience and a cumulative reciprocity of respect and care that enabled a depth of challenge that more fleeting or episodic encounters would neither encourage nor allow. Students' Weekly Reviews of both their own learning and their teacher's teaching would be one example. On the other hand, and interdependently, there were numerous opportunities to learn and be in ways that privileged the burgeoning interests of the child, most prominently and regularly through a negotiated curriculum that offered daily opportunity for choice and exploration, inside and outside the school and within mixed-age groups.

There were also iconic democratic practices, in particular the School Council that provided a dialogic context within which diversity of achievement was celebrated, unity of moral and educational endeavour affirmed, and the challenge of intergenerational learning pursued with humour and seriousness of purpose. Separately and together these ensured, not only a vibrancy of engagement and legitimacy of challenge, but also what contemporary pioneers such as George Lyward and David Wills[2] would have called a 'shared responsibility' to shape the future accordingly.

Creating and sustaining a 'consciously democratic community'

For counter-cultural developments, like Bloom's rejection of competition, to work in ways that are sustainable and productive, rather than ephemeral and decorative, they need to draw on the synergy of structures, practices and cultures expressive of a radical commitment to a 'consciously democratic community' towards which I have briefly gestured. Whilst these are not matters that a short chapter such as this can address, it is nonetheless important to note the magnitude of their importance (see Fielding 2005, 2008, 2014 and Fielding and Moss 2011).

Alex Bloom's grounded commitment to democracy as a way of living and learning together (including, let it be noted, not just a rejection of the then ubiquitous corporal punishment, but any form of punishment at all) are among the most radical, co-operative approaches to curriculum, to pedagogy, and to institutional self-government ever seen in publicly funded schools, not just in England, but anywhere in the world. Co-operation, or as I prefer to call its more fully developed form, democratic fellowship, informed and transformed every aspect of life and work at St George's, ensuring that all staff and students felt its realities on the pulses on a day-to-day basis, not selectively or occasionally as even the most developed contemporary examples of 'student voice' tend to suggest.

I end with an exhortation and a reaffirmation. My exhortation is that, within the new phase of co-operative education of which we are so lucky to be part, the movement creates space for those who wish to pursue more radical alternatives than mainstream co-operation generally allows. In doing so it needs to reconnect with and learn from its radical forebears. It needs to re-narrate a history that is too easily forgotten or marginalized in either the excitement of new opportunity or despair at the bullying arrogance and deft sophistication of a neo-liberal hegemony. It needs to tell its own story to itself and to others who wish, in the syndicalist phrase, to 'build a new world in the shell of the old'. It not only needs to connect to local, national and international movements that share its aspirations, the new co-operative education movement also needs to create a form of what Roberto Unger calls 'democratic experimentalism' (see Unger 2005 and Fielding and Moss 2011). Here schools and practitioners who have the bravery and opportunity to push the boundaries of their practice into new or uncertain territory can document their work, offer it up for critique and emulation, and on the basis of case study and emancipatory action research, help us create a better future together.

My re-affirmation returns, once again to the bravery, eloquence and lived example of Alex Bloom. Here he is, in pre-St George-in-the-East days, writing in the *London Head Teachers' Association Bulletin* at the height of the London blitz when democracy itself was fighting worldwide for its very survival:

> Man is by nature a gregarious animal. By nature, therefore he is a co-operative animal. 'Man is born free, and everywhere he is in chains,' says Rousseau. One of these chains is the compulsion of competition with all its dread effects of selfishness, petty loyalties and materialism. It should be our duty – as it would be a privilege – to break those fetters.... Let us take the good that is within (the child), and by co-operation and not by competition, show him how to use it for the common weal. Let that spirit of co-operation permeate and inspire all school activities.
>
> *(Bloom 1941: 132)*

Notes

1 In the English post-war selective system of secondary education, modern schools catered for about 80 per cent of the population, a putatively more academic 15 per cent going to grammar schools, and approximately 3–4 per cent going to vocational technical schools.
2 George Lyward and David Wills were well-known figures in the radical traditions of what we would now call residential special education. For a very fine introduction to both pioneers and to the field in general see Bridgeland (1971).

References

Anon (1947) 'Head teachers' request for more paper', *The Times*, 27 May: 8.
—— (1951)(a) 'Competition' [editorial leader], *Times Educational Supplement*, 27 July: 605.
—— (1951)(b) 'St George-in-the-East: modern school in action', *Times Educational Supplement*, 27 July: 605.

—— (1954) 'They all share the school prizes', *East London Advertiser*, Friday 23 July: 14, 15.
—— (1955)(a) '"Goodbye, Mr Chips" – the children of a London school say farewell to a schoolmaster they loved', *Daily Mirror*, 24 September: 11–12.
—— (1955)(b) '"Bloomey" goes – but his work lives on', *Evening News*, 21 September: 9
—— (1955)(c) 'Obituary: Mr A.A. Bloom', *Times*, 24 September: 9.
Berg, L., (1971) 'Moving towards self-government', in Adams, P., Berg, L., Berger, N., Duane, M., Neill, A.S. and Ollendorff, R. (eds), *Children's Rights: Toward the Liberation of the Child*, London: Elek, 9–53.
Birley, R. (1978) 'British policy in retrospect', in Hearnden, A. (ed.) *The British in Germany: Educational Reconstruction after 1945*, London: Hamish Hamilton, 47–63.
Blatchford, R. (1898) *Altruism: Christ's Glorious Gospel of Love Against Man's Dismal Science of Greed*, London: Clarion Newspaper Company.
Bloom, A. (1941) 'Equality of opportunity – for what?' *London Head Teachers' Association Bulletin*, 16, November: 130,132.
—— (1948) 'Notes on a school community', *New Era*, 29/6: 120–121.
—— (1949) 'Compete or co-operate?' *New Era*, 30/8: 170–172.
—— (1951) 'Competition in schools', *Times Educational Supplement*, 3 August: 621.
—— (1952) 'Learning through living', in M. Alderton Pink (ed.) *Moral Foundations of Citizenship*, London: London University Press: 135–143.
—— (1953) 'Self-government, study and choice at a secondary modern school', *New Era* 34/9: 174–177.
Bridgeland, M (1971) *Pioneer Work with Maladjusted Children: a Study of the Development of Therapeutic Education*, London: Staples Press.
Clark, J. B. (1907) *Essentials of Economic Theory*, New York: Macmillan.
Cohen, G.A. (1994) 'Back to socialist basics', *New Left Review*, 207, September/October: 3–16.
Dearden, R. (1972) 'Competition in education', *Journal of Philosophy of Education*, 4/1: 119–133.
Fielding, M. (1976) 'Against competition: in praise of a malleable analysis and the subversiveness of philosophy', *Journal of Philosophy of Education*, 10/1: 124–146.
—— (2005) 'Alex Bloom, pioneer of radical state education', *Forum* 47/2, 3: 119–134.
—— (2008) 'Radical student engagement: the pioneering work of Alex Bloom', paper presented at the European Conference on Educational Research, University of Gothenburg, Sweden.
—— (2014) '"Bringing freedom to education" – Colin Ward, Alex Bloom and the possibility of radical democratic schools', in Burke, C. and Jones, K. (eds) *Education, Childhood and Anarchism: Talking Colin Ward*, 86-98, Abingdon: Routledge.
Fielding, M. and Moss, P. (2011) *Radical Education and the Common School: a Democratic Alternative*, Abingdon: Routledge.
Hemming, J. (1951) 'Competition in schools', *Times Educational Supplement*, 10 August: 640.
Howerth, I.W. (1912) 'Competition, natural and industrial', *International Journal of Ethics*, 22, July: 399–419.
Jolly, W. (1894) *Ruskin on Education*, London: Allen.
Kleinig, J. (1982) *Philosophical Issues in Education*, London: Croom Helm.
Kropotkin, P. (1939)[1902] *Mutual Aid: A Factor of Evolution*, Harmondsworth: Penguin.
Noddings, N. (2012) 'The caring relation in teaching', *Oxford Review of Education*, 38/6 December: 771–781.
Spencer, H. (1864) *Principles of Biology – Volume 1*, London: Williams and Norgate.
Unger, R.M. (2005) 'The future of the left: James Crabtree interviews Roberto Unger', *Renewal*, 13/2, 3: 175–184.

3

No school can go it alone: the necessity of partnership and co-operation

Richard Pring

We are presently seeing the disintegration of the maintained system of education established by the 1944 Education Act, and, with its disintegration, the promotion of competition, rather than co-operation between schools and colleges, and indeed between teacher and teacher. The evidence would show, however, that, in order to achieve our educational aims, co-operation rather than competition is essential. This paper analyses the consequences of a fragmented and competitive system within an education market which promotes choice. It argues for partnership between schools, colleges, youth service, voluntary bodies and employers.

A bit of history

There is a long history of democratic control and responsibility for the provision of education in England, creating collaboration and partnership in different ways and in different degrees. This is well worth noting as we are presently shifting to a system which removes such democratic responsibility and concentrates power in the Secretary of State. Furthermore, the governance of the school is placed in the hands of trustees who do not answer to the local community. Indeed, increasingly they are answerable to large chains run by people from business, who seek to gain from the multi-million pound 'edu-businesses'.

The rapid expansion in the last few years of the co-operative schools' movement reflects a strong resistance to these developments – schools which are committed to local and community accountability, to public service rather than to private gain, and to the promotion of co-operation rather than competition within an increasingly fragmented system.

The implementation of elementary education, following the 1870 Act, required the establishment of school boards. Eventually there were as many as 2,650 boards supervising the elementary schools, the members of which were elected from the local community. The franchise was wider than that which prevailed at the time even for parliamentary elections – and it included women! Members were drawn, too, from local employers, religious groups and the profession. Partnerships, therefore, were developed within the community for ensuring some form of elementary education for all young people – in particular, the quantity and quality of teachers, and enough school places.

However, as educational aspirations expanded into higher level elementary and secondary education, so too did the need for a wider responsibility for ensuring adequate and fair distribution of resources. Following the 1902 Education Act, school boards were replaced by 350 local education authorities (LEAs), though under some protest from those who saw in this a reduction of local democratic responsibility and popular control (see Simon 1965: 222).

This wider power and responsibility of LEAs appeared to be necessary as urban populations grew apace towards the end of the nineteenth century and into the twentieth. Their powers and responsibilities were reinforced by the 1944 Education Act which established a 'maintained system' of education for all from primary through to secondary and further education. Essentially there was established a partnership between the LEAs, the central government which provided the overall legal framework but had few powers, the teachers and the voluntary bodies (mainly the churches). Such a partnership provided the framework for co-operation between schools and between schools and further education, even if the opportunities afforded by such a framework were not always taken up.

School and college co-operation: examples from the recent past

There are many illustrations of this approach to partnership which has not yet been entirely starved of energy. Several LEAs were noted for their innovative curriculum and organizational projects which brought the various providers together. Let me give six.

First, following the establishment of the Schools Council in 1964, teachers' centres were created within LEAs all over the country where teachers from different schools could work together in developing curriculum solutions to the learning challenges within their respective schools. I personally attended the Teachers' Centre in Highbury, collaborating with teachers from other schools as we engaged in addressing the problems arising from the raising of the school leaving age. Schools Council projects such as the Humanities Curriculum Project, Geography for the Young School Leaver and History 13-16 were 'promoted' through these centres, as teachers, encouraged to work together, became the curriculum thinkers, not (as in the current management-speak) the 'curriculum deliverers'. Unfortunately, those centres were gradually closed down as, through the influence of a National Curriculum and a National Assessment system linked to it, there was less scope for collaborative thinking, research and development.

Second, much influenced by the work of the Further Education Unit at the Department for Education and Science (DES) in the 1970s (see, for example, its publications *A Basis for Choice* – FEU 1979), schools needed to broaden the opportunities for many young people who were leaving school without qualifications and ill-prepared for entering the world of work, especially at a time when there was growing youth unemployment. They needed a better 'basis for choice'. There emerged a range of opportunities and qualifications (such as City and Guilds 365 and later Certificate of Pre-Vocational Education) which provided a more practical, though thoughtful, route into further education, training and skilled employment. But schools lacked the range of resources and expertise to 'go it alone'. They needed to co-operate, especially with their local further education colleges. Thus began a 'pre-vocational tradition' which became the basis of partnership.

Third, a significant example of this tradition, although arising from a different initiative (interestingly from the Manpower Services Commission, a quango within the Department of Trade and Industry, not Education), was that of the Technical and Vocational Education Initiative. TVEI challenged the academic/vocational dualism by supporting a mode of learning which was seen as part of a liberal education – the emphasis upon co-operative learning, the engagement in practical projects which demanded thinking and imagination, the acquisition of relevant skills, and the demand for theoretical understanding which underpinned practice. Clearly such engagement could be pitched at different levels of understanding, but the teamwork amongst both learners and teachers (reflecting different sorts of expertise) enabled that to happen. The evaluations of TVEI both locally and nationally were extremely encouraging (see particularly Dale et al. 1990). But such success depended on the close co-operation between schools and schools, between schools and further education, and between the education providers and local employers. Institutional divisions all but evaporated in the coming together of teams of teachers and employers, with an overall co-ordinator and a designated budget. But unfortunately this example of partnership was killed off by the inception of a National Curriculum and the increasing 'local management of schools'.

Fourth, we saw under the Labour Government, the establishment of the 14-19 Diplomas which, in combining liberal and vocational education and with employer involvement, were seen by Ed Balls, then Secretary of State for Education, as becoming the 'qualification of choice for young people' (DCSF 2007). The Diploma was organized around 'occupational areas', and employers and professional bodies were central partners in their development – the much needed co-operation between educational providers and local business. Indeed, the funding of the Diplomas depended on proof that schools, colleges and employers were co-operating in the development and implementation of the different courses in their respective localities. Such co-operation required common timetables for certain periods and shared funding, as well as considerable transport costs in some cases. There were some remarkable successes. The Kingswood Partnership in Bristol developed the Engineering Diploma which gave access to engineering courses in Russell Group universities. This was made possible by the amalgamation of resources, the creation of a large and attractive engineering laboratory shared by all participating schools, agreement between local schools, and the involvement of many local engineering businesses.

Fifth, in anticipation of these arrangements, there had already been important examples of education being broadened through the establishment of partnerships. In Stevenage, for example, the local secondary schools, the school for children with special needs, the college of further education and the nearby University of Hertford created a consortium, with a former headteacher as director, with common timetables between schools to enable pupils and teachers working across institutions, and with a common budget. Co-operation rather than competition between providers opened up opportunities which would otherwise have been denied.

Sixth, as an example of this growing co-operation between education providers and employers, the Centre for Engineering and Manufacturing Excellence (CEME) in Dagenham brought together employers, public sector partners, colleges, schools and universities as part of the London Thames Gateway Regeneration Scheme. World-class engineering facilities and expertise served over 20 schools in the locality, thereby providing routes for young people through school, apprenticeships and foundation degrees alongside the re-skilling of workers in neighbouring engineering and manufacturing businesses (including Ford). The pupils benefited from working with skilled technicians, using state-of-the-art machinery, on complex engineering problems (www.ceme.co.uk).

These are examples of how, within the local authority framework of responsibility and accountability for the provision of education, co-operation could be made possible through partnerships of different kinds. Such co-operative partnerships are necessary if appropriate education is to be provided for all young people. No one school can go it alone. Within the period of the last Government, over 100,000 post-14 school students were pursuing part of their studies within further education colleges. The colleges, not the schools, had the specialist teachers, such as engineers as well as the resources, for example, the trainee restaurants, to enable that to happen.

The importance of this should be clear. If educational provision is to begin with the needs of the learners, rather than with the needs of the providing institutions, then educational providers should share rather than compete. But we have seen a gradual decline of the powers and scope of the local authorities in the provision of education and training – the closure of teachers' centres where teachers were able to develop their curriculum ideas and share resources across schools, the incorporation and thereby independence of colleges of further education, the local management of schools whereby each school becomes increasingly independent of the wider local responsibility, and the transfer of schools from the local authority to a contractual relation with the Secretary of State under the academies and free schools programme. Within such an increasingly fragmented system the position in the league table becomes most important. The local authorities thereby become weaker still in ensuring appropriate and equitable allocation and sharing of resources (for example, in providing a quality advisory service). In Oxfordshire, in 2011, an estimated £29 million 'black hole' was created because of transfer of money from the Local Authority to fund the new academies (Bardsley 2011).

It is in this respect that we need to recognize the significance of the co-operative schools' movement – indeed, its 'resistance' to the fragmentation of the system and to the consequences of the demise of the local education authorities. Bearing in mind the tradition and examples of co-operation as outlined and illustrated above, it recognizes the essential need for the collaboration between schools and other educational providers in providing an advisory service which respects the values of co-operation which schools aspire to, in promoting the continuing professional development of teachers and the sharing of ideas and good practice through networks created, in making available scarce resources, in providing a powerful voice for educational values, in resisting the take-over of public provision by private for-profit companies, in curbing the powers of a centralizing government.

Inevitably, the effectiveness of such a co-operative movement will be enhanced the more that its membership becomes less scattered, and that is increasingly the case as more schools become members. In particular parts of the country there is a rapidly expanding co-operative school network. In Devon and Cornwall such networks are in many respects taking on the co-ordinating work previously once exercised by the local education authorities.

The betrayal of co-operation: begin with the institution and think in 'business terms'

There has been developing, therefore, a very different approach to the provision of education – one which, in creating schools independent of local authority responsibility and independent of neighbouring schools (and indeed competing with them in seeking to be attractive to future 'customers' through their position in the public league table), there is inevitably an emphasis on competition rather than on co-operation. Business metaphors and management language abound, as 'consumer choice' is seen essential to the 'driving up' of standards and the recognition of that in the league tables. There is a greater rate of exclusion of those who are not helping the image and performance of the school.

The changed language of education (one of 'management speak' wherein headteachers become 'executive heads' or 'chief executives') insists upon 'measurable targets', 'performance indicators', 'audits of performance', 'efficiency gains', 'curriculum delivery', 'consumers' and 'customers'. Inevitably, in order to 'hit the targets', schools and teachers in those schools engage in what is called 'gaming'. And that, according to Campbell's Law is inevitable for it stipulates that

> The more any quantitative social indicator is used for social decision making, the more subject it will be to corruption pressures and the more apt it will be to distort and corrupt the social processes it was intended to monitor

In effect, according to Berliner and Nichols (2007), Campbell warned us about the high stakes testing programme that is part and parcel of the United States *No Child Left Behind*, but which of course has been adopted within England. Mansell (2007) gives a detailed account of how that affects teaching, choice of subjects, learning and assessment.

But such management speak, appropriate no doubt to rival businesses in a competitive market seeking to attract customers and maximize profit, corrupts what we mean by learning and by education, and it militates against the co-operation and the sharing which are essential where the learner's interest, rather than the public image of the institution, is put first. This is graphically illustrated by Larry Cuban in his book *The Blackboard and the Bottom Line: Why Schools can't be Businesses*. Cuban shows how the world of business has shaped the aims and values, the governance and (above all) the language of education. But can schools be run like businesses? A succinct response to this is given through the following story told by Cuban: A successful businessman, dedicated to improving public schools, told an audience of teachers: 'if I ran my business the way you people operate your schools, I wouldn't be in business very long'. Cross-examined by a teacher, he declared that the success of his blueberry ice cream lay in the meticulous way in which he selected his blueberries, sending back those which did not meet the high quality he insisted upon. To this the teacher replied:

> That's right ... and we can never send back our blueberries. We take them rich, poor, gifted, exceptional, abused, frightened ... we take them all. Every one. And that ... is why it is not a business. It's a school.
>
> *(Cuban 2005: 3)*

A further element assumed from this 'business model' (together with its 'management speak') is the idea that targets will be more effectively reached and teachers more effectively motivated if payment follows results. 'Payment by results' is now a requirement, with an individual teacher's pay negotiated with the 'Executive Head' on the basis of his or her results. Furthermore, in some academy chains teachers are under gagging orders, preventing them from revealing to other members of staff the salary which they have successfully negotiated. It is thereby assumed that 'results' or 'targets hit' are the direct result of one teacher's efforts. Undermined thereby is the assumption that teaching is a team effort, a co-operative exercise. Undermined, too, is the assumption that the school itself is a 'community of learners', each benefiting from the co-operative work from members of a team. All this is a long way from the co-operation between teachers which prevailed once upon a time in the activities of teachers' centres as teachers became the curriculum thinkers and researchers.

Indeed, by contrast, one chain of academies (Edison Learning, a pioneer of US Charter Schools) has established rights over the 'intellectual property' arising from its Trust. Such a practice is not surprising as many of these academy trusts are, in fact, 'edubusinesses' in which educational provision, either directly or indirectly, is part of their business plan. As Glatter points out

> In some areas, school leaders report that schools that are part of the chain are choosing not to work with other local schools. Indeed, chains are apparently even starting to claim intellectual property rights for their teaching and learning model. It would be ironic if learning across an education system were stifled rather than stimulated by the arrival of chains.
>
> *(Glatter 2010)*

The need for partnership

Against this reshaping of educational discourse and practice, the need for partnership and co-operation has to be vigorously re-asserted. The evidence for this, if we put the interests of the learners first and not those of the institutions in their attempts to attract customers, is clear.

Finding the right pathways

Students need to know not only the range of possible career opportunities open to them, but also how such opportunities relate to their own abilities and aspirations. A well-informed, impartial and professional Information, Advice and Guidance (IAG) service is crucial, and should be available and indeed actively promoted from the earliest years of secondary schooling. GCSE decisions are made at 14 which affect what is possible to achieve at 16. Further choices are made at 16 and 17 which affect those at 18. For example, there are about 8000 possible combinations of three A Levels, and the choice of combination affects the kind of course and the university which the young person can aim at. There is a range of apprenticeships, with varying opportunities for progression into careers and into higher degrees.

A large sixth form college with 2000 16-18 year olds will be able to have an IAG staff of four full-time equivalent staff who would have the relevant knowledge, who would be in touch with regional employers and who would have detailed information about local apprenticeships. Schools acting on their own would not have this knowledge or understanding. Moreover, there is evidence that schools, with an eye on the league tables and Ofsted inspections, might not be impartial in the advice given to young people either to retain them or to advise them to move into further education (see Pring 2012: ch.13).

Teacher shortage

About 500 secondary schools have no qualified physics teacher. This denies the opportunity to many young people to have a balanced A Level course, both preventing them from proceeding to certain university courses and exacerbating the shortage of much needed scientists in the country. Shortages may well be developing in other subject areas such as mathematics and modern languages. To meet such a problem there is a need for expertise to be shared across schools. There are many examples of such co-operation under the local education authorities. For instance, in Abingdon, Oxfordshire, in the 1990s, the three comprehensive schools and the further education college created common timetables post-16, so that the strengths of one subject in a school could be opened up to students in another less fortunate school. There was an agreed 'division of labour' so that all subjects, with particular reference to the sciences and engineering, would have qualified teams of staff and viable groups. There was an overall co-ordinator and an appropriate sharing out of the financial costs. In the city of Oxford itself, there was a shared sixth-form centre to which each of the six high schools could send their sixth-formers to study A Level subjects which otherwise would not have been possible at their respective schools. The present Government policy to encourage both the establishment of free schools and the expansion of erstwhile 11-16 schools to sixth forms will not create the minimum number of post-16 students necessary for the proper range of viable courses.

Part of the co-operative approach to meet the problems outlined could include the use of shared online learning whereby students in physics, say, in one school might receive both resources and online tutoring from the appropriate teacher in another school. The possibilities of this are excellently revealed by the programmes developed by NISAI, which, based in Harrow, has developed programmes for young people who, for various reasons including disability, are confined to home. The programmes enable personal online tutoring, work in virtual laboratories, virtual social centres for the participants, and personal tutoring.

Employer involvement

Employer involvement with schools was crucial to the development of the 14-19 diplomas under the last Government. Those diplomas died an early death, but in mourning their passing we should not lose sight of the benefits which did arise from the partnerships established between colleges, schools and employers in different parts of the country. Reference has already been made to engineering at the Kingswood Partnership. But there are many examples. The Centre for Excellence in Industry Links (CEIL) at Weymouth's Budmouth College, a large comprehensive with a 6th form of about 400 students, has created a unique centre, funded and supported by local industries and businesses, within which students and employers are able to interact – leading to vacation apprenticeships, understanding of local needs and opportunities, practical experience of different sorts of work, and attendance at core meetings held at the Centre within the school.

Sir Winfried Bishcoff, former chair of Lloyds Banking Group, challenges why only 15 per cent of employers consider recruiting straight from school. He sees a lack of joined-up thinking between academic and vocational qualifications and a lack of good careers advice – all the more important, given the rise in university fees and the often poor employment opportunities at graduate level. Employers are looking for talent, attitude and experience – not necessarily degrees. He has helped create Careers Academies UK to make young people aware of this reality and give them the opportunities to succeed. Now working with 140 schools and colleges, 1400 employers provide support to students, thus increasing the number of paid internships and building bridges between work and school or college (Bischoff 2013).

Youth Service

One of the worst victims of the recent cuts to public expenditure has been the Youth Service. And yet, according to the National Youth Agency, approximately 28 per cent of all 13-19 year olds are in contact with some form of youth service, many of them from the most desperate of backgrounds in terms of family breakdown and potential abuse. Not only should they be seen, with their own distinctive approach to learning, as complementary to school and college, but also offering additional learning opportunities for those excluded from school or who have left school to join the ranks of the NEETs (not in education, employment or training). A properly joined-up, publicly accountable system of education would bring the local youth service into co-operative learning partnerships which are much needed if all young people are to benefit.

Continuing professional development

There is no curriculum development without teacher development, as Laurence Stenhouse (1975) argued so forcefully. That belief, however, can so easily be drowned by the management speak of the target-led approach to education in which teachers are seen as the 'deliverers' of the curriculum rather than as curriculum thinkers. But here surely we can learn from the past when teachers across schools and colleges were afforded opportunities to work together in thinking through curriculum problems and pedagogical approaches, in sharing resources and approaches and in identifying their own professional needs. Where learners come first, not the individual providers, the sharing of pedagogical experience and expertise should be a mark of the professional ethics, not dismissed under the guise of 'intellectual property rights'. But that sharing of ideas and the accompanying dialogue about educational aims requires the wider community of professionals made possible through partnership across schools and colleges.

Re-creation of partnership

How then, in the protracted death of local authority control over and responsibility for education, training and youth service, can such partnership be created? It would be difficult to resurrect local education authorities when so many schools have been taken away from them. They have inevitably lost the resources and the expertise which enabled many of them to ensure there was local accountability and to encourage local innovation across schools and colleges.

Perhaps it is time to go back to learn from the experience of the school boards, referred to at the beginning of this paper – representative of the local community which the schools served and of the employers and professions whose success depended partly on the quality of those schools. Of course, the modern equivalent would be better referred to as local education and training boards, since they would embrace schools, colleges, youth services, training providers and the local higher education institution. They would be the unit of administration and financial resources, albeit within a regional network of such units not unlike that of our present local authorities. Within such units there would be the Information, Advice and Guidance service supporting impartially all the schools, colleges and local employers. There would be the teachers' centres within which teachers from the different providers might work together on curriculum and teaching problems. There would be a sharing of specialist subject knowledge where that may be lacking in some of the providers. Schools would benefit from the resources and expertise within the colleges of further education in the promotion of more craft and vocational courses.

It could be done, but it requires a very different approach to educational provision from what presently prevails – and a rejection of the management-speak which 'bewitches the intelligence', and which disguises the 'patent nonsense' of current policy and practice. That different approach is being provided by the co-operative school movement, not simply because it is filling a gap resulting in many cases from the demise of local education authorities and not simply because it is providing valuable networks of like-minded schools supporting joint professional development and support. All that is terribly important. But rather, is it the case that the practical support provided by the co-operative movement and the resistance it provides to an ever more powerful central government, offers a different vision of education. That different vision sees the intrinsic relationship between the co-operative values nurtured in and between schools and the solidarity based on mutual respect and support of the society for which students are being prepared – a far cry from the competitive, test oriented, management ethos which currently prevails.

References

Bardsley, F. (2011) 'Education chiefs say academies rethink is needed', *Oxford Times*, 31 August, http://www.oxfordtimes.co.uk/news/9223402.Education_chiefs_say_academies_rethink_is_needed/ (accessed 1 September 2011).

Berliner, D. and Nichols, S. (2007) *Collateral Damage: How High Status Testing Corrupts American Schools*, Cambridge MA: Harvard University Press.

Bischoff, W. (2013) 'Building better bridges between our education and employment: need to know', *The Times*, 6 May: 36.

Cuban, L. (2005) *The Blackboard and the Bottom Line: Why Schools Can't Be Businesses*, Cambridge, MA: Harvard University Press.

Dale, R., et al. (1990) *The TVEI Story: Policy, Practice and Preparation for the Work Force*, Milton Keynes: Open University Press.
DCSF Press Release, 23rd October, 2007.
FEU (1979) *A Basis for Choice* (The Mansell Report), London: FEU.
Glatter, R. (2010) 'Changing organisational structures: will we never learn?' *Education Review*, 23/1: 21.
Mansell, W. (2007) *Education by Numbers: The Tyranny of Testing*, London: Politico.
Pring, R. (2012) *The Life and Death of Secondary Education for All*, London: Routledge.
Simon, B. (1965) *Education and the Labour Movement 1870–1920*, London: Lawrence and Wishart.
Stenhouse, L. (1975) *Introduction to Curriculum Research and Development*, London: Heinemann.

4
Co-operativism as an alternative: choice, assimilation and challenge

Philip A. Woods

The growth of co-operative schools is a promising and exciting development in the diverse school system that is unfolding in England. It challenges assumptions of individualism and the economic model of private competitive markets that underlie much of the thinking that dominates educational policy. What does it mean, however, to see co-operative schools as an alternative? What does 'alternative' mean in this context? This chapter explores the positioning of co-operativism as an alternative form of education in the English school system. It considers different kinds of 'strategic identity' as an alternative and different stances – 'orientations' – which alternatives may take towards boundaries and the external environment. Co-operativism is well placed to play a key role in helping to reshape mainstream policy discourse on education. There are, however, pressures and challenges towards assimilation as well as opportunities to be 'activist' in influencing educational policy. This chapter offers a framework of strategic identities and orientations to help in reflecting on these challenges and opportunities.

Educational policy in England

The public sector in the UK has been at the leading edge of international policy trends aimed at bringing about fundamental changes in the way public service provision is configured. These trends have sought to alter radically public sector values and structures by advancing privatization, public-private partnerships, market principles and managerialist reforms (Flinders 2011). They promote a market-orientated, performative logic of governance in which central government simultaneously reduces its responsibilities for direct provision of services, brings in new private providers and fosters a more entrepreneurial culture driven by an instrumental rationality and the auditing of progress against performance targets and financial goals (Woods 2011, 2013). Public services come to be dominated by a results-based legitimacy (Pierre and Eymeri-Douzans 2011: 204) that gives most attention to the measurable outputs.

The impact on the system of school education in England is particularly marked. New forms of state-funded 'independent' schools are increasing rapidly, the role of democratically elected local authorities is being further limited, and an array of new agents (as school sponsors and partners) are becoming more and more significant influencers and players in the school system (Simkins and Woods 2014; Woods and Roberts forthcoming). The direction of travel is towards what can be termed plural controlled schooling, i.e. a system characterized by multiple sources of control and education (Woods 2011). However, whilst this may seem a move that disperses power and influence in education, it is in fact characterized by a growth in both control and autonomy. There is in some ways an increase in autonomy for schools, but these autonomies are set in the context of a centralized framework which exerts strong influences (through national inspections, for example) on what is understood to be good and effective education, and on who is able and given opportunities to become sponsors and partners.

The advance of a market-orientated, performative logic of governance carries with it numerous problems and dangers that researchers and critics have highlighted (Woods 2011, 2013). They include concerns about the weakening of profession and educational values through the climate of fear that uncertainty, competition and punitive inspections promote, and the inequalities that persist or are exacerbated in a system that encourages behaviours more in line with individualistic business culture. The purpose of education tends to be narrowed to a focus on economistic ends aimed at creating individuals who fit the needs of business. Larger purposes of schooling, if not lost entirely, tend to be marginalized or overlayed by the dominant belief that school education is there to serve the requirements of a competitive economy. Where the aim of learning is viewed principally 'as the promotion of knowledge and skills deemed necessary for economic success' and dominated by 'the language of "targets", "audits" and "delivery"', development of the whole person and attention to the 'intrinsic worth of educational activities' tend to take second place (Pring and Pollard 2011: 15).

There are also, nevertheless, possibilities and opportunities within the current context. In the field of public governance, awareness of the limitations of managerialism and performative governance subservient to market principles is generating new ideas and practices in public services. Scholars discern signs of change that lead to suggestions that 'new public service' and 'new public governance' models are beginning to emerge. These signs include a revival of notions of the public interest, more examples of public services framed in a collectivist rather than an individualistic normative framework, and growing recognition of the need to move away from performance measurement as a regulatory mechanism towards evaluations that recognize broader values of social justice and sustainability (Osborne 2010; Pierre and Eymeri-Douzans 2011). In the field of leadership, considerable attention is being given to the notion of distributed leadership in the running of educational and other organizations, and it is possible to see democratic possibilities within this approach to leadership (Bolden 2011; Woods 2005; Woods and Woods 2013).

In addition, the kind of governance system that generates plural control and a more entrepreneurial culture, by its nature creates spaces and opportunities for creative agency (Woods 2011, 2013). If we see systems as emerging from innumerable local interactions as in complexity theory (Stacey 2012) – and hence as self-organizing systems in this sense – actors in the system have options to be creative as well as being constrained. They can use personal and social resources to forge alternatives. This may be at the micro-level within organizations (such as classrooms and teams), at the meso-level of organizations and networks of organizations, or at the macro-level of local, national and international systems.

What kind of alternative? The co-operative answer

If creative agency and alternatives are possible within the spaces and opportunities, the question then is: what kind of alternative do you want to create? What principles and values are most important in guiding action and innovation? Co-operativism developed as a response – an alternative – to competitive capitalism and to its accompanying social fragmentation. The original nineteenth century pioneers developed a model that could be used to create a practice and way of working together which challenged the idea that the only way possible was that of 'laissez-faire' and 'competitive political economy' (Yeo 2005: 8). The model promoted 'a set of trusting, equitable, fair human relations; a way of making society by means of Societies, open to all; voluntary, democratic, based on members who *belong* in the objective sense of *owning* as well as in the subjective sense of *feeling part of*' (Yeo 2005: 7, original emphases). The co-operative aim from the beginning was to create workable and sustainable institutions that are 'the germ of a new social life' (Holyoake 1907: 157, quoted in Yeo 2005: 6). Whilst co-operation as a human activity and way of working was not new, co-operativism in the nineteenth century was established as a practical model to give expression to ideals and principles different to those of the dominating individualistic capitalist model.

That drive to provide a practical, workable alternative to the conventional, individualistic business paradigm is the impetus behind co-operativism today in school education. The co-operative initiative answers explicitly the question about what kind of alternative to create, using the set of values that underpin co-operative practice (self-help, self-responsibility, democracy, equality, equity and solidarity). The impact of the Co-operative Group and the Co-operative College in establishing a distinct sector of schools within the diverse English school system is striking. This represents strategic and successful values-driven creative agency at the meso-level – using and making opportunities within the English market-orientated, performative governance system, but challenging the principles and values that tend to underpin that governance system. The Schools Co-operative Society describes its philosophy as 'to provide an alternative way of organizing and managing a school, that places it at the centre of its community and gives a voice to all the stakeholders that can make it and its students highly successful' (SCS 2013). Whilst there were connections between the co-operative movement and schools to promote co-operative enterprise and values in education prior to this, the first co-operative trust school was established in 2008 (Co-operative College 2013a). By May 2013, there were more than 400 co-operative trust schools, with more progressing towards becoming co-operative (House of Commons Education Committee, 2013).

These hundreds of co-operative schools are the outcomes of initiatives taken by many actors in education to establish alternatives within the evolving English education system and its schools. There is a power in the co-operative initiative, because it resonates with some of the deep-felt passion and values of many educators negotiating their way through plural controlled schooling. The promise of co-operative education is that it offers:

- *clarity of principles*, to guide practice in a turbulent and challenging policy context
- a *climate of trust* not fear, an alternative to individualistic business culture
- a concern with learning that has *intrinsic value*, not just narrow, economistic results-based measures
- a practical understanding of *accountable and balanced power and participation*, as against over centralized power and dominance by interests unaccountable to local communities.

It is important to note that in practice co-operative schooling may fall short of its ideals. Critical reflection, professional enquiry and research are essential in probing how well the reality lives up to the aspirations. It is also valuable to consider critically what it means to be an alternative in a system with a strong normalizing tendency towards very different values and aims, and some of the pitfalls and challenges associated with this stance, which is the main purpose of this chapter.

Alternative conceptualizations of the alternative

I want to propose, as a resource for this critical consideration, ideas and reflections in a piece on Māori education by Waitere and Court (2009) written for a book I co-edited on alternative education. The reflections on Māori education suggested three different *strategic identities* (my term) of the alternative position. I also want to propose that it is useful to draw on the different stances (*orientations*) towards boundaries and the external environment which were identified as a theme in the conclusion of that book (Woods and Woods 2009).

Strategic identities

The piece by Waitere and Court problematized the idea of alternative. In it one can see some parallels between the co-operativist model and Māori education. For the latter, 'the challenge is to create a counter-hegemonic space' and 'to live and work

alternative as ...	
choice	The alternative is in a lesser, abnormal, peripheral position in relation to the dominant, mainstream approach.
assimilation	The alternative acts in a way that the participants, whilst in a recognized different (alternative) educational culture, are in practice shaped into selves more in line with the dominant, mainstream culture.
challenge	The alternative exists in its own right, sustains comfortably and confidently its own integrity, and is not defined by its opposition to any dominant or other approaches in the mainstream of education.

FIGURE 4.1 Strategic identities (Based on Waitere and Court 2009. NB The labels used in Figure 4.1 are mine.)

within institutions and rules not of their own making' (Waitere and Court 2009: 205). Co-operative schools are being established within a policy framework not fashioned by educators who feel strongly that co-operative principles are a vital foundation for education and social life. Through their exploration, Waitere and Court outline three senses of the alternative, which I term *strategic identities* (Figure 4.1). Each of these is evident in different parts of Māori education over its history. They are not exclusive at any point in time, but can appear concurrently in different aspects of the alternative. This identification of the different ways of thinking about and being alternative arise from Waitere and Court's exploration of 'what has emerged as Māori have moved out to create their own parallel systems' and promoted 'the legitimacy and centrality of te ao Māori [a Māori world view] as mainstream education in Aotearoa New Zealand' (p.145). I use the term 'strategic identities' because they highlight different ways in which actors within and outside an alternative may see and feel towards that alternative in a basic sense that includes hidden or taken-for-granted assumptions about the alternative's standing in the wider society.

The first way of conceiving of and being alternative is as a *choice*, as an option on the margins of 'normal' education should the mainstream not appeal. This places the alternative in a lesser position in relation to the dominant, mainstream approach. The alternative as an option appears 'as abnormal ... as peripheral within the centered hegemonic mainstream education'.

The second way of conceiving of and being alternative is as a mode of *assimilation*. The alternative in this sense acts in a way that the participants in the alternative are shaped into selves more in line with the dominant, mainstream culture. Waitere and Court highlight 'waves of educational assimilative policies and practices' (p.145) in Aotearoa New Zealand in relation to Māori people. They point to the ways in which trying to establish an alternative – in some instances taking state funds to enable this – involves the alternative in grappling with demands for 'standards and accountability' (p.145) that emanate from the dominant centre. Through such interconnections and the assumptions that are integral to mainstream thinking, the process of being alternative can 'inadvertently reinscribe the very pathologies of difference that [alternative forms of education] attempt to negate' (p.145). The alternative imperceptibly takes on the centre's view of the alternative in two ways: firstly as other and different and, secondly and crucially, as a form of education that must aspire to develop certain (centrally defined) educational goals and identities in its students and staff.

The third way of conceiving of and being alternative is as an equal in the mainstream and as a *challenge* to mainstream assumptions. It exists in its own right and sustains comfortably and confidently its own integrity. It is not defined by its opposition to any dominant or other approaches in the mainstream of education. This sense of alternative, which is one of the ways Māori people have developed school education in Aotearoa New Zealand, 'rejects ongoing positionings of Māori people as physiologically, ideologically, or philosophically reluctant "tourists" in an educational system not of their own making: it accepts and promotes the legitimacy and centrality of te ao Māori as mainstream education in Aotearoa New Zealand' (p.145).

Boundary orientations

A second variable is the nature of the alternative's orientation to their boundaries and external relationships. Closely related to the strategic identities, the boundary orientations are distinguishable since they highlight different ways in which alternatives may view how they act in relation to those outside the alternative space. Three kinds of orientation were suggested by reflecting on a range of alternative modes of education in Woods and Woods (2009a). These are separation, engagement and activism (Woods and Woods 2009b: 228–229) (Figure 4.2).

	boundaries	**external relationships**
separation	strong – protective	weak
engagement	porous	mutually influential
activism	clear – marks base for external impact	means of fostering wider change

FIGURE 4.2 Boundary orientations

The first type – *separation* – involves the alternative 'maintaining a distance and its own protected environment' where 'the main emphasis is on creating and sustaining a separate educational environment' (Woods and Woods 2009b: 228). In this case, the external boundaries are strong in a protective sense.

The second orientation – *engagement* – is aimed at 'mitigating adverse consequences of separation and/or influencing the wider social and educational environment by building pragmatic relationships with, for example, mainstream education and governments' (op cit: 229). Boundaries are therefore porous as there is movement across these to facilitate engagement. In different ways, there is likely to be mutual influences. Woods and Woods (2009b: 229), reflecting on alternatives as diverse as Islamic schools in the US and Steiner schools in England, observed that 'engagement may lead to some alternatives being *accommodationist*, that is, practising an alternative education form but at the cost of retaining or even reinforcing key elements of the dominant, instrumentally driven culture' – in other words, becoming to some degree a mode of assimilation since inherent to engagement is 'the need for compromise'. It should be emphasized also that engagement can facilitate mutual understanding and learning that leads to positive changes and reflections within the alternative. Elsewhere, Woods and Woods (2002: 272) argued that in a diverse schooling system that values co-operation across different types and sectors of schooling, there are many fruitful opportunities to learn from different visions, interpretations and practices of education: 'Diverse "compartments" [schools] need not be fortresses against change and mutual understanding, but home bases for creative dialogue in an extended family'.

The third orientation – *activism* – involves one or both of two aims in relation to the external environment. One is campaigning to change 'conditions that give rise to any adverse consequences suffered by the educational alternative from its positioning on the margins' (which could be legislation that makes setting up alternative schools difficult, problems in accessing funding, etc.) (p. 229). The other is taking actions aimed at changing mainstream education and promoting wider social change in line with the alternative's philosophy. Examples include Māori education discussed above, and First Nations education in Canada which brings together 'Indigenous ways of knowing and being in the world [and] Eurocentric forms of education and schooling' (p. 229), as well as democratic forms of schooling that are aimed at creating system-wide participatory relationships that are different from the commodified relationships in the economy or designed to transform social inequalities by developing democratic learning communities (p. 229; see also Gvirtz and Minielle 2009; Haig-Brown and Hodson 2009; O'Hair et al. 2009). Boundaries are clear, to ensure that the alternative's practice, self-understanding and identity form a robust base for fostering wider social change through external relationships.

A co-operative anchor for alternative education

Co-operativism offers a specific kind of democratic anchoring for education. Hence in England, co-operativism – with its substantial social, cultural and financial capital – is a significant player challenging convergence around an instrumentally-driven business model of schooling and an impoverished, performative view of education. An important part of its ability to play this role lies in the set of clearly articulated and sustained principles towards which it sets its aspirations. There is also the immense practical experience it has from building and sustaining practice and institutional supports for the expression of these values. It therefore draws from a fund of cultural capital, as well as social capital through the networks of active co-operative members and staff in institutions such as the Co-operative College in Manchester. It is able to offer these cultural and social resources to support adaptive strategies (Woods 2011) that seek to overcome the dominance of instrumental rationalities by integrating values-driven rationalities into practice and working to give these prominence over purely performative and economistic goals.

Arguably, the mobilization of such resources is particularly important at the meso-level in the English school system – i.e. the level of the organization, inter-organizational relations and networks, beneath the state level. Here, potentially, they can provide a depth of resource and continuity to support and sustain developments at the micro-level. Resources such as shared values, networks of co-operative schools and national co-operative institutions are important in populating the local systems that are being filled with new players in education, chains of academies and diverse new partnerships (Simkins and Woods 2014; Woods and Roberts forthcoming). The business model of co-operativism, underpinned by wide-ranging practical experience, is a resource for reconfiguring entrepreneurialism as an expression of democratic and social justice ideals (Woods 2013b).

Co-operativism has a further advantage too. It can be seen as being in accord with the wider trends in the private and public sectors to open boundaries and enhance collaboration so as to promote innovation and learning. For example, the 'open innovation paradigm' is seen as important for industry since it recognizes the value of ideas crossing the internal and external boundaries of organizations (Chesbrough 2005); collaboration is understood as integral to creating innovative cultures in all kinds of organization (Gratton 2011) and to learning in schools and more generally (Cameron et al. 2011; Day et al. 2009; Frost 2008; Holden 2008; Slavin 2010). There is a tension between the collaborative values and those of the individualistic performative culture – tensions that cannot be ignored in developments towards new models of public service and governance, referred to above, if they are to move forward from individualistic performative culture. Co-operativism has the advantage of the robust anchor in principles that act as guides in turbulent and challenging times.

There are, however, challenges. Firstly, thinking back to the strategic identities, is the fate of the co-operative schools sector to be stuck as a marginalized choice? This is not its wish, as the co-operative conference title in Manchester 2012 suggested – 'Mainstreaming Co-operation: An Alternative for the 21st Century'. More critically still, might it become – at least in some parts – a mode of assimilation? The struggle of schools to be seen to perform as successful schools in the performative climate could lead to hard decisions that compromise the guiding values.

This is not to question the commitment of school leaders, teachers and others in co-operative schools, but to recognize the intense pressures on schools. These pressures could lead to a separation orientation, though equally – and perhaps more so – offer incentives to engagement, reflecting the attractions of collaboration and mutual learning across boundaries for innovation and learning. The underlying question concerns the ultimate purpose of engagement through collaborations – that is, whether collaborations are pursued only for instrumental purposes and the interests of the organization, or for deeper values.

The co-operative model as an alternative has parallels with attempts to promote distributed or shared leadership in opposition to reliance on the strong, heroic leader. Distributed leadership is often seen as being both more effective and fairer. However, it is also subject to the critique that it is simply a technique to assimilate teachers and others into the performative agenda and to work harder and more effectively in the service of narrow organizational goals (Woods and Woods 2013). As a result, distributed leadership has, to put it in simplified form, two manifestations. It can be used as an instrumental device to shape identities and motivations to suit the performative agenda and lacking genuine participation. Or in its deepened, more radical form distributed leadership can be an expression of democratic practice and social justice values. The latter, deepened form has overlaps with the co-operative principles.

This leads into a second challenge. How robust is the educational philosophy of co-operativism and the idea of the person that anchors its approach to education? In this chapter it is not possible to explore this in detail, and such discussion would need to go beyond the scope of the literature addressed in the chapter. However, I suggest that it is vital to raise it as a question and to register that here in the context of what it means to be an alternative. In particular, it is important to highlight the need to reflect on and understand the sustaining roots of values and ethical orientations. In part this relates to community. There is a body of work on the relationship between democratic values and community (e.g. Dewey 2005 [1916]), and the practical community dimension of putting values into practice, where co-operativism is strong: creating 'the germ of a new social life', as noted above. There is, however, a further dimension. The German sociologist, Hans Joas, critically discusses Dewey's pragmatism and suggests that, whilst Dewey recognized the significance of community for democracy, his work failed to address strongly and concretely enough the issue of 'where the deep affective roots of democracy could lie in individuals and societies' (Joas 2000: 122). It is necessary to address and understand, I would argue (Woods 2006), the deep, inner sensibilities of the person within themselves and in their relationships – often referred to as spiritual – that are not necessarily to do with religion and faith matters (Woods and Woods 2010). These are essential to nurture as they feed into the development and sustaining of values. Co-operative education describes itself as faith neutral but values driven (Co-operative College 2013b). Recognizing this, it is nevertheless well positioned to extend its concern with the human sensibilities that underlie values. The immense interest in well-being and spirituality in organizations (e.g. Benefiel 2005; Poole 2009) underpins this as an area for reflection and research, that would be important for further enhancing the identity of co-operative education as a challenge within the mainstream to the dominant instrumental rationality.

A third challenge is that of co-operativism's *activist* boundary orientation and its place as being part of the *mainstream*, rather than an option or a mode of assimilation. The strategic approach of co-operativism in education in England is not to effect a change by securing a policy change at the centre. This has the merit of practicality: waiting for a change of policy at the top, as opposed to a change in the party or parties in government, could mean an indefinite wait. In addition to this, policy cannot be understood simply as linear, top-down change. As Gibton (2013: 253) has observed in analysing policy, politicians rely too much on what they see as the power of legislation: 'The law creates an illusion of control, and when reality contradicts the illusion, the response is often further legislation'. Policy is about levers of change that include legislation and the deployment of financial, cultural and social resources to make things happen. Policy can also usefully be understood as text and discourse – that is, policy is constituted by the language and symbols in documents, speeches and policy discussions, by the meanings that policy actors create and advocate, and by the processes that affect who speaks and who is listened to in policy debates and discussions (Ball 1994). Policy is a continuous, unfolding process arising from many complex influences and interactions occurring at and across national, local, school and classroom levels. In other words, policymakers are leaders who are subject to the same limitations as leaders in all walks of life: policy and leadership are emergent phenomena rather than the products of commands at the apex of a simple hierarchy (Stacey 2012; Woods and Woods 2013). Those in positions of policy leadership in national government have power, but it is mediated in numerous and complex ways.

To the extent that this is true, it has implications for the nature of co-operativism's activist orientation and its challenge to the mainstream. The power of co-operativism in relation to educational policy is two-fold. It possesses levers of change through its ability to effect numerous practical initiatives on the ground, as with the establishment of co-operative schools. And it is has a capability to influence the 'text and discourse' of policy. Grounded in the former (effecting practical change), the latter is crucial in the strategic aim of being activist. Concepts that cross boundaries and connect with what is seen as convincing and well-grounded research can be powerful influences on policy discourse, as Miettinen (2013) demonstrates in his discussion of innovation. Such concepts can act as powerful 'directors of attention' (Miettinen 2013: 18, 19). Ideas of co-operation and collaboration are terms that link with influential ways of thinking such as 'open innovation' and distributed leadership that engage wide interest. Shaped by radical co-operative values, they provide frameworks for thinking and for the development of discourses which are alternative and challenging to the competitive, neoliberal agenda.

The crossing of boundaries is a key theme. There is strength in both mutual learning through an engagement orientation and fostering wider change through more activist relations. The point is to move between the two (engagement and activism) as needed, and to take and make opportunities for alliances that build stronger engagement relationships – as the Schools Co-operative Society has done with the NASUWT (2013). A challenge is to widen such alliances. A momentum that is able to challenge the dominant mainstream trends in policy and education requires a breadth of working partnerships which brings together in active co-operation the many organizations (trade unions, charities, faith organizations and others) that share basic values and organizational identities that promote democratic principles, fairness and the flourishing of the whole person. Co-operativism is well placed to play a key role in forging such a breadth of partnerships that can reshape mainstream policy discourse on education. The different forms of strategic identity and orientations to external relationships discussed in this chapter offer a framework for reflecting on the challenges and opportunities in achieving this.

References

Ball, S. J. (1994) *Education Reform: A Critical and Post-Structural Approach*, Buckingham: Open University Press.

Benefiel, M. (2005) 'The second half of the journey: spiritual leadership for organisational transformation', *Leadership Quarterly*, 16/5: 723–747.

Bolden, R. (2011) Distributed leadership in organizations: a review of theory and research, *International Journal of Management Reviews*, 13: 251–269.

Cameron, D. H., Gauthier, G., Ryerson, R. and Kokis, J. (2011) 'Teacher professional learning from the "inside out": studying the student experience as means to teacher action and new knowledge', paper for submission to peer reviewed journal, Ontario Ministry of Education, Canada.

Chesbrough, H. (2006) 'Open innovation: a new paradigm for understanding industrial innovation', in Chesbrough, H., Vanhaverbeke, W. and West, J. (eds), *Open Innovation: Researching a New Paradigm*, Oxford University Press.

Co-operative College (2013a) http://www.co-op.ac.uk/schools-and-young-people/co-operative-trusts-academies/co-operative-trust-schools-case-studies/ (accessed 19 September 2013).

—— (2013b) We expect to see a more diverse co-operative schools sector emerging, http://www.co-op.ac.uk/2010/12/mervyn-wilson-"we-expect-diverse-co-operative-schools-sector-emerging"/ (accessed 19 September 2013).

Day, C., Sammons, P., Hopkins, D., Harris A., Leithwood, K., Gu, Q., Brown, E., Ahtaridou, E., and Kington, A. (2009) *The impact of school leadership on pupil outcomes: final report* (Research Report DCSF- RR108), London: Department for Children, Schools and Families.

Dewey, J. (2005 [1916]) *Democracy and Education*, New York: Barnes & Noble.

Flinders, M. (2011) Markets, morality and democratic governance: insights from the United Kingdom, in Eymeri-Douzens, J. M. and Pierre, J. (eds) *Administrative Reforms and Democratic Governance*, Abingdon: Routledge.

Frost, D. (2008) 'Teacher leadership: values and voice', *School Leadership & Management*, 28/4: 337–352.

Gibton, D. (2013) *Law, Education, Politics, Fairness: England's Extreme Legislation for Education Reform*, London: Institute of Education Press.

Gratton, L. (2011) *The Shift: The Future of Work is Already Here*, London: HarperCollins.

Gvirtz, S. and Minvielle, L. (2009) 'Democratic schools in Latin America? Lessons learned from the experiences in Nicaragua and Brazil', in Woods, P. A. and Woods, G. J. (eds) *Alternative Education for the 21st Century: Philosophies, Approaches, Visions*, New York: Palgrave.

Haig-Brown, C. and Hodson, J. (2009) 'Starting with the land: toward indigenous thought in Canadian education', in Woods, P. A. and Woods, G. J. (eds) *Alternative Education for the 21st Century: Philosophies, Approaches, Visions*, New York: Palgrave.

Holden, G. (2008) 'Knowledge-building and networking: the Leadership for Learning case', *School Leadership & Management*, 28/4: 307–322.

Holyoake, G. J. (1907) *Self-Help by the People: the History of the Rochdale Pioneers*, London: Sonnenschein.

House of Commons Education Committee (2013) Written evidence submitted by Co-operatives UK, in School Partnerships and Cooperation, Fourth Report of Session 2013–14, London: The Stationery Office, 82–84.

Joas, H. (2000) *The Genesis of Values*, Cambridge: Polity Press.

Miettinen, R. (2013) *Innovation, Human Capabilities and Democracy*, Oxford: Oxford University Press.

NASUWT (2013) NASUWT and the Schools Co-operative Society Agreement, http://www.nasuwt.org.uk/Whatsnew/NASUWTNews/Nationalnewsitems/NASUWT_009742 (accessed 19 September 2013).

O'Hair, M. J., Williams, L. A., Wilson, S. and Applegate, P. J. (2009). The K20 model for systemic educational change and sustainability: addressing social justice in rural schools and implications for educators in all contexts, in Woods, P. A. and Woods, G. J. (eds) *Alternative Education for the 21st Century: Philosophies, Approaches, Visions*, New York: Palgrave.

Osborne, S. P. (ed.) (2010) *The New Public Governance?* London: Routledge.

Pierre, J. and Eymeri-Douzans, J-M. (2011) *Conclusion*, in Eymeri-Douzans, J-M. and Pierre, J. (eds) *Administrative Reforms and Democratic Governance*, London: Routledge.

Pring, R. and Pollard, A. (2011) *Education for all: evidence from the past, principles for the future*, Institute of Education, University of London: Teaching and Learning Research Project.

Poole, E. (2009) 'Organisational spirituality – a literature review,' *Journal of Business Ethics*, 84/4: 577–588.

SCS (Schools Co-operative Society) (2013) http://www.co-operativeschools.coop; (accessed 19 September 2013).

Simkins, T. and Woods, P. A. (2014) 'Understanding the local: themes and issues in the experience of structural reform in England', in a special issue on 'Structural reform in England: the new 'local' – emerging configurations of governance, leadership and management', *Educational Management Administration and Leadership*, 42, 3: 324–80.

Slavin, R. E. (2010) Co-operative learning: what makes group-work work? in Dumont, H. et al. (eds) *The Nature of Learning*, Paris: OECD.

Stacey, R. (2012) *Tools and Techniques of Leadership and Management: Meeting the Challenge of Complexity*, London: Routledge.

Waitere, H. and Court, M. (2009) '"Alternative" Māori education? Talking back/talking through hegemonic sites of power', in Woods, P. A. and Woods, G. J. (eds) *Alternative Education for the 21st Century: Philosophies, Approaches, Visions*, New York: Palgrave.

Woods, P. A. (2005) *Democratic Leadership in Education*, London: Sage.

—— (2006) 'A democracy of all learners: ethical rationality and the affective roots of democratic leadership,' *School Leadership and Management*, 26, 4: 321–337

—— (2011) *Transforming Education Policy: Shaping a Democratic Future*. Bristol: Policy Press.

—— (2013) 'Drivers to holistic democracy: signs and signals of emergent, democratic self-organising systems', in Weber, S. M., Göhlich, M., Schröer, A., Macha, H. and Fahrenwald, C. (eds) *Organisation und Partizipation: Beiträge der Kommission Organisationspädagogik*, Berlin: Springer VS: 343–355.

—— (2013b) 'Understanding the principalship: an international guide to principal preparation', in Slater, C. L. and Nelson, S. *Understanding the Principalship: An International Guide to Principal Preparation*, Bingley: Emerald: 223–241.

Woods, P. A. and Roberts, A. (forthcoming) 'The new executives in a landscape of change: the emerging reality of plural controlled schooling', in Nir, A. (ed.) *The School Superintendent: An International Perspective*, New York: Nova Science Publishers.

Woods, P. A. and Woods, G. J. (2002) 'Policy on school diversity: taking an existential turn in the pursuit of valued learning?' *British Journal of Educational Studies,* 50, 2: 254–278.

—— (eds) (2009a) *Alternative Education for the 21st Century: Philosophies, Approaches, Visions,* New York: Palgrave.

—— (2009b) 'Pathways to learning: deepening reflective practice to explore democracy, connectedness and spirituality', in P. A. Woods and G. J. Woods (eds) *Alternative Education for the 21st Century: Philosophies, Approaches, Visions,* New York: Palgrave.

—— (2010) 'The geography of reflective leadership: the inner life of democratic learning communities', *Philosophy of Management,* 9, 2: 81–97.

—— (2013) 'Deepening distributed leadership: a democratic perspective on power, purpose and the concept of the self', *Leadership in Education (Vodenje v vzgoji in izobraževanju),* 2: 17–40.

Yeo, S. (2005) 'A celebration of the modern personality of "co-op original"', in MacPherson, I. and Yeo, S. (eds), *Pioneers of Co-operation: 160th Anniversary Reflections on the Opening of the Toad Lane Store,* Manchester: The Co-operative College.

PART II
Co-operative schools

5

Co-operatives, democracy and education: a critical reflection

Gail Davidge, Keri Facer and John Schostak

Education involves drawing out the powers of individuals to think, imagine, feel and act. In particular it is about the development of the powers of communication, debate, decision and the power to form associations between people to create organizations for the achievement of common projects. How those powers to organize are shaped through social, cultural, economic, political and legal processes, practices and procedures are critical to the kind of society that results. In this sense, then, education directly addresses the question of what kind of society people want. Raging around this question of the 'desired society' or the 'good society', as it may be called, are battles of socio-economic ideas. On the one hand there are those approaches (capitalist, neoliberal, market dominated, see for example Hayek 1944; Friedman 1962; also, Harvey 2005; Klein 2008) that tend to see people as competing individuals motivated by a desire for freedom that despises equality and promotes the profit motive, often characterized as 'greed', as a key incentive. On the other are those approaches (Marxist, socialist, co-operative, communitarian, see for example Godwin 1793; Kropotkin 1904; Fraser 2007; Sandel 1982; Walzer 1985) that tend to see people as motivated by a desire for freedom *with* equality (Balibar 1994), in which collective and co-operative interests are formed on the basis of a need for security as well as friendship and feelings of care, empathy, sympathy, and even a love for others. In educational terms, such battles involve the question of how people's powers are to be applied and in whose interests they are to be directed (Schostak and Goodson 2012). In political terms, those interests, following the fall of the Soviet Union and the claim by some (Fukuyama 1992) of the 'end of history', seemed to have settled on the side of liberal market democracies dominated by business elites. However, it was short lived. The friend-enemy political logics (Strauss 1988; Schmitt 1996; Norton 2004) were resurrected as the 'clash of civilizations' (Huntington 1996), the evil axis and the 'war on terror' (see for example: Reese and Lewis 2009). Although the financial crash of 2007-8 appeared to some to herald the end of capitalism (Meltdown 2011), crisis can be viewed as the modus operandi of capitalism (Klein 2008). It can be argued that capitalism has merely accommodated to the changed conditions and, through the deployment of austerity measures, in particular by European governments, has strengthened its position (see for example, Kaletsky 2010). Writing before the crash, Immanuel Wallerstein (2003) and Giovanni Arrighi (2007) argued that a new form of capitalism might arise more influenced by the emergent powers of China, India and Latin America, one less open to democracy. According to that view, there is an urgent demand, in the light of crisis and the uncertainty of the resulting new world order, to rethink the practices and the key organizations and institutions vital for the defence, maintenance and development of democracy.

Education is crucial in this context. The role of mass schooling in reproducing the inequalities of a given social order has long been a subject of sociological and historical critique. It has also been the focus for those who have sought to 'emancipate', 'democratize' and fight discrimination in order to bring about social justice and a more equal society (see for example, Dewey 1938; Freire 1970; Moss and Fielding 2011). Such approaches to 'progressive education' were the focus of a right wing media campaign in the 1970s and 1980s that sought to counter child-centred, anti-discriminatory and democratic developments in schools (Schostak 1986, 1993) with a policy increasingly focused upon 'basics' reinforced through a core curriculum, the achievement of specified objectives, 'league tables' and inspection. The recent financial crisis has provided further impetus for an onslaught against public sector institutions generally and education and welfare in particular that had direct links back to Margaret Thatcher's election in May 1979. The cabinet documents for September 1982 released in 2012 revealed the extent of her vision of dismantling the welfare state. This included:

> compulsory charges for schooling and a massive scaling back of other public services. 'This would of course mean the end of the National Health Service,' declared a confidential cabinet memorandum by the Central Policy Review Staff in September 1982, released by the National Archives on Friday under the 30-year rule.
>
> *(Travis 2012)*

The government of the time took fright and the full vision was not implemented. Nevertheless, New Labour under Tony Blair from May 1997, then under Brown from June 2007, extended the programme through its modernization and marketization of public services. From 2010, David Cameron and Nick Clegg's alliance of the right wing Conservative Party and the Liberal Democrats reinforced the continuing shifts from public provision to private ownership, this time under the cloak of austerity.

Moreover, the move from public ownership to private ownership has been the price for European countries such as Ireland, Spain, Portugal and Greece that have been the victims of speculative financial practices, to be 'bailed out' (see for example Elliott 2011). In the US, the Occupy Movement began as a protest against Wall Street but spread around many countries of the world. It had drawn upon the symbolism of the Arab Spring of 2011 and the occupation of Tahrir Square as a demand for increased political freedoms. There was even talk of a 'shareholder spring' (Burgess and McCrum 2012). While this may not be a 'real' awakening but 'just a different class of self-interest' as Hyde (2012) points out, it nevertheless points to an alternative kind of revolution. However, the initial optimism and energy set in train by the election of Barack Obama as the first black US president, the Arab Spring, and the various recent protest 'movements' such as Occupy, the *Indignados* and UK Uncut, has been undermined by the policies of Obama himself (Roberts and Schostak 2012; Schostak and Schostak 2013), the austerity measures of Europe (Miller and Skidelsky 2013), the tragedies of Syria (Roberts and Borger 2013) and the reassertion of military authority in Egypt (Beach 2013). Protest and courageous self-sacrifice in the pursuit of democratic change is not enough. What comes after the protest, the riot, the revolution? What contemporary events demonstrate is that antidemocratic forces are powerfully entrenched at every level and are able to reassert their power through the organization of state and commerce that they control if there is nothing of solidity constructed by people that resists them. What does such solidity consist of? In a politics grounded in Spinoza (Balibar 1998; Negri 1991), the key freedom of individuals is located in their power to associate with one another to engage in mutual projects, to organize the ways in which they choose to work with each other and to engage in community with each other. That freedom, if it is to be valid for *all* people, means that no one person or group or form of organization can be privileged over another. In this sense, freedom depends on an equality of voice in decision making. This relation between freedom and equality has been called by Balibar (1994), *égaliberté* (equaliberty), a coinage to emphasize the inextricable relation between them. These principles are fundamental for democratic practice and for the formation of solidarity between people through the development of democratic organization and the aggregation of their powers to act (Laclau 2005).

We argue therefore that demands for democracy will only take off if there is a ground formed of two logics: the logic of freedom with equality (*égaliberté*); and a democratic logic of association. We will develop this argument in relation to the increasing interest being shown in the co-operative movement, particularly by schools, that is part of this process of mutual organization where people ultimately occupy and re-occupy the key economic, social and cultural sectors of their lives. This is essentially a process of creating countervailing organizations that can effectively replace the neoliberal market machines through which the few gain dominance over the many. It is, as such, an alternative paradigm for the conduct of politics in everyday life. Education, we argue, plays a vital role in the creation of the conditions for this to happen. But first, a little background.

Background to the co-operative schools' movement

Essentially, one educational outcome of the shared experience of collective ownership is 'a learnt associational identity' (Woodin 2011). It is by creating and maintaining associations with others that the powers of individuals are enhanced beyond their individual capacities for the attainment of particular goals, projects and experiences. The forms of organization through which associations are maintained and directed towards particular goals is in turn critical for the kind of society that is collectively produced.

It is important to recall that the social reformer and utopian socialist Robert Owen, a man considered 'ahead of his time' (Cole 1930), expressed *A New View of Society* (1816) more than half a decade before the first whispers of universal state education were articulated. Owen played out his own more benevolent brand of industrialism in the form of his experimental village in New Lanark, Scotland, that sought to 'replace the profit motive with the fruits of co operation, and the vices of individualism with mutuality' (Thompson in Friberg 2011: 118). Owen's thesis placed education as the primary vehicle for ensuring collective well-being and equality among his workers at the New Lanark Mill, adults and children alike. His vision sought to promote widespread social change through co-operative communities that supported the development of 'character' and secured the equitable status of its members. For Owen: 'To train and educate the rising generation will at all times be the first object of society, to which every other will be subordinate' (Owen 1830). As a pioneer of modern socialism, thereafter, Owen's commitment to mutuality inspired a variety of social, economic and educational endeavours that have responded to the competing rights and responsibilities of the individual and the community through 'co operation' (MacPherson 2011). During the nineteenth and twentieth centuries, as the 'father of the co-operative movement', Owen's dedication to educational provision remained an important tenet of the movement's fundamental values and was central to its significant international growth.

The co-operative movement enjoyed sustained growth over the first century of its existence, and in very practical terms it promoted:

- Libraries and reading rooms funded by subscriptions
- Periodicals, publications and films
- Lecture tours and adult education
- Schools
  - (1892, 107 surveyed societies (1420 societies in country) had 164 co-operators on school boards; as the Balfour Act closes school boards, the co-op focus becomes a supplementary support)
- Training and certification
- Co-operative colleges internationally

Such initiatives impacted critically upon the everyday lives of people to such an extent that it formed the basis for international developments. The co-op movement, at the start of the twenty-first century, is fully global with over one billion members worldwide. Shortly after the world's population touched seven billion, the United Nations declared that 2012 would be dedicated to raising public awareness of the movement's contribution to social and economic security and declared 2012 the 'international year of the co-operatives'. Despite this being a landmark year in promotional terms with renewed interest in the sustainability and capacity of the co-operative model across a variety of sectors, the emergent role of co-operatives is still too often invisible in formal education. In the first decade of the twenty-first century, there was a resurgence of co-operative values and principles stimulated by such initiatives as the Young Co-operatives project from 2002 and, from 2003, the Co-operative Group began to sponsor a number of business and enterprise colleges. This resurgence gathered much greater momentum after 2008 when co-operation became the driving force behind a radical move to change the governance structure of what was to become the first mainstream co-operative trust school in Reddish Vale, Stockport (Arnold 2013; Simpson in this volume). Moving into the second decade of this century, the number and variety of co-operative schools has continued to expand and develop in response to both policy reform and increasing demand from schools wishing to challenge the domination of private sector interests in school governance. What is more, co-operative schools have constituted the fastest and largest growth area within the co-operative and mutual sector so far in 2013.[1] This exponential growth has required a considerable commitment on behalf of The Co-operative College who have steered the organizational structure of this rapidly growing sector of schools since inception. If the growth of co-operative schooling continues to follow the precedent of numbers doubling year upon year, there is a distinct possibility that around 1000 co-operatively led schools may be open at the time of the British general election in 2015. It would seem therefore that the legal instruments, the will and the resources are available to provide a real alternative to state, private and corporate sponsorship of competition as the only approach to the organization of the mainstream school system. However, this is still not enough to generate the conditions of a new logic of everyday politics that could result in a new paradigm of societal organization. This depends on whether there is an alternative vision of society that these new co-operative schools are able to articulate convincingly and proliferate successfully throughout the communities they serve through the practices and projects of young people who graduate from those schools. That then is the challenge of the co-operative.

The challenge of the co-operative

What is it that the co-operative school must challenge? Historians like Brian Simon (1974) have discussed the role of schools in socially constructing 'the two nations' and sociologists like Willard Waller, as far back as 1932, have written about the essential antagonism between the child and the state school teacher as a representative both of the adult world and the social order hierarchically structured to meet the interests of the power elites. For Paul Willis (1977), it resulted in a world where the rebellion of working class lads simply reinforced the puzzle of why the working classes let the middle classes have middle class jobs. And for John Schostak (1983) the answer was essentially that schools were maladjusted to the needs and interests of young people and their communities. Such schools can be seen as young people's first introduction to the 'maladjusted organizations' they will experience in their lives. Questions of whose interests are served and of which types of knowledge are valued within contemporary society continue to be replayed within the current epidemic of educational 'reform'. Stephen Ball (2008: 57) argues that political interest in the provision of education has progressed from the 'interventionist state' of the modern era, concerned with the regulation of the urban working class to a 'competition state' at the start of the twenty-first century. The inequitable effects of neoliberal educational policies produced within the context of a 'managerial state' are mapped out by critics (see Apple, 2001; Power and Franji 2010, for example) who assert that the rise of a marketized educational discourse has served to radically alter the educational landscape and further exacerbate social inequality. Furthermore, the displacement of political anxieties that surround the dynamics of participating in an increasingly globalized 'knowledge economy' (Apple 2001) are epitomized by a reconceptualization of children in the public sphere as 'human capital' which represents 'a means of controlling the future' (Prout 2000). Indeed, Nikolas Rose argues that:

> Childhood is the most intensively governed sector of personal existence. In different ways, at different times, and by many different routes varying from one section of society to another, the health, welfare, and rearing of children has been linked in thought and in practice to the destiny of the nation and the responsibilities of the State. The modern child has become the focus of innumerable projects that purport to safeguard it from physical, sexual and moral danger, to ensure its normal development, to actively promote certain capacities of attributes such as intelligence, educability and emotional stability.
>
> *(Rose 1989: 121)*

Set this alongside the ideas of the conservative libertarian Charles Murray (2005) who invited Tony Blair to construct a 'custodial democracy' designed to contain what he termed the 'underclasses'. This was a term again employed by the Secretary of State for Education Michael Gove, following the August riots of 2011, when he called the rioters an educational underclass. Gove's cabinet colleague, Ken Clark (2011), similarly referred to a 'feral' underclass.

A school that is co-operative by name but adopts all the hierarchical forms of organization and practices of mainstream schooling remains incompatible with the vision of co-operation that is the legacy of the early pioneers. This then is the challenge. It is to present a radically alternative vision and a practice that does not reduce the young to 'an intensively governed sector of personal existence', and a large section of the population to a custodialized 'underclass' or the entire population to being the object of routine mass police surveillance in all matters (for example Ball 2013).

The steps towards democratic education

The challenge for the co-operative movement then is to construct forms of organization that meet both individual and collective needs, demands and interests (see Facer, Thorpe and Shaw 2012). In education its broadly stated aspirations include:

- Informing about co-operation – making visible the alternatives
    - Creating resources for students, activists, and politicians
    - Generating critiques of competitive capitalism
    - Increasing the visibility of alternatives to the prevailing forms of political, economic and social organization
- Experiencing and practising co-operation – building co-operative institutions
    - Engaging in free and open forms of social association for mutual benefit
    - Transforming loose associations of individuals into more enduring organizations for the accomplishment of projects and for mutual support and development
    - Developing the experience of young people with staff to create and maintain spaces within organizations for the inclusive expressions of voices and for debate in all matters concerning the organization, governance and allocation of resources and rewards
- Learning through co-operation – developing co-operative identities, practices and networks
    - Experiencing and benefitting from relationships of mutuality, equity and solidarity
    - Learning skills for effective running of co-operative institutions, developing individuals' skills and capabilities
    - Developing capacities for self-reliance, building networks of support and informal learning
- Building a movement as a condition for realizing a new vision of society

The practicalities of articulating such aspirations can draw upon legacies of democratic, 'progressive' and 'alternative' experiments and experiences (Fielding and Moss 2011). The logic such practices entail treats each voice as both free and equal. Indeed, as Étienne Balibar (1994) argues, freedom and equality are co-extensive. The principle of the co-extensiveness of freedom *with* equality, or *égaliberté*, as Balibar calls it, marks the difference between democratic forms of association and the hierarchical forms of organization essential to neoliberalism and capitalism that equate freedom only with the market freedom of private individuals to accumulate wealth competitively and thus at the expense of the freedom of others who are the losers in the competition. Co-operation thus is as essential to a notion of democracy as is freedom *with* equality of association in order to form a variety of collective forms of social living as well as specific mutual projects and the organizations that can carry out those projects. For Jacques Rancière (1995, 1999; see also May 2008; Baiocchi and Connor 2013) such a logic is the mark of the radically political where the demand for equality involves a fundamental reconfiguration of social relationships rather than a simple reform that improves pay or access to resources but makes no challenge to or change in the prevailing social order. It can be argued that contemporary forms of democracy have evolved to protect privilege rather than challenge it (Schostak and Goodson 2012; Schostak and Schostak 2013). In the search for a counter to such a hollowing out of democracy, McCormick (2011) draws attention to Machiavelli's largely overlooked political strategies to make elites accountable. These involved: the creation of 'offices or assemblies' with the power of veto and the authority to exclude the wealthiest; procedures to appoint people by election or through lotteries; and political trials involving the whole citizenry. In short, the procedures were calculated to exclude the dominance of the powerful in decision making by increasing the power of the powerless to constrain elites and hold them accountable. How then, can such a purpose be applied in contemporary education as a ground for the revitalization of democratic experience, knowledge and skills and an ethic of 'democratic fellowship' (see Fielding and Moss 2011).

To create a democratic fellowship, co-operative schools need ways of constructing a more equitable basis for assigning roles within schools, deciding upon the core activities and documenting the development of individuals within the context of the school community. Rearticulating success as an interdependent process offers scope to redefine both the purpose and the practice of 'schooling' as a collaborative endeavour. Modelling forms of evaluation based upon the historical success of 'pedagogical documentation' where events that occur at school are recorded for research and reflection in the Italian educational communities of Reggio Emilia (see: http://www.reggiochildren.it) offers a useful point of reference in this instance. It may be extended as a form of action research where individuals reflect upon their social and work circumstances in order to improve decision making and action and to increase the democratic accountability of elites by placing a check on oppressive managerialism. As argued by Michael Fielding and Peter Moss (2011), and by Fielding in this book, there is a rich and extensive historical legacy of democratic education that can be re-appropriated by people as a resource for re-thinking and re-imagining our futures, and in particular co-operative schools, as a vehicle for a socially-just education.

Is it really happening?

To what extent is democratic co-operative governance being implemented and evaluated by the schools that have adopted co-operative status? This is a fundamentally political question in Rancière's (1995; Baiocchi and Connor 2013) sense in that its implicit criterion of success involves a fundamental challenge to prevailing social relationships. Rather than hierarchy, co-operation requires an equality of contribution to decision making otherwise it falls into command and control. The challenge is to include all participants in the educational project as equals in the decision making processes.

For example, there are issues relating to trust boards as to whether young people need to be over 18 in order to vote. If so, how can this be consistent with the co-operative principle of one member one vote? What are the rights and responsibilities of young people who occupy a role on the board of trustees? Critical to whether co-operative education is *really* happening is the extent to which its ideals are driven deep into the cultural practices as well as the procedures and processes of day-to-day organization. Can the co-operative schools take on and replace, for example, the so-called 'new managerialist' obsessions with performance and attainment targets that dominate contemporary political discourses of education? Or indeed, what is the role of young people in identifying, choosing, creating and developing curricula projects?

In contrast to contemporary management and surveillance technologies frequently employed via the Ofsted inspection in the UK, the Co-operative College has developed a peer monitoring system whereby co-operative schools are able to reflect upon and celebrate how co-operation is enacted within partner schools, foregrounding 'collaboration' and dialogue rather than 'competition' and measurement. During a pilot training session for the Co-operative Identity Mark (CIM), undertaken at the College in April 2012, it was stressed that 'this is not an inspection'- a concept that some members found difficult to grasp initially. Indeed, the significance attached to a school's Ofsted rating as a primary signifier of merit was underscored by volunteer pilot school representatives who unanimously referred to their own school's Ofsted rating prior to offering any other details about the context in which they worked. The initial response of schools chosen to pilot this scheme offers a glimpse of the extent to which technologies of surveillance and market regulation have become taken for granted as a fundamental point of reference within spaces of public education. In this instance, co-operative school members appeared well accustomed to the 'usual' prescriptive approach when asked to produce evidence for a whole raft of quality evaluation initiatives such as 'Healthy Schools award', 'Inclusion Quality Mark' and 'Investors in People Award' and initially assumed that the Co-operative Identity Mark would follow a similar criteria for measurement. A significant number of participants also talked at length about the extent to which the aforementioned quality marks were often considered 'trophies' that occupied space in their school's reception area and appeared on letterheads, but in practice, were rarely referred to once the award had been granted. However, at this point representatives from the Co-operative College were keen to highlight that the fundamental rationale behind this project was to establish an enduring co-operative consciousness within schools in order to counter the superficial status that awards of this type often attract. Despite this intention, concerns were also voiced in later ethnographic engagement[2] with other co-operative school members about the significance of the assessor's level of expertise. One headteacher made the point that she felt it was unfair that some schools chose staff who were not members of school leadership teams to take on the role of CIM assessors and expressed concerns that governors or teaching assistants 'weren't qualified enough' to take on such a role. This instance highlights some of the tensions that are beginning to emerge in terms of accommodating diverse understandings and interpretations of equality of membership for such schools and their members, in particular resolving how assessment practices can move towards flattening hierarchical deference, instead of supporting it. And whilst this method of assessment offers a new language with which to talk about school improvement, it may take some time to underline the non-competitive and collaborative nature of this particular evaluation framework and reorient the purpose of the identity mark as a celebration of co-operation rather than a quantitative measure of comparison between schools. Furthermore, in these examples it can be seen how making co-operation more visible also brings with it the risk of making it more amenable to the technologies of regulation and control and neoliberal appropriation.

If the principle of freedom with equality of association is critical to democracy and thus to co-operatives, can such technologies of regulation and control be deconstructed? One school offered an example of the potential of the co-operative model to encourage collaboration and interdependency when they spoke of how they had reconfigured the usual practice of grouping students together by chronological age as a means to develop spaces for dialogue and learning across a range of age groups. One school, *Mutual High School*,[3] sees the potential of the co-op model to encourage collaboration and interdependency by reconfiguring the usual practice of grouping students together by chronological age in order to encourage conversations between peers as well as between young people and adults thus ensuring that all voices are heard as a basis for the school being able to respond organizationally.

Another co-operative academy offers a more material consideration of equality of membership within the very fabric of its school building. This new school building houses unisex toilets which are shared by staff and students alike and also incorporates a number of communal 'hub' areas throughout the school which encourage interdependent activity and engagement between students across a range of age groups. All this of course, takes place in the context of neoliberal pressures on education that demand increasing subordination to employer needs and the management of performance. Are the risks of co-option recognized? And in another school, teachers and researchers explored the extent to which it was possible to co-opt co-operative practices within conflicting agendas, reported in Keri Facer, Julie Thorpe and Linda Shaw (2012):

> I don't think it is [a political agenda]. It's just about learning, it's about helping the kids. It's a godsend. For anyone thinking of going into teaching, these structures need to be taught in universities. Because if you've got an inspector sitting in the room, these structures give you a chance to show off what your kids can do, and that's what teachers need. . . .

And to what extent is team playing just another form of surveillance?

> There's no chance to get bored, no chance to switch off. Kids know that if they're not working together as a team their team will be let down, and it ties in with the reward system, the team comes first.

And is there a subtle co-option into market needs?

> You need to start off with a history background, a little bit of an understanding of where this has come from, this is now how it's gone, it's one of the biggest organizations in the world, and look, it's a multimillion pound industry and I think that works with students, students need to know that something is successful if they're going to actually get on and do it. They don't like to be seen as a test bed. We can say, look, it's worked.

Early in 2012 the London Institute of Education hosted a seminar entitled: *'Putting the community back into community schools? Learners, teachers, parents and community in co-operative schools'* which sought to instigate a dialogue about what 'membership' of a co-operative school might entail. A range of co-operative schools presented their experiences of developing a co-operative school identity and offered examples of how they are 'finding their way' within a range of contexts. One head teacher highlighted the organic nature of establishing a co-operative identity and advised schools to embrace an emotional attachment to 'being' co-operative:

> Go with what can be achieved and grown rather than trying to get everything in place from the start. Membership is not just a practical label – to have its greatest effect it needs to be an emotional attachment.

Another delegate spoke of the transformative nature of working together as a horizontal organization and conveyed how adopting a co-operative approach to school governance and learning had transformed the direction of a school which had previously 'lost touch with the community both inside and outside of the school gates [and was] heading towards a £3 million deficit and special measures'.

In addition, one representative from a cluster of trust schools spoke of the need to harness collective resources and illustrated how 'living out' the value of solidarity enabled members to form a more powerful lobbying group in which they had started to think about wider issues that affect the school community, such as housing problems, in the hope that 'pooling our voice with others can start to make a difference'. The advantage of smaller schools developing a collaborative relationship with neighbouring schools in this instance offers an opportunity to resist the fragmentation of relationships between other schools and community groups competing for scarce local authority resources and unite all voices towards local social justice agendas. The growth of multi-school co-operative trusts in the

South West and other parts of England[4] is a case in point here as Mervyn Wilson (2012) explains:

> Many shared trusts build on existing collaborative partnerships, providing a formal legal framework through which deeper collaboration can emerge. This aspect is exemplified by the rapid growth of co-operative schools in the South West, where there are now 11 shared trusts in Cornwall alone involving a total of 86 schools, with many more preparing to start the formal consultation processes. Some of the larger trusts now provide a range of services to support schools, and are in a position to tender for services previously provided by the local authority as its role in the delivery of education steadily erodes.

Yet whilst this solution could be argued as building greater social capital and democratic voice for local school communities, the extent to which this move supports further fragmentation of local authorities remains an important concern. And whilst these examples provide small steps towards the realization of democratic and co-operative principles of practice, it is clear there is a long way to go before a coherent and comprehensive vision and practice is realized according to the principles of freedom with equality.

Can co-operatives develop a coherent and comprehensive vision and practice?

Developing a coherent discourse of contemporary 'co-operative education' depends upon drawing meaning from both historical practice and making the culture of co-operation more visible and thus subject to reflection, dialogue and re-articulation within a rapidly changing social and cultural context. This presents a distinct challenge for the under-developed area of mainstream co-operative schooling in the UK operating within a climate of competition, productivity and austerity. In order to confront dominant neoliberal notions of individualist 'freedom and choice' but *without* equality within education, schools are placed within a double bind:

> On the one hand: in order to develop a significant voice and establish an effective position as a credible alternative to the preferred academy model within the state sector, co-operative schools are compelled to operate within the confines of market driven interpretations of educational purpose and measures of success. Therefore, in order to become a school of 'choice', the credibility and sustainability of the co-op model depends upon creating 'a brand' of co-operation within schools that can be universally identified, and readily translated into 'marketable' outcomes that align with neoliberal interpretation.
> On the other hand: There is 'no blueprint franchise for co-op schools'.[5] The co-operative movement comprises a diverse collection of membership interests, needs and voices. Co-operative approaches to education strive to be

respectful of the contingent nature of equitable citizenship and, in so doing, each co-operative school retains a high level of autonomy in how it interprets co-operative values and principles according to context. This cannot be reduced to a unified 'brand' of narrowly defined educational experiences and outcomes, or fit in neatly to reductive forms of educational accountability and surveillance. Instead, co-operative approaches endeavour to reassert an ethical 'values driven' approach to education and open up opportunities for learning and democratic action which offer a deeper reading of educational freedom and choice in direct opposition to the neoliberal model.

Is it possible then to renegotiate 'evidenced based' assessment and evaluation the 'co-operative way'? In particular, are there opportunities to scaffold an alternative interpretation of 'success'? And if so, how can one address the eternal problem of defining the essence of co-operativism as a more tangible entity, thus offering a counter narrative to the individualized 'evidenced based', client centred, personalized, individualized market approach that currently dominates public sector practice (see for example, Fisher et al. 2012). Although diverse co-operative projects are united by common political aspirations, the points at which co-operative values and principles are translated from 'ideal' to action are subject to a high degree of historical, geographical and cultural variability. Whilst such diversity of approaches could be considered a significant asset in terms of extending voice and representation, this also constitutes a significant challenge in terms of navigating a more coherent group identity.

The effects of this are much more pronounced in the relatively new area of mainstream schooling. Although co-operative schools have enjoyed a period of rapid growth in number at the time of writing, the development of a co-operative school identity remains fragile and uncertain. In order to gain some consistency in the multiple ways in which co-operative values and principles are played out within diverse educational contexts, the process of establishing a co-operative identity mark scheme opens up the possibility of creating a space for these conversations to begin. It is anticipated that, as more co-operative schools engage in these practices of collaborative reflection, they will be able to share their experiences of embedding a co-operative ethos within the areas of governance and membership, curriculum, pedagogy, staff development and community engagement. Over time it is hoped that these stories and case studies will develop and expand in order to develop a richer understanding of what co-operation might mean when applied to educational contexts and offer a counter narrative to dominant neoliberal discourses.

Finally, then, to the question of whether a coherent and comprehensive vision can be developed that respects the principle of freedom with equality in all associations. At this point in time, there are no certain answers. However, recalling Waller's (1932) discussion of the essential antagonism between teacher and pupil, the radical democratic political theory of Chantel Mouffe (2005), for example, is developed explicitly in relation to the inevitable clashes of view, values and demands that occur between people. It provides a way of thinking about how to organize in ways that respect the differences, include all voices in decision making and come to courses of action that are of mutual benefit. If we are to develop organizations that are not maladjusted to the needs, values, interests and demands of people (Schostak 1983; Schostak and Schostak 2008, 2012), then we need to ensure that all voices are freely and equally included, and in Rancière's (1995, 1999) formulation, that we are faithful to the disagreements that may occur between people. To override the views of the few by adopting a majority decision is to fail the test of equality *with* freedom for *all*. Neoliberalism is by this measure, freedom *without* equality imposed by the elite few whose voices are amplified by their wealth. We are currently in uncertain times. Neoliberalism has failed to deliver democracy, social justice and freedom for all. Co-operative forms of organization in schools by including freely and equally all voices – pupils, parents, wider communities – may develop approaches, mechanisms, procedures that provide a check on elite power and thus enable the spread of democratic accountability. It may be called a Machiavellian moment in the co-operative strategy for the development of democracy. Will this Machiavellian moment be realized? As to whether the emergent sector of co-operative schools in the UK along with other co-operatives operating across the economic sectors and communities of society, could create the conditions in communities for the broader hopes of an inclusive society founded upon co-operative principles to be achieved, all we can say is, the game is open.

Acknowledgements

We are indebted to Mervyn Wilson, Julie Thorpe and Linda Shaw of the Co-op College, Manchester for information and the development of ideas relating to cooperatives that have informed this chapter and to our editor, Tom Woodin for his useful comments.

Notes

1 http://www.co-op.ac.uk/2013/03/raising-achievement/
2 This refers to a period of ethnographic fieldwork undertaken by Gail Davidge who examined the emergence of a co-operative model of education within two co-operative secondary schools in England as part of her PhD research. Ethnographic fieldwork incorporated participant observation at two co-operative secondary schools in England during the period between September 2012 and June 2013. During this time as well as noting innumerable conversations she also undertook ten formal interviews and three focus group discussions with staff and students, in addition to observing the life of the school from a range of contexts both in lessons and at break times. Her fieldwork also involved attending conferences, seminars and training events hosted by the Co-operative College where she observed the interaction between key personnel from other co-operative schools nationwide.
3 School name anonymized.
4 See http://school.coop/case-studies/co-operative-multi-school-trust/ for examples.
5 See http://www.co-op.ac.uk/2013/03/handbook-helps-co-operative-schools; www.co-operatives.ac.uk

References

Arnold, P. (2013). 'Making co-operative ideas work', *Forum*, 55/2: 245–254.
Apple, M.W. (2001). 'Comparing neo-liberal projects and inequality in education', *Comparative Education*, 37/4: 409–423.
Arrighi, G. (2007) *Adam Smith in Beijing. Lineages of the Twenty-First Century*, London, New York: Verso.
Balibar, E. (1994) '"Rights of Man" and "Rights of the Citizen": the modern dialectic of equality and freedom', in Balibar, E. (ed.), *Masses, Classes, Ideas: Studies on Politics and Philosophy Before and After Marx*, New York: Routledge. The original is: "La proposition de l'égaliberté", in Les Conférences du Perroquet, n° 22, Paris novembre 1989.
—— (1998) *Spinoza and Politics*, trans. Peter Snowdon, London: Verso.
Baiocchi, G., and Connor, B. T. (2013) 'Politics as interruption: Rancière's community of equals and governmentality', *Thesis Eleven*, 117/1: 89–100.
Ball, J. (2013) Edward Snowden NSA files: secret surveillance and our revelations so far, *The Guardian*, 21 August; http://www.theguardian.com/world/2013/aug/21/edward-snowden-nsa-files-revelations (accessed 23 August 2013).
Ball, S. J. (2008) *The Education Debate,* Bristol: The Policy Press.
Beach, A. (2013) 'This is not our country any more': gun battles rage in Egypt as death toll continues to rise, *The Independent*, 17 August; http://www.independent.co.uk/news/world/africa/this-is-not-our-country-any-more-gun-battles-rage-in-egypt-as-death-toll-continues-to-rise-8769784.html (accessed 23 August 2013).
Burgess. K. and McCrum, D. (2012) Boards wake up to a shareholder spring, *Financial Times*, 4 May; http://www.ft.com/cms/s/0/a284e414-95ee-11e1-a163-00144feab49a.html#axzz1zGDbIZ9f (accessed 30 June 2012).
Clark, K. (2011) Punish the feral rioters, but address our social deficit too, *The Guardian*, 5 September; http://www.guardian.co.uk/commentisfree/2011/sep/05/punishment-rioters-help (accessed 30 June 2012).
Cole, G. D. H. (1930) *The Life of Robert Owen*, London: Macmillan.
Dewey, J. (1938) *Experience and Education*, New York: Collier.
Elliott, L. (2011) Global financial crisis: five key stages 2007–2011, *The Guardian*, 7 August; http://www.theguardian.com/business/2011/aug/07/global-financial-crisis-key-stages (accessed 26 September 2013).
Facer, K., Thorpe, J., and Shaw, L. (2012) 'Co-operative education and schools: an old idea for new times?' Special issue, guest editor John Schostak, *Power and Education*, 4/3: 327–341.
Fielding, M. and Moss, P. (2011) *Radical Democratic Education and the Common School*, London: Routledge.
Fisher, M., Baines, S., and Raynor, M. (2012) 'Personalisation and the co-operative tradition', *Social Policy and Society*, 11: 507–518.
Fraser, N. (2007) 'Emancipation is not an all or nothing affair', interview by Marina Liakova: http://www.eurozine.com/articles/2008-08-01-fraser-en.html (accessed 28 January 2010).
Freire, P. (1970) *Pedagogy of the Oppressed*, New York: Herder & Herder.
Friberg, K. (2011) 'Negotiating consumer and producer interests – a challenge for the co-operative movement and Fair Trade', in Webster, A., Shaw, L., Walton, J. K., Brown, A. and Stewart, D. (eds), *The Hidden Alternative: Co-operative Values, Past, Present and Future*, Manchester: Manchester University Press: 115–136.
Friedman, M. (1982/1962) *Capitalism and Freedom*, Preface, London: University of Chicago Press.
Fukuyama, F. (1992) *The End of History and the Last Man,* New York: Free Press; Second paperback edition with a new Afterword, Simon and Schuster, 2006.
Godwin, W. (1793) two volumes, 4th ed., *An Enquiry Concerning the Principles of Political Justice and Its Influence on General Virtue and Happiness*, London: Robinson.
Harvey, D. (2005) *A Brief History of Neoliberalism*, Oxford: Oxford University Press.
Hayek, F. A. (1944) *The Road to Serfdom*, Chicago: University of Chicago Press.

Huntington, S. P. (1996) *The Clash of Civilizations and the Remaking of World Order*, New York: Simon and Schuster.
Hyde, M. (2012) This is no shareholder spring, it's just a different class of self-interest, *The Guardian*, 11 May; http://www.guardian.co.uk/commentisfree/2012/may/11/shareholder-spring-self-interest-high-pay (accessed 30 June 2012).
Kaletsky, A. (2010) *Capitalism 4.0. The Birth of a New Economy in the Aftermath of Crisis*, London, Berlin: Bloomsbury.
Klein, N. (2008) *The Shock Doctrine. The Rise of Disaster Capitalism*, London: Penguin.
Kropotkin, Prince P.A. (1904) *Mutual Aid: A Factor of Evolution*, London: Heinemann.
Laclau, E. (2005) *Populist Reason*, London: Verso.
MacPherson, I. (2011). 'Community, individuality and co-operation: the centrality of values', in Webster, A., Shaw, L., Walton, J. K., Brown, A., and Stewart, D. (eds), *The Hidden Alternative: Co-operative Values, Past, Present and Future*, Manchester: Manchester University Press: 203–225.
McCormick, J. P. (2011) *Machiavellian Democracy*, Cambridge: Cambridge University Press.
May, T. (2008) *The Political Thought of Jacques Rancière. Creating Equality*, Edinburgh, Pennsylvania: Edinburgh University.
Meltdown (2011) 'The men who crashed the world.' Al Jazeera Part 4; http://www.youtube.com/watch?v=osAYMnqZyZc (accessed 4 June 2012).
Miller, M. and Skidelsky, R. (2013) 'Across Europe, austerity policies have caused stagnation and despair', *New Statesman* 27 June; http://www.newstatesman.com/business/business/2013/06/across-europe-austerity-policies-have-caused-stagnation-and-despair (accessed 24 August 2013).
Mouffe, C. (2005) *On the Political*, London/New York: Routledge.
Murray, C. (2005) 'The advantages of social apartheid. US experience shows Britain what to do with its underclass – get it off the streets', *Sunday Times*, 3 April; American Enterprise for Public Policy Research, posted April 4th at: http://www.aei.org/publications/filter.all,pubID.22252/pub_detail.asp (accessed 24 May 2005).
Negri, A. (1991) *The Savage Anomaly. The power of Spinoza's Metaphysics and Politics*, Minneapolis: University of Minnesota Press.
Norton, A. (2004) *Leo Strauss and the Politics of American Empire*, New Haven: Yale University Press.
Owen, R. (1816) *A New View of Society Or, Essays on the Principle of the Formation of the Human Character, and the Application of the Principle to Practice*, Political Economy Reference Archive; http://www.marxists.org/reference/subject/economics/owen/index.htm. (accessed, 2 July 2012).
—— (1826) *The Social System — Constitution, Laws, and Regulations of a Community.*
—— (1830) *Lectures on an Entire New State of Society*, London: J Brooks.
Power, S. and Franji, D. (2010) 'Education markets: the new politics of recognition and the increasing fatalism towards inequality,' *Journal of Education Policy*, 3/25: 385–396.
Prout, A. (2000) 'Children's participation: control and self-realisation in British late modernity,' *Children and Society*, 14/4: 304–315.
Rancière, J. (1995) *La Mésentente. Politique et Philosophie*, Paris: Galilée.
—— (1999) *Disagreement*, Minneapolis: University of Minnesota Press.
Reese, S. D., and Lewis, S. C. (2009) 'Framing the war on terror. The internalization of policy in the U.S. press', *Journalism*, 10/6: 777–797.
Roberts, D. and Borger, J. (2013) 'Syria crisis: US holds talks as concern grows over chemical weapons claims', *The Guardian*, 23 August; http://www.theguardian.com/world/2013/aug/22/us-talks-syria-chemical-weapons-use-allegations (accessed 23 August 2013).
Roberts, L. and Schostak, J. (2012) 'Obama and the "Arab Spring": desire, hope and the manufacture of disappointment. Implications for a transformative pedagogy'. Special Issue, guest editor John Schostak, *Discourse: Studies in the Cultural Politics of Education*, 33/3: 377–396.
Rose, N. (1989) *Governing the Soul*, London: Routledge.

Sandel, M. J. (1982) *Liberalism and the Limits of Justice*, Cambridge: Cambridge University Press.

Schostak, J. F. (1983) *Maladjusted Schooling: Deviance, Social Control and Individuality in Secondary Schooling*, London: Falmer. Republished 2012 London: Routledge Library Editions.

—— (1986) *Schooling the Violent Imagination*, London: Routledge and Kegan Paul.

—— (1993) *Dirty Marks: The Education of Self, Media and Popular Culture*, London: Pluto Press.

Schostak, J. F., and Schostak, J. R. (2013) *Writing Research Critically – the Power to Make a Difference*, London: Routledge.

—— (2008) *Radical Research. Designing, developing and writing research to make a difference*, London: Routledge.

—— (2012). *Writing Research Critically: Developing the Power to Make a Difference*, London: Routledge.

Schostak, J. F. and Goodson, I. (2012) 'What's wrong with democracy at the moment and why it matters for research and education', Special Issue, *Schooling and Education after Neoliberalism*, guest editor John Schostak, 4/3: 257–276.

Schmitt, C. (1996) *The Concept of the Political*, Chicago: The University of Chicago Press.

Simon, B. (1974) *The Two Nations and the Educational Structure 1780–1870*, London: Lawrence and Wishart.

Strauss, L. (1951/1988) *What is Political Philosophy? And Other Studies*, Chicago: The University of Chicago Press.

Travis, A. (2012) 'Margaret Thatcher's role in plan to dismantle welfare state revealed', *The Guardian*, 28 December, http://www.theguardian.com/politics/2012/dec/28/margaret-thatcher-role-plan-to-dismantle-welfare-state-revealed (accessed 23 August 2013).

Waller, W. (1932) *The Sociology of Teaching*, London: Chapman and Hall.

Wallerstein, I. (2003) *The Decline of American Power. The US in a Chaotic World*, New York: The New Press.

Walzer M. (1985) *Spheres of Justice. A Defence of Pluralism and Equality*, Oxford: Blackwell.

Willis, P. (1977) *Learning to Labour*, Farnborough: Saxon House.

Wilson, M. (2012) 'Co-operative schools: back to a democratic future?' in Julian, C. (ed.) *Making it Mutual: The Ownership Revolution that Britain Needs*, Lincoln: The ResPublica Trust: 177–180.

Woodin, T. (2011) 'Co-operative education in Britain during the nineteenth and early twentieth centuries: context, identity and learning', in Webster, A., Shaw, L., Walton, J. K., Brown, A. and Stewart, D. (eds), *The Hidden Alternative: Co-operative Values, Past, Present and Future*, Manchester: Manchester University Press, 78–96.

6

Contrived collegiality? Investigating the efficacy of co-operative teacher development

Sarah Jones

Co-operative professional development has been a key aspect of school improvement and transformation at Lipson Co-operative Academy. It is often described as a model of good practice and has been cited by others as highly collegiate. It is certainly one of the most successful operational practices within our co-operative philosophy. This chapter critically analyses the notion of collegiality when applied to teachers' co-operative professional development. The focus of the study is a team of teachers that was set up to operate as a democratic co-operative social enterprise. Their goal was to develop strategies to effect school improvement through a co-operative pedagogy. Lev Vygotsky's ideas of the Zone of Proximal Development and the More Knowledgeable Other were used in the conceptualization of the team, known as the school improvement group (SIG) and, over time, it has been successful in terms of teacher and learner satisfaction. Such is the success of the model, that all teaching staff are now engaged in a range of self-generated SIGs. However, we have also observed weaknesses in the ways that relationships form and outcomes are achieved. Within the SIG it is possible to identify elements of 'contrived collegiality' (Grimmett and Crehan 1992; Hargreaves 1991). In order to study this assertion and to get 'under the skin' of its functionality, I focus on particular aspects of collegiality, and highlight the tensions that appear. Conflicts and strains are inevitable in the transformation process, and they cannot be aligned with collegiality. The internal tensions and contradictions seen in the operation of the group are not necessarily destructive events and, whilst they cannot be aligned with collegiality, they can be a possible force for change. Understanding why co-operative professional development 'works' contributes to a more thoughtful and complex approach to leadership built on internal principles of self-help, democracy and solidarity in addition to a sustainable model of teacher emulation.

Lipson Co-operative Academy is a large inner-city secondary school based in Plymouth. The Academy draws its students largely from the immediate residential communities many of which score highly on indices for multi-deprivation. There exists within this local authority one of the widest range of school typologies found in England: sponsored academies; converter academies; faith schools; selective schools (three single sex grammar schools and some ex-grammar schools masquerading as comprehensive schools); independent schools; a UTC (university technical college); and free schools. Lipson Co-operative Academy is one of two local city secondary schools to be designated as a co-operative academy. At the time of writing, all the secondary schools find themselves attempting to recruit from an ever-decreasing number of students as the demography of the city changes. Despite schools collaborating to reduce their planned admission number, with the exception of the UTC and grammar schools, they have to work in a context of market driven competition. Notwithstanding these challenging circumstances, the Academy remains very popular and has been the recipient of multiple awards for excellence, including those for the collective academic performance of the students; its outstanding commitment to, and performance in, continuing professional development and research; and its ethos. It has also been awarded three 'outstanding' judgements by Ofsted and is the subject of one of their best practice reports (Ofsted 2008, 2010, 2012).

Since becoming a co-operative trust school in 2009 and then a converter academy in 2011, Lipson Co-operative Academy has sought to foster and promote the values and principles of the International Co-operative Alliance (1995), reproduced in the appendix to this book. The aim was to 'go deep' and embed the co-operative values into day-to-day practice rather than to embark upon a multi-school co-operative trust with a very wide membership base as a starting point. In other words, we wanted to explore a co-operative solution within the world of neoliberal educational assumptions. The values are brought to life on a day-to-day basis through pedagogical practices, governance and leadership, the curriculum and through engagement in social and ethical enterprise. One example of the alternative approach to leadership seen in the Academy is the development of democratic and co-operative practices of professional development. As the senior vice principal in the Academy, part of my role is to ensure that professional development has a substantial impact on teachers at all stages of their careers, and of course in the classroom. To be effective this means that its impact must be seen in the learning and progress of the students, both individually and collectively. A co-operative pedagogy is dominant in the school and is centred on dialogue and interaction in order to develop both interdependence and independence in learners. We have a background in promoting participatory democracy in design and research, so it appeared natural to me that staff development should follow the same model. Experiments in embedding the principles of co-operation were to be the starting point from which to improve our work and to transform collegiate behaviours beyond notions of support and challenge. It was also envisaged that this would challenge more traditional methods of top-down or externally led models of professional development. I particularly wanted to focus on the impact of democracy and self-help at all stages, from inception to participation through to output. I wanted to avoid the exploitative practice that some schools undertake by recruiting junior members of staff to run professional development without the underpinning principles described above, and without authority or authenticity. I aimed to create space for co-operative values to be explored, mediated and interpreted as transformational practices for teaching and learning. I hoped to be able to make this kind of approach sustainable through co-creating a methodology for professional development that nurtures participatory democracy and solidarity. In short: I aimed for high quality collegiality.

Collegiality and co-operation

Collegiality is the relationship between people who are united in a common purpose (Eun 2010). At Lipson, the collegiate aims were to promote democratic leadership through participation and dialogue. Fundamental to these aims was recognition of the autonomy and professional freedom of teachers, along with a desire to draw upon the breadth of experience and creative thinking already in existence. Teachers are no more 'empty vessels' to be filled than are students. We drew on a model provided by Andy Hargreaves (2008) who describes collegiality as:

- Spontaneous: it should emerge primarily from the teachers themselves.
- Voluntary: participation should be non-coercive with no constraint or compulsion.
- Development oriented: the group should choose external mandates and reject others, or effect change from within themselves based on their needs.
- Pervasive across time and space: not administratively planned or regulated.
- Unpredictable: collegiality is incompatible in implementation-oriented systems. Collegiality should have high unpredictability in its outcomes.

It is my contention that collegiality arises from co-operation and that when considered together they have the potential to enhance one another. Collegiality can exist without co-operation but it is more fragile and open to mutation. Although we might define co-operation by the values and principles of the ICA, in the context of professional development, I am referring to any activity that results in mutual benefit derived from behaviours that are ethical and open. This is in sharp contrast to forced development by fear and surveillance. The tools for evaluation in both paradigms may be the same, for example lesson observations, but the purpose and ideology are different. Through structured co-operation we nurture a 'growth mind set' (Dweck 2006) to enhance and strengthen collegiality where we accept talent is not 'gifted' to anyone. It is instead a result of many hours of purposeful practice, opportunity and plenty of self-motivation. It is about taking risks, responding to criticism and valuing effort. Work undertaken together has the potential to be co-devised, co-critiqued and co-evaluated. The dialogue of multiple voices facilitates the development of common goals and effective planning and, by exploiting the members' desire to learn, a willingness to embrace new challenges emerges.

TABLE 6.1 Co-operation and collegiality

Collegiality	Co-operation has the potential to add:
Spontaneous	An understanding of *self-help* and *self-responsibility*. The growth mindset develops resilience so members learn what to do when they encounter problems.
Voluntary participation	*Membership is open.* The values are explicitly defined and tested.
Development oriented	*Solidarity* is supported through dialogue. Group goals are generated. Mutual development strategies are created and emulation is a founding principle.
Pervasive across time and space	Little interference from the leadership team. Mutuality is developed as co-operatives have their own terms of reference. They are *owned by their members*.
Unpredictable	Co-operatives are *democratic* organizations that serve the needs of members. They support the value of *equity*.

The 'peer' factor in evaluation encourages this. Staff should not be in competition with each other, nor be slaves to praise by external sources, or the leadership team. Teachers should not feel threatened by the success of others. Through co-operation we assume that all participants act as autonomous agents and that they will seek to improve their work as well as that of others. In short, there is value in the activity for everyone. It is possible to draw upon the values of equality and equity to ensure equal participation and solidarity in letting no one fail. The sense of well-being that is unleashed by paying attention to these values is created and nourished by genuine power-sharing and purposeful and transformational dialogue. As Table 6.1 summarizes, co-operation has considerable potential to enrich and develop the practice of collegiality.

However, there are a number of barriers to collegiality which operate across schools despite their contextual differences. Even schools and organizations that define themselves as 'co-operative' in nature struggle to define and achieve this practice of collegiality, and are victims of 'micro-political tensions' (Blase 1991) that undermine their wider purpose. When this thinking is factored into the dominant discourse of the neoliberal world of competition, individualism and autonomy, attempts at school improvement through collegiality can easily be undermined. Hargreaves (2008) contributes a great deal in explaining obstacles to school improvement that he describes as presentism, conservatism and individualism, all of which detract from a meaningful and sustained practice of collegiality and attempts at teacher development programmes. He notes that many teachers facing pressures of conservatism and individualism, which are often culturally and historically derived, will only 'do what is desirable to them'. Teachers' notions of professionalism may be based upon specific criteria of effectiveness that correspond to their own capacities and interests rather than the needs of their particular educational context.

Teachers sometimes doubt the existence of future rewards for which they are reluctant to sacrifice present opportunities and, as a result, tend to work collaboratively only for short periods of time. Hargreaves (2008) explains that teachers concentrate on short-range outcomes as a source of gratification. He describes a real attempt by leaders of schools to develop greater collaboration in which 'interactive professionalism' demands robust collegiality and where teachers make active enquiries into their schools while also using achievement data to guide collective efforts. The fact that many teachers embrace only short-term outcomes may be due to 'endemic presentism' and the way we organize learning. In this country we generally arrange large groups of children with a sense of urgency in one place for a short time and get instant success or disappointment. The business of performance and endless surveillance and accountability measures can easily undermine our concentration on long-term initiatives and effort. This persists with the Ofsted 'fear factor' even though many enlightened school leaders try hard to address it through cycles of inquiry, school self-evaluation, and 5-year strategic improvement plans to name just a few initiatives. Of course, long-term plans can also collapse due to a change of leadership or wider political changes.

Collaborating towards a common cultural goal encourages people to co-construct new knowledge by building on each participant's contribution (Eun 2010). However, working within the standardization agenda that regulates schools and narrows their focus on 'performance', allows teachers much less planning and thinking time and involves them in more detailed accountability. Adaptive presentism (Hargreaves 2008) has grown as teachers have engaged in short-termism, abandoning time for reflection, professional reading and discussion. Although this short-termism provides momentum, it can put a lid on development. These are strategies that become entrenched as they have the 'rush' of success, but they do not reach the core of teaching and learning. Thus, we might consider this approach to be more closely aligned to what Hargeaves calls 'contrived collegiality' which is useful in providing a frame to define, or counter-define, collegiality. Contrived collegiality tends to be:

- Administratively regulated.
- Compulsory: declared as voluntary in principle but is often not at all voluntary at the level of practice, for example, through mandatory collaborative planning.
- Implementation-oriented: teachers are persuaded to work together to implement the mandates of others. Fixed in time and space.
- Predictable: if we seek to develop collaborative cultures we do so for political reasons and not in order to develop human relationships.

Grimmett and Crehan (1992) suggest that contrived collegiality occurs in schools because it is designed to increase predictability, leading to attempts to secure co-operation by contrivance rather than by the teachers themselves. However, it is not so simple. Collegiate relationships are often transient in secondary schools due to changing priorities and different team conflicts. The framework of collegiality described above was a starting point for considering the efficacy of our model of professional development, but it did not allow me to 'get under the skin' of the functionality, and apparent dysfunctionality, of its collegiate nature. Whilst acknowledging the benefits of co-operative professional development, the mutation into contrived collegiality remained a persistent danger.

Co-operative professional development at Lipson

The issues outlined above were the guiding ideas for organizing professional development at Lipson Co-operative Academy. A group of teachers formed the Learning School Improvement Group (LSIG) which was set up originally as an alternative to traditional professional development to explore and develop long-term and sustainable practices in pedagogy and learning. It was anticipated that teachers would contribute directly to its development and welcome the control and autonomy offered by a mutual model. The bottom-up approach and collegiate accountability was to be a sound basis for trust and self-regulation. We believed that teachers would naturally value the absence of forced participation and seek a model of emulation to replace it. Consideration was given to a social-cultural framework based upon the work of Lev Vygotsky (1978) in which it is assumed that knowledge is both constructed through dialogue and between people and 'reality'.

In the most recently evolved structure, membership of a SIG is not voluntary, but there is choice as to which one you may join. There are seven individual groups, often referred to affectionately as SIGlets. The groups fluctuate in membership and size but are consistently heterogeneous in terms of age, experience, specialism and role of constituents. Early in the development of this work, when we had only one SIG, about a third of the teaching staff were members. They were largely teachers who had a desire to improve their practice in the classroom or those who had it suggested to them that this was the forum in which they could improve their teaching. Far from seeing this form of professional development as an 'easy option', they were colleagues who challenged each other's thinking and evaluated practice. Leadership of the group was not driven by the 'fear factor' of surveillance and judgement but rather by the 'peer factor' where teachers held themselves and others accountable for improvements.

The members of the SIG had access through peer mentoring to the 'More Knowledgeable Other' (MKO). This provided everyone with a 'base group' in which to work where there existed a range of experience on the topic under consideration. It was envisaged that the idea of the Zone of Proximal Development (Vygotsky 1978), in which participants with more experience improve with the support of others, could be utilized by the SIG to help create a collegiate, interdependent team, reflecting a truly co-operative enterprise with respect to professional learning. Using the ZPD prevented the wide range of expertise becoming a gulf between members, and allowed everyone access to both coaching and support. This had to be managed by the group members to ensure that no-one was pushed beyond the 'stretch' zone of their development into the 'panic' zone. This has been much easier to achieve in small base groups than it would have been with larger groups of teachers.

A strong initial steer was given to the group to develop the use of co-operation as a pedagogical device based on the work of Spencer Kagan (2006), Robert Slavin (1980) and David W. Johnson and Roger T. Johnson (1998). This provided the original scaffolding for our co-operative approach. In addition to the use of base groups, advocated by Johnson and Johnson as a class management tool, we adapted a wide range of techniques to the needs of Lipson. Lesson planning was based upon Kagan's PIES: positive interdependence, individual accountability, equal participation and simultaneous social interaction. We used active questioning to develop a rich dialogue and reduce competitive stagnation as described by Slavin (1980). The work was personalized and evaluated in order to gauge the impact on the progress and engagement of students. Over a four-year period the SIGs have continued to reflect on this practice; refine and extend it to suit the context of the school; evaluate its impact; and shape its development. All participants are expected to carry out action research projects. These are referred to as PDSAs (Plan; Do; Study; Act). The PDSAs are usually small scale action research projects, but many morph into larger inquiries. Once PDSAs have been evaluated for use value by the members, they are selected by a democratic collective decision making process to form workshops where SIG members train other teachers, and some teaching assistants, through a dedicated professional development programme. The members provide support and individual coaching where it is required. Opportunities are given to the participants to engage in a Master's level programme based around the specific work they are undertaking, and this is funded by the Academy. At the time of writing, we have taken eight participants on the programme, and five have just completed, four of them with distinctions. In total, 42 per cent of the staff have gained a Master's level award through tutoring in the Academy.

At first sight, and at a superficial level, the SIG group works well, with new and experienced members being paired up. Co-constructed professional learning takes place, and the quality of teaching and learning has improved. Evidence for this is not explored in depth here but exists in the form of performance data; feedback from the team's motivational behaviour and performance; student satisfaction groups; external assessments; and Ofsted reports. At Lipson we talk positively about our contribution to democratic renewal.

Creating tensions

Despite purposeful outcomes, all is not rosy in the garden. There are occasional tensions and conflicts when questions are asked about the true co-operative nature of this form of professional development, especially with regard to its collegiate nature. Our model of professional development proved to be more complex than anticipated. The most persistent barrier was a reluctance to sacrifice present benefits in favour of a long term solution. In teaching, rewards are scarce and teachers are vulnerable to factors they cannot always control. The SIG workshops that seemed quick to implement new ideas were often the most popular, but could be superficial. The underlying thinking was based on a growth mindset, democratic principles and self-responsibility but these could easily be lost in translation as people looked to simpler 'strategies' rather than 'ideas'. Short-termism could be addictive, fed by visible and compelling outcomes and leading to mutual celebrations rather than reflecting on the shared learning. The first challenge was seen in *leadership*. There are times in the year when the teams appear to lose momentum in remaking co-operative relations within a wider hierarchical educational setting. They can 'stagnate', a situation which may require a resurgence of leadership external to the team. A disappointing dependency hangs over from previous years when the confidence to make decisions and take risks declines, and members look to the senior team for direction. When we suggested that those who had run successful workshops in the previous year evaluate the impact and lead SIGlets, so being part of the new leadership development process, there was support for the proposal but many wanted to link up with a 'more powerful other' to be confident in this process. This led me to consider that the collegiate approach might only be skin deep and that much more effort was required to bring about cultural change in co-constructing, confirming and re-learning the role.

Although the objectives of the SIGs are meant to be co-constructed, tensions arise from variable levels of engagement and participation by members. Teachers may be keen to mutate their goal into something that allows them to continue doing what they have always done such as using traditional methods in assessment to support learning (peer assessment) but passing them off as 'new co-operative approaches'. In the SIGs these tendencies are evident in observing who determines the objectives of the group, who chooses whom as their MKO, and who does what in realizing these objectives. The activity is at times fragmented and causes disruption. Others in the SIG can find it difficult to 'break in' to existing partnerships and sub-groups. Some staff felt 'excluded' and some even rejected the group claiming that it was an elite team, so far had their practice developed. Crisis! This was anti-co-operative. Many hours were spent puzzling over how this could be resolved. The answer came from within the team itself. The Academy consequently spawned seven newly constructed SIGlets which were the result of the bigger original SIG recognizing that the group was too large now to meet its aims. In fact, this was a predictable response that reflected new thinking. The 'subjects' were attempting to maintain control within the group. It became clear that both conflict *and* co-operation were a part of goal achievement. Some habitual actions on the part of experienced staff could prevent the embryonic actions of others. The hierarchy of practice meant that more experienced members could easily undermine the effort and initiatives of the less experienced who were not always valued unless supported by more senior participants. There were cases of deference in terms of *who* speaks to whom and in *how* they spoke. For instance, the introduction of peer appraisal into the SIG was short-lived. Initially co-created and determined by the group, with the planned use of MKOs, some members of the SIG rapidly lost confidence in peer appraisal and wanted a return to a hierarchical system where they could show their progress to someone who 'mattered'.

A small number behaved in the opposite way and strategically ensured that their ideas for this systemic change 'worked'. It indicated that much more than hope and belief in humanity must be considered when applying co-operative approaches. Time and effort must be employed to work on aligning thinking as well as practice. Otherwise, scratch the surface and we return to the old 'fixed' mindset of striving to out-compete each other by trying to be 'the best' for the leader. People may, therefore, have different objectives within the same activity system even if they are articulated through a common language and this can lead to unintended consequences. Despite the loss of stability, it is actually at this point of heightened tension and conflict that the objective can be co-constructed and substantial transformation take place. This is important as it informs us that we should accept the conflict and tension rather than seeing it as a dysfunctional measure of the democratic work we are undertaking. Leaders need to be aware that interfering less is an option that should be considered even where hierarchies are being reproduced.

A further question centres on *relationships*. In co-operative activities, such as learning in the classroom we might expect to see an 'apprentice and master' model appear. However, the apprentice, just like any growing teenager, gradually begins to find their feet and develop their own ideas. They sometimes outperform the master and this is when tensions start to emerge. The resultant power dynamic causes strain and some fractures appear in the carefully constructed heterogeneous teams. When I first observed some genuinely-heated arguments between colleagues, my first instinct was to intervene. How could an inexperienced colleague turn on and criticize their mentor? This was, again, anti-co-operation! However, I soon discovered that, over time, if left alone, this turmoil and argument has often righted itself and newly co-constructed ideas have flourished. As explained above, new SIGlets were born as these ideas were no longer found suitable for the original groups. But it left me with more questions to be answered about the nature of these relationships and the interconnections between collegiality and co-operation. The process of co-constructing depends on repeated dialogue. This cyclic approach is exploited through the 'plan, do, study, act' (PDSA) development tasks in which the SIGs are actively engaged. Further conflicts arise when, having moved together in a differentiated but coherent learning activity, sub-groups within the SIGs are asked to abandon their learning outcomes in preference for others that 'fit' the overall strategy. Disagreements need to be articulated and debated openly if progress is to be made towards creating new forms of knowledge and practice. In reality, this rarely happens openly in the SIGs, despite 'openness' being one of the ethical co-operative values. Tensions wax and wane over time. Leadership must therefore recognize that this is not really a loss in momentum but a necessary prelude to the next stage of development.

Returning to collegiality through this argument, we can see how we might explain the loss of spontaneity and decline in development oriented approaches. Not all experience leads to knowing; something remains emotional, unarticulated and subconscious. Actions that are habitual, including ways of thinking, are disturbed, and a commitment to collective inquiry is activated. The division of effort is made more complex by recognizing Hargreaves' notion of presentism among people who have made initial changes and can see the impact. They do not typically now display the same effort or support for others in the development of concepts and projects that they enjoyed earlier on in their evolving practice. Early adopters of co-operative learning are sometimes reluctant to accept new or more transformational practices, even when they are co-constructed, so remain hostages to their past. They have taken retrogressive steps, and mutated newer approaches back into what was once new and innovative, but has now been superseded. We do things we are unaware of. The negotiation of power on this level drives the conflict between the group objective and the members of the team. The contention that people can be at one time co-operative in a common enterprise and at the same time rivals for the material and tangible rewards of successful competition is valid and accurate (Blase 1991). But activity-based teams need them both to achieve mutual benefit through social change. People use strategies such as compliance patterns and socialization in the division of effort. This is because opportunities for choice will bring to the surface different views on goals and micro-political interactions. As a result both conflict and consensus underpins relationships in the SIG. Power may still be the common currency of all negotiation and the basis for all social and organizational behaviour. Personal motives for participation will vary and include the potential for career enhancement through action research. Despite the open articulation of a democratic approach, hierarchical relationships and forms of action are still very much in evidence at Lipson.

Our understanding of collegiality can be deepened by considering the links between the activities and the identity of participants. Members interact and engage in common activities, help each other, and share information. They build relationships to learn from each other and this learning creates and transforms human *identity*. This has been particularly powerful in motivating and sustaining teachers' enthusiasm and commitment early in their careers. Yet, there are a number of factors which work to challenge this growth. The SIG community has rules to follow about meeting times and deadlines so that their activities are not pervasive through time and space, despite the aspiration for 'anytime, anywhere' learning. Confidence comes from members of the SIG who meet deadlines and get praise rather than transforming broader outcomes. In addition, it is through the act of *participation* that identity is constructed: it is not what you know but who you are and what you become in the practice. This has serious implications for the use of peer mentors in the SIG as these are already largely based on the MKOs. When people are knowledgeable in one area but not experienced or actively participating in others, conflict can arise and, as a result, the validity of dissemination workshops has been challenged. Those who stand up and run workshops 'voluntarily' in the SIG sometimes affect the identity of others in a destructive way in a new context where one's mentee takes risks and gains accolades leading to a sense of inadequacy amongst those who originally were seen as pioneers.

Moreover, the SIG does not operate in a vacuum and identity can be constructed in relation to imposed performance criteria such as the Teachers' Standards or external government-driven statements and policies. The regular (planned?) changes to the examination system, curriculum, inspection framework and other surveillance mechanisms can cause alienation resulting in a sense of crisis and of loss. Tensions, both temporal and emotional are seen to pull members of the SIG in conflicting directions leading to exasperating questions, for instance, whether they should be focusing on the 'learning game or the results game'. Members often test the viability and achievability of their own work and beliefs by making comparisons to those around them, and teams will have passed through different processes of both self-determined and socially-determined professional identity (Stoll et al. 2003). In this context, the ability to change quickly, rather than applying known wisdom is a valuable asset.

The SIG community has both explicit and implicit rules which help to define the position of members and their activity. In order to understand participation, implicit socio-cultural factors (Lloyd and Cronin 2002) play a significant role alongside the articulated rules. All teachers operate under regular legal rules but this SIG also developed rules about collegiality and how pedagogical tools can and cannot be used. Over time, as these rules were agreed, and formed the basis for achievements in the school, a vested interest emerged to perpetuate them. Such conservatism and contrived collegiality can undermine innovation and spontaneity. Thus, rules can stimulate creativity as well as prevent further pedagogical change. In looking at the ways in which rules can be changed it is not always easy to determine if co-operation has been elicited by skilful micro-politicizing or through freely given collegiate action. When new teachers are inducted into the SIG, they may negotiate rules and build new consciousness but may, at the same time, be operating in a destructive way. By speaking and listening to others, a co-operative identity can be constructed which resists surveillance tools and naïve judgements about their effectiveness. People position themselves in relation to the social and cultural context. They use the value of self-help and self-responsibility to enhance participation. They do this best when they are given adequate space and time. Solidarity emerges in 'bargaining' relationships about strengths and weaknesses.

Summary and conclusions

Lipson, the school in which the SIG was fashioned remains a culturally strong school, aligned in its constitution and heart to the co-operative ideal. It does not have 'collaborative pretence' (Grimmett and Crehan 1992), even if collegiality is somewhat contrived. We have seen this in the areas of leadership, relationships and identity. This culturally strong school is built upon tightly structured belief values and norms with loosely-coupled organizational structures, causing one to think less and feel more. However, to establish a strong culture, more work in developing collaborative interdependence is needed. To do this we need to find answers to the problems that remain for us concerning the distribution of power, not over people but over accomplishments; the methods to foster experimentation and risk-taking whilst maintaining strength over norms to encourage and be open to feedback; and continuing a process of self-monitoring in a socially-constructed context in order to stimulate further developments while avoiding surveillance and damaging power dynamics.

Democratic professional development takes professional learning beyond mere reflection and dependence upon outside experts into an arena where teachers develop new ideas together. It creates a greater readiness to experiment and a commitment to continuous improvement. Transformation occurs as new leaders emerge, with or without legitimacy. There is a need for greater attention to the *co-operative* as opposed to the *conflicting* dynamics of micro-politics in schools, as favoured by Blase (1991). Leadership must adapt and be allowed to grow rhizomatically through the emulation of those who succeed. The co-operative practice illuminated above has the potential to develop and re-form the elements of collegiate practice.

However, conflict is where transformation can occur, and provides an opportunity to explore issues of divergence and creativity. Learning, after all, *is* change. In exploring the work of the SIG, the barriers of conservatism, individualism and presentism suggested by Hargreaves (2008) actually give way to more challenging issues, and unforeseen consequences relating to conflict, power struggles and identity. Much of the work written on contrived collegiality tends to argue that teams are functional or dysfunctional with the focus on the individual; this has not been useful in exploring the SIG. It is not helpful to suggest that we can explain peoples' actions singularly within a collaborative setting. Using one team as a contextually based example, I have shown that, conflicts and tensions are inevitable in the change process. Through co-construction it is possible to challenge the limits that Hargreaves presents. We can collectively produce a culturally mediated and democratic version of professional development that embraces internal tensions and contradictions and use them as a force for improvement. In doing so, it is necessary to pay attention to continuing transitions and transformations within any given activity system. Hierarchical assumptions regularly clash with individual goal-driven behaviour. It is also necessary to think in holistic ways and to avoid separating out components of identity, practice, outcome and object from a co-operative enterprise – small fluctuations in any component will cause wider changes.

Within the co-operative enterprise of the SIGs, only some of the conditions defined by Hargreaves (2008) have been met. We have to accept that collegiality is difficult to implement and will only be seen sporadically. School culture is influenced by sub-cultures and values that bind people together but are overlaid with, sometimes contrary, personal perspectives and career trajectories. Collegiality is in fact culturally and organizationally induced and when we promote bottom-up problem solving supported by co-operation, there is some hope of moving the SIG to interdependence. This does not deny the potential role for professional recognition, professional involvement and reward which can also help to create a high sense of efficacy.

But it may be necessary to ignore or make compromises with constraints and surveillance mechanisms, notably the inspection regime, that have superimposed different forms of potentially innovative collegiate practices, thus further marginalizing co-operative work. In this sense, Hargreaves' notion of collegiality is unrealistic in schools in the current educational framework. There are some factors that are part of the wider political context that are external to schools but have a determining influence on internal practices. Under the Coalition Government, educational policies swing wildly from one extreme such as wholesale structural reforms like free schools and academies to political interference in the minutiae of how children should be taught to read, such as synthetic phonics. The marketization of schools is destroying, or reimagining, the relationship between professionalism and knowledge; this 'assault of audit culture' is actively changing identities. Hargreaves (2008) encourages our thinking to be a little less focused on initiative overload and micromanagement, and a bit more 'Finnish'. In Finland steadiness is praised and teachers are more likely to be trusted to find best solutions without having one's motives questioned.

Questions can be raised about the rights of the individual in the face of group pressure. Norms of collegiality could be seen as another form of imposition, and the protection of individuality and discretion of judgements, as a protection of their right to disagree and reflect critically on what they are being asked to collaborate on. Is it acceptable to commit, not to developing and realizing purposes of one's own, but to implement purposes devised by others in organizationally-contrived collegiate activities?

References

Blase, J. (ed.) (1991) *The Politics of Life in Schools*, London: Sage.
Dweck, C. (2006) *Growth Mindset: the New Psychology of Success*, New York: Random House.
Eun, B. (2010) 'From learning to development: a sociocultural approach to instruction', *Cambridge Journal of Education*, 4: 401–418.
Grimmett, P. and Crehan, E. (1992) 'The nature of collegiality in teacher development: the case of clinical supervision', in Fullen, M. and Hargreaves, A. (eds) *Teacher Development and Change*, London: Falmer Press.
Hargreaves, A. (1991) 'Contrived collegiality: the micro-politics of teacher collaboration', in Blase, J. (ed.) *The Politics of Life in Schools*, London: Sage.
—— (2008) 'The persistence of presentism and the struggle for lasting improvement – an inaugural lecture', Institute of Education: University of London.
Johnson, D. and Johnson, T. (1998) *Learning Together and Alone: Co-operative, Competitive and Individualistic Learning*, London: Pearson.
Kagan, S. (2006) *Co-operative Learning*, California: Kagan Publishing.
Lloyd, M. and Cronin, R. (2002) 'A community of teachers: using activity theory to investigate the implementation of ICTE in a remote indigenous school', in Proceedings AARE 2002, Brisbane, Queensland.
Ofsted (Office for Standards in Education) (2008) Inspection report – Lipson Community College, www.ofsted.gov.uk
—— (2010) Inspection report – Lipson Community College, www.ofsted.gov.uk
—— (2012) 'Best practice guide – Lipson Community College', www.ofsted.gov.uk
Slavin, R. (1980) 'Cooperative learning', *Review of Educational Research*, 50: 315–342.
Stoll, L., Fink, D. and Earl, L. (2003) *It's About Learning*, Abingdon: Routledge Falmer.
Vygotsky, L.S. (1978) *Mind and Society: The Development of Higher Mental Processes*, Cambridge, MA: Harvard University Press.

7
Co-operative democracy in practice – a learner's perspective

Ashley Simpson

This chapter offers a case study perspective of someone who has been a student at a co-operative school and is now working with other co-operative schools across England. I will analyse the effects on a school before and after the adoption of co-operative structures, values and principles and will chart the ways in which both the school, and the individuals within it, including myself, were transformed through the initial development of democratic ideas and co-operative structures. On school, community and personal levels, this process has wrought significant changes. In outlining some key themes of successful co-operative schools, I will argue that connections need to be made between these various aspects of school organization and wider aspects of social life.

The first co-operative trust school was established at Reddish Vale, Stockport, in 2008. There was a widespread feeling that the status quo had to change in the ways that the school related to the pupils and wider community. Critically, there was a need to engage and empower the previously isolated and disillusioned sections of the Reddish community, as low aspirations and lack of cohesion were being expressed inside the school and the effect was disengagement by pupils. The proposed solution was a democratically controlled co-operative school, where parents, pupils, staff and community members had a voice. The theory became a reality in 2008 when the school became the first co-operative trust school in the country and, with it, an effective framework for an education to be underpinned by the values and principles of co-operation was developed. The problems that faced my school were common to many other schools, problems that remain today. There is an often held perception by scholars of radical and democratic educational traditions that mainstream schools operate as battery-caged hen coups and are rigidly divided by institutionalized boundaries (Fielding and Moss 2011). Elements of this tendency could be identified at my school which were pitted against the prospect of change at Reddish Vale. This chapter will explore the ways in which co-operative schooling was adopted as a means for individuals and communities to improve and change their lives. The first section will explore the linkages between civil society, citizenship and the desire to create a critically-aware democracy. The context of Reddish Vale before 2008 will be considered alongside the processes through which the school was transformed from a state comprehensive school to a co-operative trust school in 2008. Co-operative structures and pedagogies were created by embedding co-operative values and principles throughout all aspects of school life. However, co-operative schools have faced a number of difficulties which reflect the complexities of this transition in relation to the interests of a number of different stakeholders. Finally, I will document some longer-term issues inherent in the co-operative schools' movement.

Co-operative education promises to have a significant impact on improving people's lives, and it is this approach to education and learning which has the capacity to meet the needs of young people today. My personal participation in the Reddish Vale Co-operative Trust inspired me and created new opportunities. I actively engaged with the ideas of a democratic civic society, and became politically involved with the Co-operative Party of which now I am the North West representative on the national youth committee. My participation in a co-operative school further catalysed my involvement in the supporters' trust movement in football. In 2012, I chaired the Stockport County Supporters' Co-operative, seeking to give a democratic and representative voice to supporters. Most importantly however, it enabled me to go to university, to study politics at the University of Leeds. In September 2013, I started a Master's degree in international relations at the University of Manchester. I accredit my personal journey through activism and higher education primarily to the skills, knowledge and foresight I obtained during the foundation years of England's first co-operative trust school.

Education as emancipation for young people

Co-operative education is widely seen as a way in which young people can more actively engage with civil society and politics. The context of young people's status and the ways they interact socially, politically and economically are complex. Education is not simply bound by economic factors, but directly connects to the social and political roles that young people play, what Gert Biesta calls the 'political role of education' (Biesta 2012: 690). A critical form of education that engages young people locally at a community-based level is an essential precursor to an active civil society. Involving young people in a pluralistic form of schooling, with ownership and democratic structures embracing the whole community, will have societal benefits. This is why Hannah Arendt maintained that 'plurality is the condition of human action' (Arendt and Canovan 1998: 8), a notion that connects to what Michael Fielding has termed an inclusive emancipatory community (Fielding 2001). Co-operative education, through its values and principles, can offer an emancipatory alternative contributing to a dynamic civil society with young people at its centre.

Democracy, pluralism and co-operation do not exist in a vacuum but have to contend with the forces of political and social conformity within the dominant discourse of neoliberal economics. New relationships within the public service sphere have given rise to 'citizen-consumers' in which market principles are widely accepted (Biesta 2012: 685). The on-going privatization and de-politicization of public spaces and places, not least in education itself, has resulted in growing political apathy (Biesta 2012). In my experience, a deep sense of entrenched disillusionment pervades many young people today. This disenchantment in our education system cannot be plastered over by a few school trips here, a few extra-curricular activities there, it is embedded in our culture, in our institutions and the very walls of our schools.

One way forward is to engage and empower young people to build a practice of participation and a critical approach to knowledge over a sustained period of time. This is not only about creating a critical learning and education system, ultimately it is about creating a healthy and responsive democracy. Education and learning should openly embrace the wider world and young people should not be isolated from wider forms of political action. By political action I mean issues that can be solved through democratic discussion and pluralist action, whether that be protecting youth services, holding referenda in schools or initiating social outreach programmes. As a young person myself, the disenfranchisement of a sizeable group of young people, is visible. To get to the root of these issues, we need to assert the responsibilities of educators, teachers and the whole society to engage them in meaningful action. Significant social benefits would also accrue from politicizing young people within a healthy and pluralist democracy (Mouffe 1992). As Jurgen Habermas argued, culture and education should not be 'restricted to the ethical dimension of personal attitude', but rather, form a rich understanding of the world (Outhwaite 1996: 42).

In South Manchester, the co-operative approach to education was perceived to be a significant way of addressing these issues through pluralism, co-operative values and the empowerment of young people. The personal interactions, relationships and processes at the heart of this educational initiative offer fascinating insights into democratic change in schooling.

Reddish Vale Technology College

Reddish Vale Technology College is situated on the outskirts of Greater Manchester in the Metropolitan Borough of Stockport. White British is the predominant ethnicity, the human poverty index, including, longevity, literacy, unemployment and income for Reddish is 14.4, exactly the national average. However, it is important to note that Reddish compares poorly to the other parliamentary constituencies of Stockport: for example, Hazel Grove is 10.9 and Cheadle is 7.9 (Seymore 2000: 147-156). Throughout the time of my secondary school education (2003-2008), Stockport Metropolitan Borough Council had a Liberal Democrat majority at a local government level. By contrast, Reddish's main catchment areas, the Reddish

North and Reddish South council wards, plus the parliamentary constituency, were all occupied by Labour councillors and a Labour MP. From 2007, the relationship between the school and this wider context would change significantly.

As a year ten student in 2007, school was enjoyable but frustrating. Personally I had no issues with attendance and attainment but a significant number of people at the school did. My general feeling of frustration was borne out of a general feeling that the status quo was stagnant, there was little to energize and enthuse. School trips and extracurricular activities focused on replicating the same endeavours year-on-year. Nothing was new, and importantly, nothing was being done to address the issues in the community. At the time Reddish Vale had an Ofsted inspection and received grade two: 'Reddish Vale Technology College is a good school. Some aspects of the College's work, such as the provision for care, guidance and support, are outstanding' (Ofsted 2007:4). However this did not reflect the real picture of how socio-economic issues had infiltrated the school; problems in the external community were now reflected within the classroom and on the playing fields. The combination of low aspirations, a lack of community cohesion which prevented young people from taking an active role in the community, and limited opportunities for young people, meant that many young people were 'left behind' or, more critically put, were 'failed'. Moreover, there was a general consensus among students that traditional forms of representation within the school were neither efficient nor effective. Those 'elected' onto the school council were in effect nominated by teachers, the 'good' people or the 'popular' people mainly, which was not democratic. This is what Fielding (2001) has characterized as a traditional and safe form of 'student voice' as opposed to the 'radical inclusion' of voices that are seldom heard. There was a need to go beyond the traditional paradigm of student voice and student councils. At that time, many of the questions we posed ourselves were based on inclusion: how could we open up these structures to nurture an active democracy; how could we include all the stakeholders of the school through new forms of representation; how could we put this new approach into practice on the ground; and who would take the lead? Moreover, this sense of ineffective representation was not merely felt by the young people but also among others in the community, parents and staff.

A number of people came together in order to address issues of social and political neglect. I remember vividly being asked to stay behind one evening after school. I shared a sense of malaise and was asking critical questions, but, at that time, was not aware of an alternative. I was told to go to the library where discussions on the nature of the school, the problems it faced and the ways to combat them, were taking place. There were three of us in the room, the director of college improvement, a friend of mine and myself. We articulated our sense of disillusionment, neglect and frustration and began to develop a response. We argued that the education and learning at Reddish Vale had lost its purpose. True, young people continued to get qualifications year after year, but there was little purpose to it. In developing an alternative strategy, the problems of our present predicament became clearer as we realized that the exclusive focus on results was leading schools away from their role in citizenship and local communities. I was presented with a yellow sheet of paper on which were written the key values and principles of the co-operative movement. These values and principles instantly fused with me, they seemed rational, reasonable, and a good basis on which to run a school. They provided a clearly defined structure which meant that people were able to identify tangible outcomes as part of an alternative approach to education. This meeting was significant on a number of levels. We rediscovered a wider social purpose of education beyond the institutionalized school targets and assessments. A new approach had to ensue. On a personal level this would put me at the epicentre of a new movement in co-operative schooling. I committed myself to a project which would be built steadily over time. This marked the start of a personal journey of experiences, responsibilities and beliefs that have transformed me personally, notwithstanding the transformation of the school and the young people who have since walked through the doors of the school.

However, it was not all plain sailing and what seemed obvious to me met with varied opposition elsewhere. During 2007, I was involved with stakeholder consultation with various organizations. Without doubt, some of them were against change, in particular I remember a meeting with a feeder primary school who were vehemently against my participation in the meeting. In such cases, the fear of democracy from those in established positions and not wanting to lose control, were tangible. Resistance during the consultation period was widespread across all stakeholders, from teaching staff, senior management and community stakeholders alike. The fears and insecurities ranged from staff who were concerned about pensions and pay, senior management and parents who were worried about changes in admissions procedures, to key members of the community such as local politicians who felt the school should not be taken out of local authority control and justified this on the grounds of democracy. Resistance to change at Reddish Vale also resulted from a fear of embracing democratic ideals and how they could be practised. For example, the headteacher and some other senior leaders were initially opposed to student input in the running of the school, whether that be participating in staff appointments or leading campaigns. This passive resistance partially undermined the co-operative project and reflected Noam Chomsky's claim that the fear of democracy is 'entrenched' across society (Chomsky and Macedo 2000: 44). A forum was established to represent the various stakeholder groups within an emerging democratic structure. It provided a way of airing and discussing concerns and issues and also provided a way of mediating those who feared the democratic direction of change. However, from the stakeholder forum the views/decisions/strategies of the project would be enacted through a small working group who were committed in developing democracy within the school. Crucially, the senior leadership team (SLT) held reservations about the transition to democracy and deployed tactics of passive resistance by ignoring or disassociating themselves with certain aspects of the change within the school. These issues highlight the fragility of building democracy at moments of transition. It became clear that the reticence of the SLT could not be resolved in these early stages of development but had to be managed as part of a process of democratic change and improving standards within the school.

Under the 2006 Education and Inspections Act, being a trust school meant that the governance of schools, and control of the land and assets, increasingly shifted from local authorities to the governing body and community stakeholders. At Reddish Vale, young people latched onto the sense of ownership, identity and belonging which opened up on becoming a co-operative trust school. In 2008, despite the consultation teething problems, Reddish Vale Technology College became the UK's first co-operative trust school. In essence this meant Reddish Vale became a multi-stakeholder co-operative made up of voluntary members from staff, community, parents and carers as well as partners from public, private and third sector organizations. Importantly for me, and what made it different, was that we were including the learners as full members of this – 'our' – co-operative. Young people now had the same rights as any of the other adult members involved. These rights, and a commitment to a co-operative approach, were enshrined in the articles of our new charitable trust. One person-one vote democracy and a right to parity of voice was integral to our vision. Gradually, the relationship between students and the school changed as young people gained a sense of belonging that resulted from the shift in ownership. The transition was an essential first step in building a democratic values-based school.

The values and principles of the co-operative movement had an umbrella effect over the school, protecting our identity through a clearly defined framework, bringing everyone together as part of a shared project. Creating spaces within the school for the recognition and participation of the wider community helped to bring about an important shift in attitudes and practices. We deemed it essential to ground our approach in mutual self-help and collectively agreed common goals by working together, contrary to the dominant trends towards privatization and competition. We aimed to fuse personal and social development by giving participants an equal status and creating a harmonious school where relationships with teachers, students, parents, or even a community group on the periphery, would be underpinned by trust and mutually-defined goals. Chomsky has summarized this impulse in explaining how democracy needs to be based upon a broad conception of human development,

> Human beings whose values were not an accumulation of domination but, rather, free association on terms of equality and sharing and cooperation, participating on equal terms to achieve common goals that were democratically conceived.
>
> *(Chomsky and Macedo 2000: 39)*

Prior to conversion, the school was marked by a lack of democracy in which the voices of young people were severely limited, a fact that frustrated me considerably. When I subsequently thought about the role of the parents and the teachers, that same sense of disenfranchisement was evident; the school showed little 'concern for publicness' (Biesta 2012: 685). By contrast, becoming a co-operative trust school gave stakeholders a degree of self-determination. The question we asked ourselves was, how can we develop and expand democracy in the school and in the community? Central to this rationale was a concern to listen to the community and our perceived need to engage publicly with wider constituencies. Within the school, this sense of publicness was initially built on international grounds when Reddish Vale set up an Ethiopian Fairtrade coffee co-operative in 2008, owned and run by the young people at the school. Within the community of Reddish, pupils established a creative arts co-operative which included the performance of drama, dance and music. While many co-operative schools run these types of community out-reach programmes, I believe this is inadequate as a basis to develop a co-operative culture, embed co-operative pedagogy or bring about change within the community.

Within a year of conversion, an organization called Youth Space would be set up by my friend who had also been at the key meeting in the library. The broad aim of Youth Space was to enact change through the ethos of co-operation, a concept designed to give young people a 'space' which they could use as a platform for reaching their goals and to exceed society's expectations. The aims were to change the relationship young people had with civil society by empowering them democratically through local politicized action, to challenge negative media stereotypes of young people by presenting them as role models in their community, and to provide a collective voice for young people by creating a forum where they could meet, socialize and discuss their grievances. Youth Space had a major impact upon the school in nurturing new forms of youth support that became widely accessible. Some young people became 'self-helpers' able to challenge competitive orthodoxies while contributing to civil society. Energies have been channelled through the use of social media and new technologies in order to develop projects that connect with the broader constituencies. The future leaders programme aimed to inspire and encourage young people to take a lead role in community activism by learning the skills of community organizing including promoting community and applying for grant funding. Students themselves organized a community fun day to launch Youth Space. The initiative fed back into the success of educational strategies in the school itself by working in collaboration with Human Utopia, a social enterprise which aims to raise the aspirations of young people, staff and communities by directly addressing Ofsted outcomes. These workshops focused on the emotional wellbeing of young people and aimed to create a sense of commonality and belonging by addressing the simple question, 'What do I owe Reddish Vale?' All of these projects were enacted as a direct result of being a co-operative school and by giving young people a voice through community activism.

In 2012, Reddish Vale Co-operative Trust school was converted to a co-operative academy trust school and we had to agree the composition of the governing body and other associated committees. This process was the next evolutionary step in a democratic process which also enabled the school to achieve a greater sense of autonomy. One immediate practical impact was a series of referenda within the school whereby students voted on an array of issues, including school uniforms and the toilets, and although these issues were not that significant, they nonetheless engaged the young people in ways that had not been done previously. Furthermore, to embed democracy, those driving the co-operative project argued that students needed to be at the heart of decision making through staff appointments, referenda, in addition to having the freedom to initiate and manage specific projects, campaigns and social enterprises. Giving young people these responsibilities would be an anathema to most in society, but the Reddish Vale approach of putting young people first resulted in increasing numbers of students participating in the decision-making process. The momentum behind the stakeholder group continued to emphasize the creation of opportunities for participation, engagement and empowerment which could not be confined to narrow or technical issues. For example, we felt it was essential to have a young person's voice at governors' meetings. As there was an age restriction on current students serving as a governor, a former student who had previously helped to set up the co-operative trust, and who was still running projects at the school, took on the role.

This youthful dynamism and promotion of democracy has resulted in better internal relationships, especially between students and teachers. It also fed into the results achieved by the school. In 2012, Reddish Vale received its highest ever GCSE results: 62 per cent obtaining five A*-C including maths and English. The democratic foundations we built back in 2008 can be credited with some of this success. This is a long-term process which must respect the various interests of all stakeholders if they are to contribute to a vibrant and successful school.

Challenges facing co-operative schools

From my experience at Reddish Vale, and in working with other schools within the co-operative network, it has become clear that a number of long-term issues could pose significant challenges to the movement. My aim is to highlight some problems which I hope can be avoided at other schools. Teaching is a fundamental concern for these schools. The general insecurity of teachers which is already fuelled by rapid social and educational change can, in certain cases, be compounded by a further transformation in a co-operative direction. Teachers are already under considerable pressure to meet targets and the fear of a potential economic impact on their position can undermine progress. Co-operative models are also sometimes identified with neoliberal trends which facilitate the privatization and marketization of public services and assets. By contrast, other teachers have accepted neoliberal assumptions and, for example, question any attempt to introduce alternatives to the mainstream business and enterprise curriculum.

Indeed in developing co-operative schooling, it is essential to create co-operative pedagogy within the classroom to help illustrate the practical and ethical advantages of co-operation. It will be crucial for co-operative schools to capture a sense of democratic transition in the school as a whole as well as the classroom in particular, as a stepping stone to deeper co-operative engagement, across the whole of the curriculum and pedagogy. Undoubtedly, this is a hard area to address.

Beyond the classroom, there are considerable advantages in focusing upon the needs of young people. At a number of schools, students have generally found it easy to pick up these ideas and run with them by translating co-operative ideals and values into tangible, practical, actions which result in campaigns and projects on the ground. Yet, embedding a meaningful co-operative structure poses further significant problems. Even though co-operative trust schools call themselves co-operatives, hierarchical assumptions may continue to be felt. The tensions between a group of pupils and teachers at Reddish Vale, in comparison with the reservations of some staff at senior management, illustrated this clearly. In this case, there was a need to carefully negotiate the relationships between pupils, teachers and governors. Bottom-up demands for change can lead to disagreement with those who would prefer to slow the pace of change. Managing and resolving these debates is crucial if co-operative values and principles are to be embedded in schools.

The actual structures of co-operative schools are often focused on one person, whether it be someone in senior leadership or on the general teaching staff. The actual management in some co-operative schools is not always devolved throughout the structure of the school. In fact, the management side of the school can easily become isolated from the co-operative approach. As a result, there are a lot of co-operative trust schools which only have 'co-operative trust' in their name. I recall visiting one school which had been converted to a co-operative school for nearly three years, and at the time had not set up a membership structure in order to encourage the participation of stakeholder groups. Developing a system of membership is essential in building feelings of belonging and association with the co-operative. Ultimately, for the co-operative to succeed, people need to opt in, and the school needs to convince potential members that this cause is worthy of their support. Many successful co-operatives offer specific benefits and incentives to members. But membership can also help to articulate the wider reasons for favouring democratic schooling. Stakeholders are able to air grievances and develop a sense of common purpose. In short, membership provides a key democratic principle which provides students, parents, staff and community with a democratic voice.

One would be naïve to suggest that communities have yet fully embraced this potential. The apathy of the community is often based upon a mistrust of schools and low expectations. Reddish Vale's stakeholder engagement is still emerging and has faced difficulties in implementing a coherent community dialogue. However, the stakeholder forum does have the potential to release democratic energies by bringing together students, parents, staff and the community for the good of all. The forum allows for elections and open, transparent and accountable ways of running a school. The Brigshaw Trust in Leeds has effectively embraced primary schools, a secondary school, a language college, children's centres and a vast array of community organizations, for mutual benefit.

A further internal tension relates to the rapid growth of the movement. Expanding too quickly, especially in response to politically-imposed targets, and without a sufficient resource base, carries significant dangers for the emerging democratic nature of these schools. It is important not to dilute the prospect of democracy and the potential impact that can have on transforming individuals and communities. A mutual network of successful schools sharing practice across regions is a logical development but it takes time to build trust and co-operation. My fear is that, in responding to both positive and negative policy directives, some co-operative schools start to fail without adequate support from a movement that has not sufficiently built up its capacities for support.

Co-operative schools not only face internal pressures but also operate within a very challenging wider context. The undermining of public and community services has impacted on the social fabric and caused considerable disruption over a number of generations, processes that have been exacerbated exponentially since the 2008 banking crisis. A co-operative school can be a mechanism to help address elements of this disruption by tackling community issues on its doorstep. The Reddish Vale approach was based upon creating a responsive network of people of all ages, whereby community actors could respond effectively to local issues. Young people in particular emphasized the lack of local and youth services. Reddish Vale became an active partner in the Reddish ROC (Redeeming Our Communities) café which opened in April 2010 and provided a place for young people to socialize after school. It developed in the wake of the decline in existing services and aimed to address anti-social behaviour. Community groups and individuals started to co-operate on joint community projects and funding applications such as an allotments project to produce locally sourced food. I felt a strong sense of citizenship and ownership emerge among those active in this process which helped us to see the school as about much more than the young people who entered and left every day, as the beginnings of a much more inclusive, responsive and more just local community.

I am under no illusions. The co-operative schools' movement to some extent is working against the direction of current education policy. While some have actively embraced democracy and a bottom-up approach, and all the co-operative practices that go with it, other schools have been unable to do so, especially where there has been an over-reliance on a management perspective and on one or two individuals. Building a successful co-operative management structure is as important as building a pedagogy for learners. There needs to be a convergence in leadership, where top-down meets bottom-up, through new forms of dialogue. Such relationships take time to change, a shift which has been facilitated by the visible success of co-operative schools. In Reddish, this can be seen in relation to local politicians who were, at the start, wary about our proposals. Initially, the local Labour MP did not support it, but gradually became more supportive of the school and its endeavours. The local councillors were a little more responsive but their attitude could also be lukewarm. Over time, these attitudes shifted with the success of the initiative in developing a democratic response to the rapid and deepening changes in schooling.

Conclusions

This chapter has offered a case study perspective from a personal point of view. I outlined the synergies between education, learning, citizenship, and how these elements can be part of a healthy and critical democracy. In mapping out the processes and key practical ways in which Reddish Vale School was transformed from a state comprehensive to a co-operative trust, I emphasized the importance of the voice and action of young people as well as other stakeholders. Co-operative structures and pedagogy were developed by embedding co-operative values and principles throughout all aspects of school life. Co-operative schools aim, in theory, to democratically empower an array of stakeholders. If this is to become a reality, new structures, systems and technologies are needed to support young people in breaking out of competitive and elitist educational practices. Through their experience at a co-operative school, young people should develop the ability to change their lives, their communities, and the wider world in the future. But the long-term consequences of these processes are unclear and co-operative schools continue to face many difficulties. From the beginning, the transition to a co-operative school can be complex in dealing with multiple stakeholders. The rapid expansion of co-operative schooling has left many questions that still need to be answered.

Co-operative schools do, however, raise some fundamental issues about education and the way we live now. They offer the potential to develop democratic education by reinforcing the principles of liberty and social justice. Co-operative education has the potential to address not only educational issues but also, as part of wider strategies, those relating to poverty and wider social issues. Social justice as a concept raises the crucial issue of the purpose of education. Chomsky talks about the aim of education being to help create 'wise citizens of a free community', that encourages a combination of citizenship with liberty and individual creativeness (Chomsky and Macedo 2000: 38), a claim which fits closely with my vision of co-operative education. It offers a chance for the construction of inclusive communities across lines of difference within a pluralistic democracy rather than fostering a competitive 'them' and 'us' situation (Mouffe 1992: 32). A healthy parliamentary democracy will always depend upon a broader pluralistic democracy based upon active citizenship which acts as a safeguard for shared values and principles. Political identities should be constituted from these wider collective forms of political identity and democratic demands (Mouffe 1992:31).

Throughout my journey as part of a co-operative school, and in later years working in the network of co-operative schools, the sense of liberty and citizenship has resonated strongly with me. Fundamentally, being part of these value-driven democratic processes has made me become aware politically and socially. I developed as a person and became critically conscious of the injustices that prevail in society. Importantly, I became able to identify these injustices, and more importantly, to actively challenge them. Being part of England's first co-operative trust school has convinced me that positive change for the benefit of individuals and communities can happen. That people coming together for mutually beneficial causes can change the world and improve the prospects of people's lives.

References

Arendt, H. and Canovan, M. (1998) *The Human Condition*, Chicago: University of Chicago Press.
Biesta, G. (2012) 'Becoming public: public pedagogy, citizenship and the public sphere', *Social & Cultural Geography*, 13 (7), pp. 683–697.
Chomsky, N. and Macedo, D. (2000) *Chomsky on Miseducation*, Lanham, MD.: Rowman & Littlefield Publishers.
Fielding, M. (2001) 'Students as radical agents of change', *Journal of Educational Change*, 2/2: 123–141.
Fielding, M. and Moss, P. (2011) *Radical Education and the Common School. A Democratic Alternative*, London: Routledge.
Mouffe, C. (1992) 'Citizenship and political identity', *October*, 61: 28–32.
Ofsted (2007) Reddish Vale Technology College, inspection report, OFSTED.
Outhwaite, W. (1996) *The Harbermas Reader*, Cambridge: Polity Press.
Seymore, J. (2000) '"Appendix 4, Human Poverty Index for British Parliamentary Constituencies and OECD Countries", Poverty in Plenty: A Human Development Report for the UK', [report] London: Sterling Earthscan Publications Ltd.

8
The impact of co-operative skills and approaches on young people's development and attainment: an ASDAN perspective

Dave Brockington

Over three decades, an organization called ASDAN, which I helped to found, has promoted co-operative skills and co-operative learning and teaching which have had a direct impact upon the personal development and the academic attainment of young people. In answer to W. B. Yeats' question, paraphrasing Plutarch (1992: 50), whether education is more like lighting fires or filling pails, ASDAN has generally favoured the former although there is a bit of both processes going on in any educational encounter. In fact ASDAN has helped to light a few fires and succeeded in keeping some burning. It is a national educational charity and also an approved national awarding body which has promoted learning-to-learn skills, skills for employability and skills for life since its inception in the early 1980s. Annually, over 200,000 learners follow one or another of a wide range of curriculum programmes and qualifications that we have developed. Most secondary schools in the country are registered with ASDAN, almost two-thirds of further education colleges and many post-16 training and apprenticeship providers. The ASDAN pedagogic model emerged originally from responses to the raising of the school leaving age policy intervention in the early 1970s and the questions which arose at the time concerning appropriate teaching and learning within secondary education (Brockington and White 1978). The emerging model drew also on theoretical insights informed by Bernstein's work on framing (Bernstein 1971), Bloom's work on the taxonomy of educational objectives in the cognitive and affective domains (Bloom 1956, 1965) and, more latterly, on Dweck's work on motivation and mindset (Dweck 2006, 2012) as well as Watkins' work on learning orientation (Watkins 2010).

In the last five years we have worked with the Co-operative College alongside teachers from co-operative trust schools, now the fastest growing and largest network of schools in the country besides the Church of England and the Roman Catholic faith school networks, to develop curriculum support and accreditation materials for co-operative studies from Key Stage 2 to Key Stage 5. Co-operative studies is based upon the application of co-operative values to an educational setting and has a widespread potential in the English school system. Topics and activities covered in these materials include explorations of democracy, Fairtrade and ethical enterprise, the nature of co-operatives and ideas for planning and developing co-operative businesses and practices (ASDAN 2014a, 2014b). Co-operative approaches to teaching and learning are also being disseminated to a wider audience through the national network of co-operative schools represented by the Schools Co-operative Society (SCS).

Co-operative education has helped us to connect narrow definitions of skills to wider contexts. The recent international banking and financial services crisis, which has adversely affected the lives of millions of people across the globe, was arguably not caused by any deficit in the teaching and learning of 'maths', no doubt to the relief of teachers who are often blamed for social and economic failures. More credibly, it might be proposed that a deficit of 'values' had something to do with it. So what values might we now wish to include in any future prioritization of the aims of education and the policies to achieve them? My personal answer to that question, would most certainly include the definition of co-operative values by the International Co-operative Alliance (ICA) in their Statement of Co-operative Identity (ICA 1995) which includes equity and equality as well as honesty, openness, social responsibility and caring for others as aims to strive for and build upon.

We could take equality as a current example where shadows fall between policy rhetoric and the actual reality. The contemporary use of language and discourse on 'social mobility' pays limited attention to fundamental inequalities in income and wealth distribution. Certainly the current government seems reluctant to address such underpinning income and wealth inequality issues in any serious way. In contrast, the work of the epidemiologists Richard Wilkinson and Kate Pickett, and their Equality Trust, have highlighted the overwhelming research evidence that more equal societies across 23 countries and 50 US states perform better on a spectrum of social and wellbeing indices, including educational attainment (Wilkinson and Pickett 2010). Yet the Coalition Government have distanced themselves from such arguments within the overall context of a relentless focus on state expenditure cuts to budgets for welfare, health and also education services which have been precipitated by the global financial crises.

Co-operative values help to highlight some interesting features of current education policy and debate as we stand, in 2014, in the midst of a far reaching so-called education 'reform' agenda promoted by the Coalition Government. Far from being a technical or a purely procedural matter, the teaching and learning of co-operative skills has to be placed within these wider philosophical and policy frameworks.

What is it we want education to do? Who is education for? Do we want different sorts of education for different groups of people? What, as the recent Nuffield Review of 14-19 Education and Training posed as a fundamental question, does it mean to be an educated 19-year-old coming out of compulsory education in the UK in the twenty-first Century (Pring et al. 2009). For many years, education policy has not been responsive to unpacking or specifying such questions of broad aims. This chapter will address these fundamental issues through an analysis of ASDAN's educational approaches and their effectiveness. In doing so, I will also draw on personal experience and reflections since my own background includes the teaching of philosophy in application to social welfare and education at the University of the West of England where I was a head of faculty for 17 years, running a research and training centre.

Despite the marked shift away from articulating aims, purposes and values in education over recent years, governments continue to focus upon measurable skills and implementing policy, based putatively upon strong evidence. For example, the Programme for International Student Assessment (PISA) statistics have provided much of the current rationale and impetus for educational policy changes relating to curriculum, assessment, governance, management and control of schools. Yet these are now the subject of considerable debate and critical scrutiny. Michael Gove, the Secretary of State for Education at the time of writing, has been criticized for 'cherry picking' evidence from PISA to suit his ideological preferences (Stewart 2011, 2013). Perhaps all governments are prone to such biases. The last Labour government certainly claimed to base policy decisions upon 'what works', a notion which begged a prior question as to the aims and purposes of policy.

Despite these tendencies, the dichotomy between broad values and specific educational targets is not unbridgeable in relation to co-operative learning. Two recent research projects have connected co-operative teaching and learning to the raising of attainment. These research findings serve to confirm ASDAN's work in promoting 'learning to learn' which is mediated through collaborative and experiential learning and teaching. The first example is the research exercise conducted by Steve Higgins, professor of education at the University of Durham, on behalf of the Sutton Trust Education Endowment Foundation (EEF) in 2011. The Sutton Trust, under the leadership of Peter Lampl, has developed sustained research on the fundamental educational divide resulting from the English private school system. In pursuit of more effective policy and practice, the Trust has also outlined the critical role that social disadvantage plays in the arena of educational attainment, progression and access to higher and further education, and ultimately into rewarding employment; in other words, to what is now increasingly referred to as social mobility. The background research summation by Higgins, 'What works in raising attainment and closing the gap: research evidence from the UK and abroad' highlights the 'promising classroom strategies' to raise attainment and close the gap between those groups of learners who do attain according to current criteria and those who do not (Higgins 2011). These 'promising classroom strategies' include collaborative and co-operative learning, peer involvement and making learning explicit. Without exception, these have all consistently been core design features of the ASDAN methodology. Moreover, the national assessment standards for the 'Working With Others' qualification, which ASDAN led the field in developing, continues to be acknowledged as significant by both employers and higher education alike. Indeed, the ASDAN methodology, by combining skills assessment with knowledge assessment, represents an important antidote to the systematic and continuing polarization between vocational skills and the academic acquisition of knowledge and understanding.

The second, and related, piece of good news for mainstreaming co-operative education and co-operative teaching and learning approaches is the national research undertaken by the University of the West of England (Higgins 2011; UWE 2012). This examined the impact that ASDAN's Certificate of Personal Effectiveness (CoPE) qualification has had on learner attainment in GCSE core curriculum subjects including English and maths. Researchers interrogated the DfE national pupil database of over 500,000 learners spanning a two year period, which represents a considerable baseline dataset. In particular, it considered the impact of the ASDAN qualification vehicle, with its in-built co-operative and 'learning-to-learn' approaches on learner attainment in GCSE core subjects. The overall finding was that the completion of the ASDAN Certificate of Personal Effectiveness (CoPE) at Level 2 had a statistically significant association with improved attainment in English and maths GCSEs. The research has also been highlighted in a recent seminar by the Education and Employers Taskforce and demonstrates the impact of ASDAN's 'learning to learn' approach on core subject GCSE attainment including maths and English (James and Harrison 2012).

Firstly, undertaking CoPE at level 2 in a wide usage school, where it is followed by 25 per cent-100 per cent of the cohort, is associated with an estimated 10 per cent increased likelihood of achieving GCSE English at A* to C, compared to similar young people in schools not offering CoPE. Secondly, undertaking CoPE at level 2 in a wide usage school is associated with an estimated 5 per cent increased likelihood of achieving five GCSEs at A* to C including English and maths, excluding GCSE equivalent qualifications, compared to similar young people in schools not offering CoPE. In addition, the other main findings on ASDAN and closing the attainment gap, include significant improvement for low-attaining pupils, black and minority ethnic pupils and those with special educational needs.

In order to see the full picture, it is necessary to move beyond 'what works' into the context of why and how ASDAN's co-operative values and teaching and learning methodology, actually does 'work'. The contributing key features include the 'hidden curriculum and the process of listening and reflecting' within teaching and learning; the 'personal challenge curriculum' and the 'encouragement/challenge equation' and the 'psychology of failure, learning styles and models of intelligence and assessment'.

Hidden curriculum and the process of listening and reflecting

Educational innovations, such as co-operative approaches to teaching and learning, cannot be isolated from their social context. Thinkers such as John Dewey, Jean Piaget and Lawrence Kohlberg have all recognized in different ways that, within systems of social relationships, people obey the same obligations not out of fear but from mutual respect. For example, in *Democracy and Education*, Dewey (1916) placed the school at the heart of the rapidly evolving and diverse society of the USA. He laid out an educational philosophy that was required to inherit and effectively adapt American democratic traditions. Richard Pring has pointed out that Dewey held a particular view on the relationship between school and society which was far from a simplistic and causal relationship:

> The school had to embody, in its very relationships and teaching methods and exercise of authority, the values that, in theory at least, typified the new state of America. If you want a just society you have to create just individuals. But if you want to create just individuals, you need to create just institutions and relationships within which they can learn justice
>
> *(Pring 1984)*

I would add that if you want to develop individuals committed to justice you need to create, model and perform justice. This is all about performative ethics which need to be lived out through real educational and social relationships. We do not simply want to encourage a society of people who just 'know and recite' ethical principles they have learned from Kant or Hume or Mill. People who not only understand and analyse but also practise, perform and live ethics will be in a position to make a much stronger contribution to social justice within their communities.

In defining co-operative approaches to teaching and learning, one must take account of both the taught and the untaught, or hidden curriculum (Hargreaves 1982). This hidden curriculum might be described as the operationalized values of any school, including its form of governance, the manner in which it promotes relationships between teacher and learner, between learner and learner, between teacher and teacher, and also with the outside world of parents and wider community. Of course this will all be strongly influenced by the current political landscape in which we are witnessing the transformation and dismantling of the existing structures of state education through, for example, the 'academization' policy. As a response to this situation, it is necessary to address the fundamental questions alluded to earlier in order to achieve the maximization of happy, healthy and positive relationships in schools and society. We must be aware of the ideological assumptions and wider social and market influences which are driving national government policy and constricting democratic local government.

The ASDAN response to this changing context has been to develop meaningful forms of learning in ways which also take account of longer-term and deeper educational factors. ASDAN's successes have not resulted from complex solutions but rather from listening carefully to both practitioners and learners, and then reflecting that listening back into the programmes and qualification materials. In doing so, we too have followed a learning cycle. These materials and approaches tend to work because of the very practice employed in their creation which is co-creation, trialling and then listening to feedback and incorporating and reflecting it back to learners and practitioners. This ASDAN approach parallels what is found in many co-operative schools where stakeholder groups find a voice through membership forums. These forms of governance embody the process of listening carefully to the voice of the stakeholders and users. Such 'listenings' also represent good practice in the private sector where the focus and motivational need is for the gathering of market intelligence.

Moreover, our 'listenings' to practitioners have been honouring in a way that has supported professional practice and autonomy over a period of 30 years, during which time the political and educational landscape has centralized, and, if anything, has tended towards taking professional autonomy and decision making away from teachers. This centralizing trend is even reflected in the popular language for describing curriculum as being 'delivered' by teachers in a way that a postman or woman would deliver a parcel or package, not interpreted or mediated by them. An educational world where the role of the teacher is to 'deliver' what has been agreed elsewhere, packaged up and sent down the line, is rather mechanistic (Pring et al. 2009). However, listening attentively is not just good for evidence gathering in research, or as an effective business or professional practice. At its best, it is therapeutic, because essentially it is an affirming process. The Chinese sixth Century BC poet Lao Tse, author of the Tao TeChing, as quoted by Carl Rogers, wrote:

> *It is as though he listened,*
> *And such listenings as his enfold us in a silence*
> *In which, at last, we begin to hear,*
> *What we are meant to be.*
>
> *(Rogers 1980)*

You hear what you are meant to be in a holding silence. While not all listening is deeply therapeutic, the notion of 'holding' is useful in exploring mindful and reflective listening which is shared between people. This is rather a-typical of much of the dynamic of contemporary teaching and learning, in which the dominant pattern is often for teachers to speak rather more than listen. Co-operative models of teaching and learning tend to exemplify a different proportional balance.

The personal challenge curriculum and the encouragement/challenge equation

In contrast to the Fordist, centralized and industrialized 'delivery of the curriculum', ASDAN's approach has always been to work collaboratively with teachers and learners. It is essential to start from a place of relevance to the learner while nurturing new interpretations among both teachers and learners. For example, ASDAN was highlighted in Mike Tomlinson's Working Group on 14-19 Reform report 2004 as one of the originators of the 'personal challenge' methodology alongside the International Baccalaureate (Working Group on 14–19 Reform). This 'personal challenge' approach enables the teacher to co-produce with the learner, an activity and a 'task set' of challenges which can be negotiated and then assessed within overall guidelines. This activity starts from the learners' personal interests and enthusiasms, and can then provide the experiential 'learning by doing' which enables the development of both knowledge and skills. It can also provide opportunities for performative ethics through caring for others and participating in community service. By negotiating appropriate challenges, teacher/learner co-production can take place and this is in itself a context in which the teacher can become the facilitator for learning not just the transmitter, didactically, of facts or knowledge. Indeed, through discussion, learners and teachers are able to create and write their own personalized challenges for themselves.

By propagating and practising this message, we have supported the consolidation of teachers' professional standing and professional judgement. Over the last 20 years, nearly a quarter of a million teachers have been reached by this ASDAN message through our programmes of inset workshops and continuing professional development (CPD) training for 'learning-to-learn' processes. This contribution, which has been kept alight in recent times, is essentially about teaching styles and modes of teaching and learning. It has some echoes back to Mode 3 CSE in giving back professional judgement to teachers for co-designing and constructing some aspects of the curriculum.

In learning and teaching, the balance between encouragement and challenge is a further core feature of the ASDAN approach which contains an important message about learning and teaching styles. The politician, Tony Benn, once said, 'You get the best out of people by encouraging them'. Fundamentally that seems to me to be spot on, and any first year undergraduate in psychology or social psychology would be able to cite you the overwhelming research evidence for the truth of that proposition. So how interesting that the research evidence for getting the best out of people at a basic human level stands in stark contradistinction to macro level national pre-occupations with the adoption of league table measurement systems which are used to name and shame, and to highlight failure in order to produce the competitive motivation to change through fear. Underpinning this dominant management model are deeply held assumptions about the need for competition to 'drive up standards' with little or no consideration of how one might use co-operation and the sharing of effective practice to achieve the same desired results. So getting this balance right at the micro level in teaching and learning, between challenge and encouragement, is at the heart of professional judgements teachers have to make every day. It is also incumbent upon politicians to strike the right balance between challenge and encouragement at the macro 'systems level' although, notoriously, this often does not happen. As a result, bullying and undermining, for example, now appear to be incorporated into the national schools inspection system operated by Ofsted. At their Easter 2013 Conference, the 28,000 strong, National Association of Headteachers (NAHT), announced the launch of a national alternative schools inspection service, named INSTEAD. This reflected the deep frustration, disquiet and perhaps even desperation, experienced by many teachers and school leaders with the dominant inspection model.

Within the constraints of this educational policy context, ASDAN has promoted a facilitating pedagogy that achieves a judicious balance between encouragement and challenge in practice. A very impactive poem, often wrongly attributed to Apollinaire, gets movingly close to expressing the essence of this basic educational equation. It is called 'The Edge' by Christopher Logue (1968) and it describes how a 'Muse' encourages and cajoles learners to 'come to the edge' although they are deeply afraid of falling from a great height, but at last and with patient encouragement and firm assurance there is progress and movement:

And the Muse said:
Come to the edge

And they came
And he pushed them
And they flew.

We are talking here about something quintessential in teaching and learning. I am moved personally because, as a child, my own experience was of failure and near failure. I failed the 11+ examination and I remember vividly how, in my secondary modern school that I subsequently attended, I didn't recognize myself as the subject of the sentence when a supportive and encouraging teacher said to me: 'Well, you'll be thinking of going to university'. At first I looked over my shoulder to check the remark was not directed elsewhere, because I did not conceive of myself as destined for university.

We are touching here on themes of self-esteem and self-identity. And tellingly, within the overall theme of co-operation, identity itself is co-produced and socially constructed, as well as maintained, through social interaction and a complex tapestry of social dynamics. We know this, and we know that human beings are social animals whose social and individual identities are forged together.

The psychology of failure, learning styles and models of intelligence and assessment

My belief in certain educational values, represented through ASDAN, is closely connected to basic issues of social justice and the phenomenon of failure. Part of the 'psychology of failure' is that one can so easily 'fail by default'. It goes like this: first suppose that you do not succeed at a particular task, intellectual, or physical, and out of fear and embarrassment at the possibility of further failure, avoidance tactics are then adopted, *not to try again*. Of course, if one does not try, does not continue to engage with the problem, there is an immediate kind of self-protection from the consequent shame of failing again. The psychological 'pay-off' for not trying any further is that, at the very least, one can say: 'Well, I didn't fail . . . I just didn't bother to try'. And for many young people, and indeed people of any age, that position is the most acceptable one. My experience is that this 'failure by default' mechanism is deep rooted. Human beings can so easily be de-motivated by an experience of failure, and can become utterly frozen and stuck, resulting in a kind of physical, emotional and intellectual limbo. I know this, because I have been there myself, and, to a greater or lesser extent, I expect have we all at certain times. In matters of teaching and learning, we ignore at our peril this psychological phenomenon of 'adaptive preferences', the human propensity to fail by default through fear and shame. But the phenomenon of failure is not just about pathological individual failure.

The English education system has systematically failed hundreds of thousands of young people over the years through the administration of an ungenerous and limited view of what it is to be able and to be intelligent. The social construction of those realities has served to consolidate inequalities. By contrast, ASDAN materials and programmes incorporate design features which provide a systematic nurturing of confidence to combat failure. For example, 'small steps of achievement' help to maximize rewards in a way that builds confidence incrementally for all learners. These small steps to achieving are very similar to the principles of David A. Kolb's experiential learning cycle which is basically 'Plan, Do and Review' learning, in which, at the point of review, one begins the cyclical process of planning, doing and reviewing once again (Kolb 1984). This process encourages a co-operative social interaction between learner and teacher. Alongside 'formative listening' which is essentially an affirming process for learners, formative assessment through small steps of achievement similarly enables learners to recognize their progress through co-operative and enabling interactions between teacher and learner.

However, the chilling truth remains that, despite some advances in perspective that have occurred in the last fifteen to twenty years, our dominant view of ability and intelligence, as encapsulated in successive government policies on raising attainment and achievement, is still predominantly based on a flawed and very limited construct of intellectual performance. In this model only a narrow range of human dispositions are valued while many others are positively devalued. This dominant definition of intelligent performance is still based upon what Gilbert Ryle, the Oxford philosopher, referred to in his seminal book *The Concept of Mind* as the 'intellectualist legend' (Ryle 1949). According to this legend the defining properties of mind are characterized by theorizing and no behaviour could be described as intelligent if it were not prefaced by a theorizing process. Our society's basic view of intelligence is still caught up in this ludicrous conceptual muddle. And ludicrous it is, since by implication, on this model of intelligence one could not very easily or appropriately refer to intelligent football playing or to intelligent plumbing. This model of intelligence reflects a false assumption built into the very fabric of our educational system, that those of a 'practical' disposition, who 'know how' to do things, are somehow inferior in comparison to those who 'know that' certain facts are the case. Moreover, we go on to assess these 'knowings that' by testing memory, and regurgitation of knowledge, usually in a written essay form. In other words we fail an awful lot of people. We call and label them as less than clever because they do not measure up when they are judged by this very narrow academic view of what it is to be clever. All this is propped up by narrowly defined assessment tools and procedures which utterly fail to recognize a very wide range of intelligences and learning styles, as exhaustively outlined by academics and researchers ranging across several decades, from J.P. Guilford to Howard Gardner (Guilford 1967; Gardner 2011).

Essentially we are dishonouring people. It is all so hugely damaging, as if we can afford to waste our children's talents, and to treat a significant proportion of our population as if they were unlikely ever, really, to excel at anything very important. Many ASDAN qualifications represent a middle ground between the vocational (skills and their application) and the academic (knowledge and understanding). In the popular and often polarized debate between the two, this middle ground remains significant, as representative of an 'education for capability' approach, as the RSA Manifesto expressed it (RSA 1979). ASDAN has implicitly and explicitly espoused a generous view of intelligent performance and has promoted the development of a balanced skills and knowledge based assessment. These include generic 'learning-to-learn' skills as well as other social, personal and co-operative skills alongside the more traditional types of assessment for knowledge and understanding. So significant are these skills, experiences and applied knowledge perceived to be for entry to higher education and to employment that, for over a decade, the UCAS Guidance to Applicants on completing their 'personal statement' has referred specifically to the achievement of ASDAN's Level 3 Certificate of Personal Effectiveness as a means of demonstrating independent learning and wider experiences, flair, enterprise, commitment and the courage to stick with a task often beyond immediate comfort zones.

The English educational divide is also, of course, a social one. We would be doing a very great favour to the promotion of social justice if the Government, backed by co-operative schools and other networks, were to publicly re-assert the equal value of 'knowing how' alongside 'knowing that' since these modes of knowing are mutually dependent and mutually beneficial. They represent an essentially co-operative rather than divisive and polarized approach to teaching and learning, and to the development of rounded, caring and socially responsible young people educated for the twenty-first century. If this could happen, alongside a more equitable distribution of resources for the development of these different and equally valuable modes of knowing, they might at last contribute to what I believe would then be a brighter and more creative and productive future, let alone a more equitable one.

Currently, we are witnessing considerable change to the national schools performance measures and there is a danger that ASDAN's work will be undervalued and sidelined by political priorities. The combined effects of these changes will be retrogressive and will narrow the number of subjects and skills taught as well as the range of assessment methods. All of this is a thousand miles away from recognizing the multi-dimensional nature of the human intellect.

Originally we developed the 'Working with Others' qualification, and others like it, such as 'Improving Own Learning and Performance', and 'Problem Solving', with

Tim Oates, then of the National Council for Vocational Qualifications (NCVQ) and now more recently the Chair of the Coalition Government's Expert Panel on the National Curriculum Review. I spent seven years working with the Department for Education and its predecessor bodies, to get recognition for this fundamentally co-operative qualification (Brockington 2002). These qualifications were developed not just to be owned and offered by ASDAN but as national qualifications which could be, and indeed are, offered by all the national awarding bodies who wanted to be involved. It is a small unit sized qualification which, taken alongside two other unit sized qualifications, 'Problem Solving' and 'Improving Own Learning and Performance', are currently 'equivalent' to a GCSE. But because of the rising political battles over GCSE equivalents, a notion which was historically never about asserting equivalence, but rather about establishing a framework for comparison, this is one of the qualifications lined up to be dropped from the all-important 'Headline Performance Measures' by September 2014. Alison Wolf's *Review of Vocational Education* (Wolf 2011) criticized schools' manipulative use of certain types of vocational qualifications which she believed had little intrinsic value to learners but were instead being used by schools to gain league table points, particularly through the use of so-called 'multiple equivalence'. The unit qualifications I am speaking of here were never ascribed point scores that amounted to 'multiple equivalency' and were therefore not susceptible to this manipulative use. And although 'gaming' of the system of multiple equivalence qualifications did take place, the overall system of league table performance measures, when changed, will itself remain substantially intact and will continue to be 'gamed'. The results of all this for learners are no less damaging. Gaming to achieve performance targets and league table points can easily shift the focus of teaching time and resources from wider groups of pupils to smaller numbers of borderline learners whose results have a disproportionate effect on the school.

Assessment, especially when it is used to develop and enhance learning, is at the heart of the education process. There is a sense in which the very process of assessment can, if we are not careful, serve to solidify the differential power relationships between learner and teacher, and this can be very destructive if one is not mindful of these delicate issues. It is one of the reasons that 'assessment for learning', where the assessment process is itself a tool for encouraging learning, often undermines power differentials in promoting a collaborative and co-operative dialogue between learner and teacher. We need this inclusivity in assessment more than we need systems that tend towards devaluing the talents of what John Newsom in his influential 1963 report on English education referred to as 'Half our Future' (CACE 1963) It was the Spanish poet, Antonio Machado, who wrote that, 'The eyes that you see, are not eyes because you see them, but because they see you' (Machado 1983). This is a powerful reminder always to try to honour the person in the process of assessment.

It is at the end of *The Winter's Tale* that Paulina says to the mourning and broken Leontes: 'It is required you do awake your faith' (Shakespeare 1963, Act 5, Scene 3). For a significant body of people, our faith is firm and already awake. We know that co-operative values are coherent and both resonate and sing to people, especially in our secular world. They are as rational and as justified as any values based on common sense and common utility. We should continue with all our efforts to promote them. And if there was a line from popular culture which epitomized the strength of the co-operative movement, I think one could do worse than consider the lyric sung by Michael Jackson as a very young performer:

> "I used to say: I am me
> Now, it's us
> Now, it's we."

It is a declension which although no doubt intended originally as a descriptor for loving couples, is actually full of hope for mutuality and the co-operative process.

Alongside this I would like to conclude on an international and multicultural note because a similar declension is also found in South African philosophical liberation theology. It is the notion of Ubuntu which is espoused by Desmond Tutu and represented in his wide ranging reconciliation work (Battle 1997). The Ubuntu concept recognizes that persons and groups form their identities not in isolation but in relation to one another. It is crystallized in the equation, "I am because you are". It invites us to face up to our collective interdependence rather than the more solipsistic western focus on the individual as worker and consumer.

References

ASDAN (2014a) 'ASDAN and co-operative studies' http://www.asdan.org.uk/Co-operative (accessed 15 January 2014).
—— (2014b) 'Co-operative studies' http://www.asdan.org.uk/media/downloads/asdan_co_operative_brochure_spreads.pdf (accessed 15 January 2014).
Battle, M. (1997) *Reconciliation: The Ubuntu Theology of Desmond Tutu*, Cleveland: The Pilgrim Press.
Bernstein, B. (1971) 'On the classification and framing of educational objectives', in Young, M.F.D. (ed.) *Knowledge and Control*, Basingstoke: Collier Macmillan.
Bloom, B.S. et al. (1956) *Taxonomy of Educational Objectives,* Handbook 1: *Cognitive Domain*. Handbook II: *Affective Domain*, See Krathwohl et al. 1964.
Brockington, D. (2002) *Key Skills Within the National Qualifications Framework: 14–19*, Oxford and Warwick Universities.
Brockington, D. and White, R. (1978) *In and Out of School: The ROSLA Community Education Project,* London: Routledge and Kegan Paul.
CACE (1963) *Half Our Future* (The Newsom Report), London: Her Majesty's Stationery Office.
Dewey, J. (1916) *Democracy and Education,* London: Macmillan.
Dweck, C.S. (2006) *Mindset: The New Psychology of Success,* New York: Random House.
——(2012) *Mindset: How You Can Fulfil Your Potential*, New York: Constable & Robinson.
Gardner, H. (2011) *Frames of Mind: the Theory of Multiple Intelligences*, New York: Basic Books.
Guilford, J.P. (1967) *The Nature of Human Intelligence*, New York: McGraw-Hill.
Hargreaves, D. (1967) *Social Relations in a Secondary School*, London: Routledge.
—— (1982) *Challenge for the Comprehensive School: Culture, Curriculum and Community,* London: Routledge.

Higgins, S. (2011) 'What works in raising attainment and closing the gap: research evidence from the UK and abroad', Presentation to the Sutton Trust Education Endowment Fund. See: http://educationendowmentfoundation.org.uk/library/what-works-in-raising-attainment-and-closing-the-gap (accessed 15 January 2014).

ICA (1995) *Statement of Co-operative Identity* http://www.uwcc.wisc.edu/icic/issues/prin/21-cent/background.html (accessed 15th January 2014).

James, D. and Harrison, N. (2012) 'Education and employers working together for young people; the impact of a skills led qualification on GCSE attainment: the case of ASDAN's Certificate of Personal Effectiveness', http://www.educationandemployers.org/research/research-seminars/professor-david-james-and-neil-harrison---16th-october,-2012/ (accessed 15th January 2014).

Kolb, D. (1984) *Experiential Learning: Experience as the Source of Learning and Development*, Englewood Cliffs, NJ: Prentice Hall.

Krathwohl, D.R., Bloom, B.S. and Masia, B.B. (1964) *Taxonomy of Educational Objectives: The Classification of Educational Goals. Handbook 2 Affective Domain*, London: Longman.

Machado, A. (1983) *Selected Poems, Times Alone*, Translated by Robert Bly, Middletown, CT: Wesleyan University Press.

Plutarch (1992) 'On Listening', in Waterfield, R. (ed.) *Essays by Plutarch*, London: Penguin.

Pring, R. (1984) *Personal and Social Education in the Curriculum*, London: Hodder and Stoughton.

Pring, R., Hayward, G., Hodgson, A., Johnson, J., Keep, E., Oancea, A., Reese, G., Spours, K. and Wilde, S. (2009) *Education for All: The Future of Education and Training for 14–19 Year Olds. The Nuffield Review of 14–19 Education and Training, England and Wales*, London: Routledge.

Rogers, C. (1980) *A Way of Being*, Boston, MA: Houghton and Mifflin.

RSA (1979) 'The Education for Capability Manifesto', London: Royal Society of Arts, http://www.heacademy.ac.uk/heca/manifesto (accessed 15 January 2014).

Ryle, G. (1949) *The Concept of Mind*, London: Hutchinson.

Shakespeare, W. (1963) *The Winter's Tale*, Kermode, F. (ed.), New York: Penguin

Stewart, W. (2013) 'Is PISA fundamentally flawed?' *Times Educational Supplement* (TES) 26th July. http://www.tes.co.uk/article.aspx?storycode=6344698 (accessed 15th January 2014).

Stewart, W. (2011) 'Mr Gove fixes PISA's new problems by ignoring them.' *Times Educational Supplement* (TES) 7th October 2011. http://www.tes.co.uk/article.aspx?storycode=6115609 (accessed 15th January 2014).

UWE (2012) *Building a Culture of Achievement*, Bristol: ASDAN and UWE. Summary Report at http://www.asdan.org.uk/media/downloads/ASDAN%20summary%20Report.pdf (accessed 15 January 2014).

Watkins, C. (2010) *Learning, Performance and Improvement* (INSI *Research Matters* No 34). London Centre for Leadership in Learning: Institute of Education, University of London.

Wilkinson, R. and Pickett, K. (2010) *The Spirit Level: Why Equality is Better for Everyone*, London: Penguin Books.

Wolf, A. (2011) *Review of Vocational Education* (Wolf Report), London: DfE.

Working Group on 14–19 Reform (2004) *14–19 Qualifications and Curriculum Reform. Final Report*, London: DfES. http://webarchive.nationalarchives.gov.uk/20130401151715/https://www.education.gov.uk/publications/eOrderingDownload/DfE-0976-2004 MIG839.pdf (accessed 15 January 2014).

9

Co-operative schools: putting values into practice

Tom Woodin

The co-operative schools movement is stepping into an already fast-moving stream of educational activity. In doing so it pinpoints a number of long term tensions and contradictions central to the nature of schooling. Co-operative schools respond not only to the unremitting onslaught of new policies and initiatives but to an earlier educational framework. They have drawn upon both historical resources and contemporary opportunities while promising a new vision of education based upon the values of self-help, self-responsibility, democracy, equality, equity and solidarity (Woodin 2011, 2012; Woodin and Fielding 2013).

Although it is a new development, co-operative schools relate to historical trends. Over the last century and more, the expansion of schooling represents a major social transformation. Soon after the advent of compulsory universal schooling, which marginalized other models of education, assumptions began to move beyond schooling for the 3Rs. The extension of compulsion through the raising of the school leaving age to 14 in 1921, 15 in 1947 and 16 in 1972, was met with initial opposition and recalcitrance that soon subsided over the years following the reform. Despite significant disillusionment with the institution of schooling, its popularity has nevertheless grown incrementally. Complementary social forces have placed education systems at the heart of modern societies: subject to ever-closer official and political scrutiny and also more firmly lodged within popular expectations and aspirations. For much of this history, schooling was regarded as a progressive social force embracing ever-wider constituencies. Rising democratic expectations supported the emergence of schooling for all. Pupils, parents and communities have become central to this educational crusade even though their role has often been constrained (Woodin et al. 2013).

Recently, the need to measure and compare schools and whole education systems has been asserted. Technical definitions of learning have been deployed with great effect by international bodies such as the OECD, with the PISA league tables being held up as the way of judging 'standards' and 'competitiveness'. Critics have pointed out that the single-minded adherence to these measures causes cheating and gaming on the part of schools and can skew the whole educational process in the pursuit of results (Glatter 2013; Roach 2013). Standards may meet the theoretical needs of government and the labour market in the medium term, but pupils are also humans, (emerging) citizens, friends, children and employees among other roles. Standards do not always speak to the problems of the here and now – poverty, inequality, family relationships, friendships, and community well-being to name a few preoccupations of young people.

Over previous decades, the post-war structure of education as a 'national system, locally administered' has been called into question. Policymakers have come to perceive local education authorities as the 'problem': bureaucratic, inefficient monolithic state enterprises that imposed fixed ways of educating rather than responding to a diversity of educational needs (see Lowe 2002). From 2010, under the Coalition Government, the gradual process of undermining LEAs turned into an avalanche with the extension of converter academies and free schools which are directly responsible to the Department for Education (DfE). The imposition of academy chains has stripped many schools of their independence. One headteacher (2011) described feelings of despondency and the consequent need to 'collaborate or die' among educators who are eager to defend their schools against the predations of these academy chains. Centralization and 'nationalisation' (Newsam 2011; Mortimore 2013) have created logistical problems given that the Department now has to manage contracts with a plethora of institutions. In undermining LEAs, little thought was given to a potential replacement. Belatedly, political parties have been consulting on this issue and a number of options have emerged including commissioners, partnerships and 'middle tier' structures which might potentially fill the void (DfE 2014; Labour Party 2014).

Despite the mass of evidence and academic commentaries that emphasize the singular direction of education policy since 1988 (Chitty 2009, Stevenson 2011), divergent, albeit muted, trends can be identified. Marketization, diversity and choice have unleashed strong competitive tendencies between rival educational institutions. However, the unravelling of one model of public education for common benefit does not intrinsically lead to the polar opposite of full scale privatization and profit making institutions. The nurturing of diverse and autonomous institutions has in fact resulted in unexpected forms of schooling. The loss of local democracy and accountability, previously achieved through local education authorities, has not produced a uniform acquiescence. Co-operative schools have grown within the spaces of contemporary education policy, and, while recognizing the role of competition, differentiation, choice and specialization, have concentrated upon co-operation, collaboration, networks and shared governance. Many of them are achieving improvements in standards as well as promoting citizenship and social action (Audsley et al. 2013). Although the co-operative schools movement represents, in part, an attempt to reconfigure community schooling along lines of egalitarianism and local accountability, it does not represent a simple return to the past. In fact, co-operative education is increasingly being conceived as part of the 'commons' from which different educational models can be developed, within and beyond the state (Boden et al. 2012). Indeed, co-operative education adds new complexities to the contemporary neoliberal context in which universal state provision has been problematized (Gamble and Wright 2004).

The growth of co-operative schools can also be explained by looking at the nature of the co-operative movement with its blend of business acumen and focus upon values. The established consumer movement does not fit easily into the categories of the voluntary sector, third sector or civil society organization which are often assumed to be comprised of small-scale, fragile organizations. By contrast, until recently, the Co-operative Group had a turnover approaching £14 billion although this strength was severely challenged in 2013 (Co-operative News 2014). Significant financial, cultural and historical resources were brought to bear in cultivating co-operative schools. The Group actively supported the drafting of new legal models through a firm of solicitors and made financial contributions to conferences, meetings and the formation of the Schools Co-operative Society. In turn, these legal and financial resources were grounded in, and guided by, co-operative values. The Co-operative College has played a crucial role in directing this growth by ensuring that co-operative values and principles were at the heart of all developments. The coming together of financial and legal resources with strategic vision and know-how ultimately created a model that schools could adapt for their own autonomous development (Co-operative College 2014; Schools Co-operative Society 2014).

It remains a paradox that co-operative schools are not, in the full meaning of the term, co-operatives. Co-operative trust schools have to establish charitable trusts to involve external stakeholders while co-operative academies, which are more independent with direct lines of accountability, are part of a 'public' system of education. Nevertheless, they embrace co-operative values and principles and develop membership schemes to encourage the participation of key stakeholder groups in teaching, learning and governance. Co-operative schools, then, can be understood as hybrid or embryonic co-operatives which operate within a specific educational and legal framework. What is fascinating are the ways in which values have been transferred and adapted to schools and the changes in practices and understanding which are beginning to emerge from this interaction. Ascertaining the relative strengths, successes and limitations of these trends is one of the challenges facing anyone wanting to understand co-operative schools (Breeze 2011; Facer et al. 2012; Woodin 2012; Woodin and Fielding 2013). The research for this chapter was based upon visits to schools and interviews with a range of stakeholders, carried out between 2011 and 2013, as well as organizing seminars at the Institute of Education and attending events, conferences and meetings.

Values and democracy

Beyond their spatial and cultural rootedness, co-operative schools have positioned themselves as part of a global network of co-operatives. The presence of this broad movement has directly benefited schools, not only in relation to curriculum development, on such issues as Fairtrade, but also in terms of identity. One headteacher noted how the material reality of the co-operative movement bolstered values, ethos and feelings of safety within the school:

> I think the important thing about the co-operative ethos is, it links to a bigger set of ethics than just the school ethics. So it links to a national and an international movement, a bit like the church schools ... So it's not just your own school's ethos ... you are a part of something much bigger ... behaviour has improved and student attitude has improved, and that co-operative ethos has helped us with that – the way that they treat each other.
> *(headteacher 2012)*

This secular sense of belonging to an inclusive and widespread value-led community has indeed stimulated considerable enthusiasm among co-operative schools which are forging links between everyday school life and a global movement.[1] Schools have used the Statement of Co-operative Identity to chart their way through an educational world inundated by new legislation and initiatives. The focus upon results, league tables and data-driven measures has displaced a fuller awareness of the educational purposes of schools which have consequently become more opaque. By contrast, embracing co-operative values brought latent ideas out into the arena of debate, discussion and action. One school leader welcomed the coherence, clarity and logic of the Statement which countered a fear of fragmentation:

> The values were always with us ... but we hadn't articulated them in those clear words and those clear words are what makes it easier for us to move forward in the direction of co-operative learning and co-operation generally
> *(Jones 2011)*

Previously, within this school, Lipson Co-operative Academy, the search for vision and coherence had created 'a blancmange ... I'll have one of them, oh that looks fantastic, oh look at what they are doing. We threw too much into the mix and this [co-operative values] has helped give me discipline ...' (Baker 2011). Rather than offering a prescriptive model, co-operative values represent a set of guidelines within which there is scope for flexibility. The particular conditions, context and the ways that values are conceived and utilized, will all impact differently upon any given school. Co-operative values may be introduced and debated on enrichment days, in assemblies and in the classroom. Groups, guilds and houses are named after values such as equality, democracy and solidarity. These discussions can set in train a journey of debate and change.

Co-operative values and principles have also widened the avenues of accountability to pupils and communities. Schools have used the Statement to make a public proclamation of what they stand for. The values extend the school beyond a limited coterie of leaders and open up the potential for accountability to the main stakeholders and the general public. Adopting such a set of values and principles leaves any organization vulnerable to the counter claim that values are not being implemented and that other directions and initiatives are possible. Co-operative values may even allow those lower down any given hierarchy the possibility of appealing to a higher documentary authority (Arnold 2013) which is also starting point for democratic renewal.

Co-operative values have stimulated dialogue and exploratory action within a culture that celebrates authoritarianism and the panacea of the 'super-head'. Leaders in co-operative schools have had to balance their own authority with encouraging action from below in working towards alternative conceptions of the professional leader (Gunter 2011). Two headteachers, in emphasizing the importance of 'leadership at all levels' and 'giving away power to get things done', were consciously remoulding leadership as a more mutual set of relations based upon notions of shared governance and distributed leadership (Stoll et al. 2006; Woods 2011). Leadership was seen as a flexible practice that should elicit challenges to top-down authority: 'We have had that leadership where I went in and introduced the different types of co-operative learning and they've taken it in another direction' (teacher 2011). In these emerging models it is accepted that leadership, while focused upon outcomes, does not simply reside within the individual mover and shaker, but rather points to the need for shared responsibility and joint action for social responsibility (Nemerowicz and Rosi 1997). Crucially, in co-operative schools this is increasingly done in active dialogue with young people, parents and communities.

However, co-operation, like democracy, can be 'thick' and 'thin'. Indeed, conflict may arise from the multiple interpretations derived from co-operative values. Some groups of pupils have become excited by the opportunity to change things only to find that those in positions of power, even following a period of fruitful co-operation, are subsequently unwilling to go ahead with decisions (see Simpson in this book). The recoil from democracy and the reassertion of hierarchy, can clearly harm the way in which co-operation is viewed – as a fig leaf covering authoritarian relations rather than as a conduit to more equal relationships.

Moreover, while the whole range of values must be accepted as part of becoming a co-operative school, in practice teachers will inevitably emphasize and work with the ones that most closely complement their current practice. Given the flexibility of the co-operative approach, it may be possible to be selective about which values to adopt and to what extent. For instance, a surface acceptance of equality along with a focus upon respect, honesty, trust and caring for others can be identified in most schools which may not necessarily encourage democratic participation. On the websites of some co-operative schools, it can be difficult to identify their alignment with co-operative values. Co-operation can be perceived as a technical mechanism and governance structure rather than as a means of defining the content and purpose of education. In some religious schools, co-operative values are integrated into existing values which may again have the effect of toning down their distinctiveness. From one perspective, co-operative values are hardly revolutionary as the practices of school leadership are often saturated with values

(Gold et al. 2003). When educators are introduced to the Statement of Co-operative Identity, many respond by saying, 'this is what we already do!' and 'co-operative values are our values!' To some extent this common language testifies to the close historical connections between co-operative ideas and public institutions, an association that accounts for some of the initial success of co-operative schools.

Membership and participation

One conspicuous element in the co-operative educational message has been that of membership which represents a crucial way in which co-operative ideas are being transferred to schools. The word membership runs like a snake through the text of the Statement of Co-operative Identity. Members establish co-operatives to meet their common needs, are the *raison d'être* of a co-operative and take responsibility for putting co-operative values into practice. Yet, within the co-operative movement, the meaning of membership has been much debated. Actually existing examples of membership vary considerably despite the commonality of member ownership and control. Smaller worker co-operatives may enjoy active and continuous member participation in comparison with larger consumer co-operatives where representative structures mean that member control is more sporadic and formalized. However, on the face of it, membership in schools speaks to a number of contemporary agendas including a democratic deficit, apathy about civic and political participation and the breakdown of collective ties of belonging.

Membership has triggered debates about the ownership of schools. The formal models for co-operative trusts and academies put various categories of members at the heart of schools. Pupils, teachers, parents, community and, potentially, alumni can elect representatives to a school forum which, in turn, directly advises senior leaders and the governing body and, in some cases, appoints governors. Proponents of co-operative schools argue that this is a new form of democracy. The promotional video, *Co-operative Schools – Where Values Make a Difference,* is introduced by two pupils who inform us that they are 'co-operators'; one goes on to say that 'I am a member of a co-operative school which is owned and democratically controlled by its members' (Co-operative College/Group 2012). This is a powerful message which calls upon members to take responsibility for their 'own' schools and to 'own' their education.

Co-operative schools have embarked on membership schemes whereby individuals from stakeholder groups are encouraged to pay a membership fee of £1 to join their school co-operative. Membership champions recruit members and, depending upon their enthusiasm and their networks, they have met with varying levels of success. The Cotham Co-operative Academy in Bristol tied its membership development to a specialism in performing arts and organized elections in parallel with those taking place in the city as a form of citizenship education. In order to underline the importance of this scheme, the school produced T-shirts, postcards, stickers, pens, and other branding material, for their launch in September 2012. Student reps were given space and time to consult their peers and senior leaders in the school while minutes of meetings were published for all to view. Initial consultations with pupils revealed concerns about lunchtimes, uniforms, mobile phones, school trips and offering more opportunities in outside spaces. More profound issues were also probed such as homophobia and inclusion, admissions, engaging parents, making the forum more representative, developing a school vision and initiating projects that make co-operative values more visible. By June 2013, member groups included 829 students, 164 staff, 16 alumni, 45 community members and 325 parents (Cotham Co-operative Academy 2013). In other schools, developing surface participation on a range of issues such as the use of mobile phones has encouraged them to delve deeper, for example, consulting on a policy document relating to the single equalities legislation. In this case, pupils emphasized the importance of anonymity in a school which employed many local people.

By stimulating loyalty, membership has the potential to exert an influence across school life. Small-scale co-operative enterprises, known as Young Co-operatives, have been established to meet needs and generate an income that can be reinvested. Such economic activity has educational and social benefits and represents, in some cases, an active form of community engagement, from Fairtrade to music and dance. One pupil recorded the real benefits of membership and noted that, 'the teachers sit down, we run it' (pupil). The divisions between the technical and measurable aspects of schooling and wider conceptions of learning and environment are regularly traversed by such groups. One teacher worked with a small group of co-operative enthusiasts in an inner city school:

> I want them to come up with the ideas and own them because it's about them owning the school and then owning the co-operative trust side of their school as well and having pride in their school ... which was slow to start with ... It's about planning it and working out how they can do it practically ... now they've started to realize they can make a difference, not only in the school but also in the community ... it has given them a new lease of life, that school is about more than what they just learn in the classroom although that's important. The way that they're learning is changing as well – they are starting to think further and outside the box a bit. Want to get all kids to do that really ... Just talking to them, they say, "Oh, we learnt so much more in this lesson because we did it this way than another way", so it is really starting to have a big impact not only on the teachers planning their lessons and delivering them but also the way that they are learning and absorbing ... the information that they need to pass their exams
>
> *(teacher 2012)*

Co-operation and participation were coming to be seen as central to results and standards rather than the two being antithetical forces. Previously at this school, it was argued, a strong focus on community education had been separated from school improvement (headteacher 2012). Traditions of community education were being reworked in order to link them into central school processes.

In addition, transitions from small scale ginger groups to engaging larger numbers of learners in school and community life have been made. Corelli College in south east London, has involved upwards of 150 students in a wide variety of leadership roles. Having developed this scheme with advice from a Cambridgeshire village college, pupils have been given opportunities to define and engage in multiple leadership roles. Young people take on responsibility for change including having an input into teaching, curriculum and even interviewing applicants for jobs; the very process of dialogue represents a form of deliberative democracy in which young people become familiar with addressing issues that directly affect them. A seminar at the Institute of Education, at which groups of students led presentations, sparked off a number of ideas and individuals sub-sequently joined the Youth Parliament and other organizations (Jaffe and Cronin 2013). In these experiments, leadership is thus being conceived as a mechanism for mass participation.

However, membership schemes are in their infancy and their significance has not yet crystallized. Membership is being reinterpreted in new conditions. The members of such schools are often transient in that students, parents and staff may only be associated with their school for a short period of time and it remains unclear how membership will develop in the long term. In addition, participation and membership are commonly viewed as coterminous with one another so that participation in school life can be seen as the essence of the co-operative approach (Scargill 2014). Co-operative schools may represent a new amalgam of co-operative membership based upon ownership and control and the voluntary participation found in a broader set of civil society organizations. For example, individuals have been included in one-off projects such as specific school events, visits and consultations, and building poly-tunnels and greenhouses which have also involved community groups.

Membership represents a crucible in which compulsion and voluntarism are being brought together in new ways. Pupils are already compelled to attend school where they are expected to participate in various activities, a fact which makes the co-operative principle of voluntary and open membership somewhat ambiguous. The notion of exclusive 'member benefits' found in co-operatives is potentially problematic if they are not available to all pupils. Explaining the purpose of membership can then become a protracted process. It is also possible for member groups, which are sometimes comprised of the 'usual suspects', to become more focused upon the concerns of active participants rather than stimulating action among the school community and beyond.

In one school, the forum had stopped recruiting and used their available energy to develop services for the whole school. It was not clear why they needed to recruit further members if key organizing committees were now occupied. Formal membership and recruitment had fallen by the wayside within a few years and the school had, to some extent, used co-operative ideas for a short term gain. In this scenario, co-operative ideas might be treated as a temporary measure to activate new constituencies. Another school that was struggling with the notion of membership stepped back from voluntarism with an opt-out system for teachers and automatic entry for pupils – membership by stealth. A headteacher reported that they had 'not got membership yet':

> We are going to assume that every member of staff is a member unless they say no ... Then we are going to make sure that every student signs up and pays a pound. We're probably going to do that with a non-uniform day on the last day of term
>
> *(headteacher 2012)*

The representative committee structure implied by the legal documents could be overwhelming:

> It's quite burdensome and bureaucratic I think. There's this fancy diagram of who goes here and you know ... the trust structure is quite complicated. You have a trust meeting and you're supposed to have representatives from the stakeholder forum that go to trust meetings. And each stakeholder group is supposed to attend the trust meeting. That – we've not really cracked that yet and I don't think we are the only ones who haven't cracked that
>
> *(headteacher 2012)*

Infusing structures with a lived dynamic may take some time to achieve. In this school, it has been difficult to sustain the number of members attending forum meetings, particularly among the staff. Following a challenging Ofsted report, the headteacher felt compelled to operate in an 'autocratic' manner in order to move the school out of special measures which further limited the scope for consultation and made staff wary of additional voluntary activities that may be implied by membership schemes. In such a context, the 'old methods continue' with staff expressing doubts through the local union branch. Within a context of performativity (Ball 2013), co-operative values have had to mingle with the exercise of power from above, resulting in mixed messages about co-operative working.

Member recruitment and development with parents and communities has also been pursued but, for obvious reasons, this has proved more difficult to address. Sean Rogers (2012) of the Co-operative College has argued that the movement is 'putting the community back into community schools'. Schools increasingly want to project a 'friendly' image and are actively working to address the fear and recalcitrance that many adults feel about schools when reflecting on their own pasts. The need to go beyond superficial involvement enters the realm of re-socializing parents to engender their trust and to facilitate effective involvement. For example, one school had employed outreach staff who supported parents to develop research and evaluation skills in order that they could more effectively participate in school life – a forerunner of the complex 'capabilities' that may be required in the future (Sen 1999; headteacher 2012). Schools also have to deal with the unrealistic assumption that they become hives of community action overnight – in itself a difficult move to make given that schools only have a limited capacity for such action. Mervyn Wilson of the Co-operative College has noted the impatient demands of policymakers:

> the short-termism of politicians who think that you become legal on Friday so you can give us the evidence of impact it's making by Monday morning ... we need to be judged in 5 to 10 years' time and the acid test in those communities, do people speak of 'our' school or talk of 'the' school, that's the journey we're on ...
>
> *(Wilson 2011)*

This journey has extended well beyond the boundaries of individual schools into the wider networks of schools.

Networks and partnerships

The co-operative schools movement has indeed facilitated joint working among schools on the basis of co-operative values. Co-operative schools represent one aspect of a widespread impulse for collaborative action (Hargreaves 2010; Richard Pring in this volume). A strong 'instinct for mutuality' (Wilson 2014) has been reflected in the urge to share the co-operative vision as widely as possible – literally, that it should be available to all:

> Our aim is not to keep it specialist to us, just for us or to show it off. It's actually to help others be part of the Schools Co-operatives Society ... it isn't just something that we want to keep for ourselves. It is something we would hope would grow because that would help education generally.
>
> *(Jones 2011)*

Paradoxically, co-operative education has exerted contradictory pressures in creating structures which diminish the role of local authorities while simultaneously bringing them back into the educational arena on new terms. The three academies that are directly sponsored by the Co-operative Group have worked closely with local authorities in Stoke-on-Trent, Manchester and Leeds, somewhat to the initial dismay and chagrin of certain policymakers given that academies had been purposely located outside of local authority control. Other co-operative trusts and academies have involved local authorities in governance arrangements as both necessary and useful partners. But building such relations has, at times, been strained given the sustained and purposeful attack on their existence. Tensions have been exacerbated if schools previously had a thorny relationship with local authorities. Where co-operative schools have not been favoured, they have sometimes been viewed by local authorities as a 'least worst option'. This has caused added difficulties. For instance, one local authority which encouraged all schools to go down a co-operative route was subsequently rebutted by headteachers now jealously guarding their autonomy and distrustful of local officials (Wilson 2011).

Among co-operative schools themselves, new modes of collaboration have emerged. As schools took on a co-operative identity, it soon became a 'network' and established the Schools Co-operative Society which then organized itself into regional structures, paying attention to the principles of autonomy and independence. These secondary membership networks bear a strong resemblance to the practices of the Co-operative Group, the historical structures of the labour movement as well as voluntary and business federations. At the same time, many people welcome the possibility of re-establishing an element of local organization to bring logic, efficiency and democracy back into public schooling. Local identity is particularly strong in some rural areas where common schooling was widely accepted given the existence of dispersed populations and small school rolls. Successful co-operative partnerships have built upon a history of collaboration and addressed a tangible need to work together. For example, in Devon and Cornwall, a large number of co-operative trusts have formed, some with more than 15 schools. The local authority was a key player in developing this strategy which acknowledged that alternatives to traditional models had to be developed in response to the impending crisis created by the Coalition Government. These trusts appear to have aspirations to operate as mini LEAs and retain a vision of community education. A strong awareness of common purpose, of defending schools and existing relationships, pervades these partnerships and collaborative working arrangements have emerged on a range of issues including pedagogy and curriculum (McGovern 2011). In part, this shift represents a subversion of the intentions behind education policy which clearly identified local authorities as the cause of inefficiency and poor educational performance.

Elsewhere different configurations have resulted. Schools have been aware that, in the past, LEA services were of a variable quality with some being highly valued while others were considered poor. Accordingly, schools have specialized their services responding to local experience and conditions. At the Brigshaw Co-operative Trust on the outskirts of Leeds, a highly effective network has enriched existing partnerships in bringing together a number of institutions across the age range. By personalizing and sharing welfare services provided by schools within the trust, responsive services have evolved based upon dialogue and communication between service providers and individuals within local areas. Pooling such welfare support services has resulted in dramatic improvements:

> So that when a head says we have a problem, the guidance support team can respond to family needs very rapidly. Whereas formerly you could have a crisis situation where it might take much more time for a tradition local authority-based team to respond, we can often be providing support within hours.
> *(Laurence 2011)*

As the trust took on a greater range of extended services, the local authority in effect 'decentralised a range of accountabilities and opportunities'. Incrementally expanding co-operation enabled new thresholds in understanding and activity. At the same time, despite having the support of the local authority, the values of self-help and self-responsibility could give rise to ambiguous feelings:

> We now need to make relatively few referrals into the centre of children from our schools ... But that can be a bit scary because what we are saying is 'actually we can be less reliant on external support because we are doing more ourselves'.
>
> *(Laurence 2011)*

Schools have been keen not to simply recycle old models which could be perceived as bureaucratic and authoritarian. Instead, flexible, slimmer and leaner bodies have been envisioned which are receptive to the changing needs of schools. In some areas, business opportunities and collective buying arrangements have been trialled by schools through joint purchasing. The Schools Co-operative Society has begun to look into the possibility of providing joint services at reduced cost although this cannot be done through compulsion, as in academy chains, but requires the common consent of schools.

Moreover, co-operative schools have added to the diversity of schooling. Co-operation can engender isolation within rapidly changing local ecologies of education. By evolving distinct ways of working, schools may foster a sense of separateness, especially if they are located in highly-populated areas containing many types of school within close proximity. Two co-operative schools I visited have developed their special educational needs provision and have offered a welcoming atmosphere for pupils with special needs which other schools were happy not to take on in a competitive climate. As a result, real differences as well as public perceptions can affect the intake of one school which in turn impacts upon others.

We should also be alert to the potential drawbacks of regional structures and the contested meanings of the local which are apparent in these developments. Co-operative arrangements have strengthened partnerships but new relationships can take a long time to establish. For example, after a number of years negotiating with the DfE, SCS was finally allowed to sponsor schools as an improvement partner; how far this can been expanded is an area of active discussion (Hatcher 2013). While regional arrangements have worked in the South West and parts of Yorkshire, where there was a history of common action among groups of schools, similar arrangements have not resulted elsewhere. In some regions it has been easy for expectations to spiral unrealistically. Regional structures can at times appear as a further burden, a top-down imposition based more upon hope than realistic action; one teacher complained of a regional networking event, that 'the whole tone of the day meant it was a top-down model and no one is going to go away and do anything ... you could just tell it was not going to happen' (headteacher 2013). In the short run, regional organizations may be perceived as creating extra work for few educational or material benefits – quite a risk for schools given the pressures on them to focus exclusively upon improving standards. The resources which have been provided by the Co-operative Group, and other co-operative and mutual enterprises, has been a significant feature of this development but, in areas where there is a limited history of co-operation among schools, more than short term support may be required to have a lasting impact. As local authorities have been consciously undermined, schools have had to organise themselves with few supplementary means at their disposal. In the meantime, new models have emanated from policy circles which promise quick solutions to the problem (DfE 2014).

However, as alluded to at the beginning of this chapter, co-operative schools have also benefited from national and international links within a global co-operative movement. In such circumstances, the concentration upon the 'local' can be constraining. A history of competitiveness cannot always be wiped off the slate with the introduction of a co-operative school and many factors may make it hard to generate genuine collaboration within geographical areas. Local inequalities have led to certain schools being perceived as 'better', having more influence in local and regional forums and resulting in a lack of trust. Competitive market tendencies continue to exert an influence which may create difficulties for co-operation with schools down the road, for instance, in terms of sharing data. 'Local democracy' carries a strong resonance and, while essential to any vision of the future, should not blind us to the interaction that may be developing on a wider canvas. Learning can be enriched by associations between pupils and educationists nationally and internationally – such alliances can provide a sense of purpose and confirmation of one's own practice. In addition, visits of teachers to co-operative schools and networks in Spain and Italy have provided ballast for a co-operative identity. The co-operative schools movement may well be prefiguring new forms of networks that tie together local, national and international spheres.

Conclusions

Co-operative schools can be seen as working within the confines of education policy while also challenging it. Despite the lukewarm reception of co-operative schools by the Coalition Government since 2010, the movement is actively reconfiguring the intentions of policymakers. To some extent, the co-operative model is necessarily a top-down one given that structures had to be developed before schools could take advantage of them. Co-operative schools thus represent creative and opportunistic responses to new legislation which are building upon and developing supportive relationships. The varied fortunes of membership schemes illustrate how too direct a transference of the co-operative model carries dangers of being misunderstood in the educational context. Equally, it is possible that continuing educational forces may neuter any long-term effect of co-operative practices and values. Democratic expectations thus have to be balanced against the real daily pressures, external and internal, felt by schools.

A strong motivation behind education policy has been to lever external resources into education given that, on their own, schools can be vulnerable. Yet, as some private sponsors of trusts and academies have been aware, finance is not enough – in the case of co-operative schools, knowledge, innovative organizational thinking and values based upon a sustained tradition were just as important. Embedding co-operative values across a school, it is hoped, will prevent subsequent leaders from simply discarding co-operative values. Thus, in looking forward to more equitable education systems (Ainscow et al 2012), both resources and values will be necessary to sustain and expand the bonds of collaboration and co-operation.

The rapid growth of co-operative schools has taken place alongside the gradual extension of understanding as new ideas are imported and adapted to an existing situation. Historically and conceptually, co-operation is like an onion which can reveal multiple layers of depth and significance. As Ian MacPherson points out in his contribution to this book, co-operation can sometimes lack the simplicity of ideas to make it truly popular. In some schools, there are numbers of people who simply do not 'get it' which can lead to confusion and misunderstanding (Davidge 2013). Adopting a co-operative label is only a starting point. Advances can be checked and slowed by those who are less sure about the direction of travel. Over time, with the succession of new staff and leaders, co-operative schools will again have to reinvent the meaning of co-operation if it is to flourish. It will need to emphasize the 'co-operative difference' as part of a wider picture of education for all and not simply good schools for the aspirational, a tension running through contemporary educational thinking (reflected in Adonis 2012). In its very nature, co-operation requires the support and sympathy of many different people so can only be achieved in practice through concerted action. The co-operative schools movement has re-emphasized schools as democratic and community based institutions and re-asserted the role of common values within the arena of public debate. It is developing a rich but complex inheritance for the future.

Note

1 The contrary of this process is of course also true – that recent scandals and economic losses affecting the consumer co-operative movement in the UK can have deleterious influences upon this wider movement. The co-operative movement inevitably bears a burden of representation which suggests that perceived failure in one area must necessarily reflect upon all co-operatives – in the way that the failure of capitalist firms rarely lead us to question the whole capitalist system. Nonetheless, despite this adversity, co-operative schools have continued to multiply.

References

Adonis, A. (2012) *Education, Education, Education. Reforming England's Schools*, London: Biteback.
Ainscow, M., Dyson, A., Goldrick, S. and West, M. (2012) *Developing Equitable Education Systems*, Abingdon: Routledge.
Arnold, P. (2013) 'Making co-operative ideas work', *Forum*, 55: 245–254.
Audsley, J., Chitty, C., O'Connell, J., Watson, D.M. and Wills, J. (2013) *Citizen Schools: Learning to Rebuild Democracy*, London: IPPR.
Baker, S. (2011) Interviewed by Tom Woodin, 19 September.

Ball, S.J. (2013) *The Education Debate*, Bristol: Policy Press.
Boden, R., Ciancanelli, P. and Wright, S. (2012) 'Trust universities? Governing post-capitalist futures', *Journal of Co-operative Studies*, 45: 16–24.
Breeze, M., Wilkins, A. and Bickle, R. (2011) (eds) 'Co-operation in education', *Journal of Co-operative Studies*, special issue, 44.
Chitty, C. (2009) *Education Policy in Britain*, Basingstoke: Policy Press.
Co-operative College/Group (2012) *Co-operative Schools – Where Values Make a Difference*, Accrington: Huckleberry Films.
Co-operative College (2014) Website, http://www.co-op.ac.uk/ (accessed 21 March 2014)
Co-operative News (2014) Community impact index report, *Co-operative News*, 14 January, 14.
Cotham Co-operative Academy (2013) Presentation to Co-operative Education in Wales, Institute of Welsh Affairs, 28 June.
Davidge, G. (2013) 'Some "get it" more than others: cultivating a co-operative ethos in uncertain times', *Forum*, 55: 255–268.
DfE (2014) The role of the regional schools commissioner, http://www.regional schoolscommissioner.com/sections/about_the_org (accessed 2 March 2014).
Facer, K., Thorpe, J. and Shaw, L. (2012) 'Co-operative education and schools: an old idea for new times?' *Power and Education*, 4: 327–341.
Gamble, A. and Wright, T. (2004) *Restating the State*, Oxford: Blackwell.
Glatter, R. (2013) 'To whom should our schools belong? Towards a new model of ownership', in Julian, C. (ed.) *Making It Mutual*, Lincoln: ResPublica, 166–170.
Gold, A., Evans, J., Earley, P., Halpin, D. and Collarbone, P. (2003) 'Principled principals? Values-driven leadership: evidence from ten case studies of "outstanding" school leaders', *Educational Management and Administration*, 31: 127–138.
Gunter, H. (2011) *Leadership and the Reform of Education*, Bristol: Policy Press.
Hargreaves, D. (2010) *Creating a Self-Improving School System*, Nottingham: NCSL.
Hatcher, R. (2013) Co-operative trusts, Alliance Against Birmingham Academies, 21 January, http://allianceagainstbirminghamacademies.wordpress.com/2013/01/21/cooperative-trusts/ (accessed 24 March 2014).
Jaffe, T. and Cronin, K. (2013) Interviewed by Tom Woodin, 23 September, 2013.
Jones, S. (2011) Interviewed by Tom Woodin, 19 September.
Labour Party (2014) *Review of Education Structures, Functions and the Raising of Standards for All*, London: Labour Party.
Laurence, P. (2011) Interviewed by Tom Woodin, 16 September.
Lowe, R. (ed.) (2002) 'A century of local education authorities', *Oxford Review of Education*, special edition, 28.
McGovern, P., Bryant, D., and Bacchus, L. (2011) Building a co-operative alternative, presentation to Schools Co-operative Society Conference, 9 November.
Mortimore, P. (2013) *Education Under Siege. Why There is a Better Alternative*, Bristol: Policy Press.
Nemerowicz, G. and Rosi, E. (1997) *Education for Leadership and Social Responsibility*, London: Falmer.
Newsam, P. (2011) The nationalisation of schools in England, Local Schools Network. http://www.localschoolsnetwork.org.uk/2011/06/the-nationalisation-of-schoolsin-england/ (accessed 25 July 2013).
Roach, P. (2013) 'Reasons to co-operate: co-operative solutions for schools', *Forum*, 55: 269–277.
Rogers, S. (2012) Presentation at Institute of Education seminar, 'Putting the community back into community schools', 13 March.
Scargill, V. (2014) Presentation to Leadership for Learning Nework, University of Cambridge, 11 February 2014.
Schools Co-operative Society (2014) Website, http://www.co-operativeschools.coop/ (accessed 21 March 2014)

Sen, A. (1999) *Development as Freedom*, Oxford: Oxford University Press.
Stevenson, H. (2011) 'Coalition education policy: Thatcherism's long shadow', *Forum*, 53: 179–194.
Stoll, L., Bolam, R., McMahon, A., Wallace, M. and Thomas, S. (2006) 'Professional learning communities: a review of the literature', *Journal of Educational Change*, 7: 221–258.
Wilson, M. (2011) Interviewed by Tom Woodin, 27 July.
—— (2014) Presentation to Leadership for Learning Nework, University of Cambridge, 11 February.
Woodin, T. (2011) 'Co-operative education in Britain during the nineteenth and twentieth centuries: context, identity and learning', in Webster, A., Brown, A., Stewart, D., Walton, J.K. and Shaw, L., *The Hidden Alternative: Co-operative Values, Past, Present and Future*, Manchester: Manchester University Press, 78–95.
—— (2012) 'Co-operative schools: building communities in the 21st century', *Forum*, 54: 327–339.
Woodin, T. and Fielding, M. (2013) 'Co-operative education for a new age?' *Forum*, 55, 2: 179–184.
Woodin, T., McCulloch, G. and Cowan, S. (2013) *Secondary Education and the Raising of the School Leaving Age – Coming of Age?* New York: Palgrave Macmillan.
Woods, P. (2011) *Transforming Education Policy. Shaping a Democratic Future*, Bristol: Policy Press.

PART III

Co-operative education in co-operatives and higher education

10

The co-operative university? Transforming higher education

Stephen Yeo

> Co-operatives are voluntary organizations, open to all persons able to use their services and willing to accept responsibilities of membership ...
> *1st principle: voluntary and open membership, International Co-operative Alliance (ICA) Statement of Co-operative Identity 1995*

> If manure be suffered to lie in idle heaps, it breeds stink and vermin. If properly diffused, it vivifies and fertilizes. The same is true of capital and knowledge. A monopoly of either breeds filth and abomination. A proper diffusion of them fills a country with joy and abundance.
> *Poor Man's Guardian, 3/15, 1 June 1834: 146*

> Sooner or later this country must face a comprehensive form of education beyond school ... and make it available to all ... This will be achieved through a bloodier battle than that for the comprehensive reform of secondary education.
> *Eric Robinson, 'A Comprehensive Reform of Higher Education', in Higher Education Review, 3/3, Summer 1971: 1927–2011*

Knowledge, states and markets

There are many reasons for thinking that now is a good time to be considering – more than that, acting on – the idea of transforming higher education (HE) in Britain in a co-operative and mutual direction. In this essay I will select just one reason and use it to identify some of the wider issues involved: it is that ideas matter more and more in this century, as do the forms of association through which ideas are produced and distributed. My approach to co-operation, which is committed as well as conceptual, is illustrated with historical and current instances as well as my own experience. Ideas and examples are clustered in five overlapping sections which are not linear or chronological.

In 1969, Boris Ford, professor of education at Sussex asked 'what is a university?' (Ford 1969). He regretted that this is 'a topic which most of us who work in them seem content to avoid'. This is no longer so. 'The idea of a university' is in play as it has not been since Newman's work in 1854, or before him that of Humboldt (Anderson 2006; MacIntyre 2009; Shattock 2012; Swain 2013). Deeply felt answers have been coming from academics with very different points of view (Barnett 1990; Scott 1993; Bailey and Freedman 2011; Collini 2012; Holmwood 2011). In working through this issue from the point of view of co-operative and mutual enterprises (CMEs) we have much to learn about the intellectual as well as financial diffi-culties that any coherent, ethical *idea* of a university, with its own values and principles, continues to face in 'the West'.

A definition of co-operation relevant to HE is a good place to start. The ICA's *Statement of Co-operative Identity* (1995) contains one (see appendix). Reading the whole *Statement* with a single university or a global HE network in mind, key concepts jump out: autonomy; voluntary and open membership; and member ownership and control. Cooperation is relevant to education because by its nature learning is a two-way, mutual activity. Knowledge is something you can give to others without losing any of it yourself. 'All education which is worth the name involves the relationship of mutuality' (Thompson 1968: 4). A *de haut en ba*s system, particularly in England, has always been marked by a fear from the top that too much 'Higher' for too many of the 'Lower' involves either a waste of money or a loss of position. As the Master of the Rolls asked during the legal battle preceding the 1902 Education Act, which abolished School Boards as rare examples of direct democracy in Britain and prevented them controlling any Higher Grade work beyond elementary education: 'why should I teach my ploughboy Greek?' (Eaglesham 1956).

I have spent much of my life in or near education, from entering a Parents National Education Union (Cholmondley 1960) pre-school in 1945, to retiring from Ruskin College Oxford as Principal in 1997. I taught at the University of Sussex from 1966 to 1989. Since 1997 I have worked in a variety of ways with the Co-operative College, and now with the Co-operative Heritage Trust. In each of these places the form as well as the content of learning has been a central concern (Yeo 1970, 1990, 2000). In opportune times for CMEs, it may be time to follow Brecht's advice, 'nor should you let the Now blot out the Previously and Afterwards' (Willett and Manheim 1976: 307).

For most of my time there, Sussex represented an innovative and, in retrospect, a co-operative and mutual idea of how a new university should organize itself and how that connects with what it teaches, learns and writes about. Yet Asa Briggs's inspirational 'New Map of Learning' (see below) lasted no longer than twenty-five years. Ever since it was dismantled I have recognized that 1960s and 1970s enthusiasts like myself, assuming a 'secular trend towards increasing academic self-government' (Moodie and Eustace 1974: 58), neglected the internal work necessary to sustain a *different* model of the university, based on co-operative and mutual *membership*, in competitive, market-convergent times.

We tended to use our pre-1996 Research Assessment Exercise habitus (Lucas 2006), defended as 'academic freedom', to work externally: in my case organizing for community and labour history in associations like the Federation of Worker Writers and Community Publishers. We resisted Planned Programme Budgeting *(Final Report* 1973: 27-38) but allowed management to marginalize the ideal of cross-grade, communitarian self-government. Our radicalism tended towards *alternative* rather than fully *oppositional* construction. Academics continue to disdain management as 'admin' and are wary of 'teaching loads' in order to defend their 'own work'. It may be that intellectuals, like the Professional and Managerial Class more generally, have little elective affinity with CMEs. Writers as they would like to be, non-scientific academics prefer on-the-page connections to on-the-ground constructions, whole systems to knowable, slow-cooking Societies. But this may point us in a particular direction as far as transforming higher education is concerned.

These tensions are discernible historically. It would be worth considering how far 'adult education', treated as an isolated department rather than as the whole HE enterprise, unintentionally functioned to let a comprehensive, democratic transformation of HE off the hook between 1945 and c. 1979 (Goldman 1995; Taylor and Steele 2000). It was a rare and famous strike in 1909 about the nature and direction of knowledge, led by staff, which lay at the heart of Ruskin's history (Waugh 2009; Ree 1984; Pollins 1984). And the idea of specifically workers' equivalents to universities underlay the pre-history of Ruskin as a College founded in 1899, as it did the Co-operative College in 1919 (Dale and Dodd 1899; Merry 1899). Such notions floated in the European air during the late-nineteenth century. *Universites Populaires* had been encouraged by the followers of Emile Durkheim in France, and Marcel Mauss' work remains central to theorizing mutuality (Mercier 1986; Mauss, 1922). The central *intellectual* problem for any co-operative university has to be knowledge itself, the power which flows from and into its dominant *divisions of labour* in the sense in which Durkheim used that term (Durkheim 1893).

In what ways are our times good as well as opportune? More and more, ideas are seen as material: the 'knowledge worker' and a 'knowledge economy' have been current since the 1960s (Drucker 1959). This hardly needs saying in universities nowadays. It has long been assumed in co-operatives: 'bread, knowledge and freedom' as William Lovett, the storekeeper of the First London Co-operative Trading Association wrote in the title of his autobiography (Lovett 1876). In this way, CMEs can be seen as movements for lifelong learning which offer models for brain-workers today (Maccaferri 2011). The generation of new knowledge and consciousness through these co-operative forms is becoming essential to sustaining modern, 'economic' co-operatives *as* cooperatives. There is a sense in which large-scale co-operatives and mutuals, for instance in the financial sector during times of capitalist crisis, need to become learning organizations – specialist universities – in themselves. The alternative is to take the line of least resistance – the capitalist road.

Member-consciousness is the (organic) capital of cooperatives and mutuals, a point well understood among successful networks of co-operatives and credit unions across the world where education was seen as coterminous with co-operation (Arizmendiarrieta 1984; Culloty 1990; Bajo and Roelants 2011).

During the early twenty-first century, universities are commonly defended by their funders and managers in terms of bread rather than truth, generating useful knowledge for Britain's competitive position in a global race. They might equally be evaluated in terms of the originality, morality or sustainability of the ideas they produce, distribute and exchange. Or in terms of the special relations between the private freedoms and public responsibilities which their charters and statutes, including their licence to confer degrees, are drawn up to incorporate – by no less an arm of the state than the Privy Council. How universities are governed matters. Put another way, it matters to what extent people in them dare to make states, but not quite as they choose, rather than submit to abstract notions of 'the state' and 'the market'. The fully 'public university' makes its own 'circumstances', its own markets and states of affairs, changing as well as understanding The Market and The State.

Complex relations between the public and the private to make things differently and to make things happen, are the stuff of present-day co-operatives and mutuals. CMEs are full of externally-derived, market and state contradictions in and against which their members make spaces to produce, distribute and exchange goods, social relations and ideas. Such enterprises are economic, yes, but for what kind of economy? An economy of the common good? They are businesses, yes – no more heavily state-funded than, say, British Aerospace – but also voluntary and open associations of members. 'A co-operative', says the 1995 *Statement*, 'is an autonomous association of persons united voluntarily to meet their common economic, social, and cultural needs and aspirations through a jointly-owned and democratically-controlled enterprise'.

Co-operative characteristics: possibilities for universities?

As suggested at the start, autonomy, ownership, and control by members in 'voluntary and open membership' characterize co-operatives – how far can we re-think universities and HE systems along these lines?

Autonomy?

It matters whether we conceive of autonomy in terms of individual institutions or federated activities across a wider system. Certainly, there is a long history of institutions striving for autonomy, whether that be in terms of civic status or, more recently, in status groups such as the Russell Group which promote league-table autonomy. Universities seek autonomy as fast as they reasonably can, whether from local authorities, the Council for National Academic Awards, or joint ownership by 'parent' universities. Reading, Exeter and Southampton all gained their independence from University of London or Oxford examinations. Former components of the University of London regularly 'win' degree-awarding powers. Currently, Suffolk University Campus wants its 'freedom' from the academic, research and financial underwriting it has so far enjoyed from the Universities of Essex and East Anglia. Imagine a minimalist 'university', on a regional or even national scale, to which autonomous units prepare and present candidates. Why go it alone rather than help to form an open, co-operative university network designed for learners and learning in our times? There is potential for students, teachers, managers and support staff to *socialize* massive, open online courses (Moocs), to prevent autonomy at single institutional level working for competitive sameness rather than for co-operative difference. Imagine a university – 'universal' was a favourite Owenite word – as a complex local *and* global cluster of federally-linked mutual societies of diverse sizes fit for their purpose and for meeting members' needs. Some might be as small as seminar rooms; others as large as science parks and with no social or technical obstacles to communication between them or, for that matter, with anyone else who wishes to learn to follow the argument wherever it leads.

From the point of view of forming co-operatives with organic, meaningful memberships, CMEs could provide universities with services (teaching, assessment, research or any other type of supply) for purchasers across an open system rather than within one closed institution. The North East Music Co-operative (NEMCO), providing instrumental tuition across the North East is one example from the school sector. Once there are enough such co-operatives (in language learning, world-market literacy, study skills, public history, memory-work and life-writing), and once they have been shown to engage their members in mutually improving, productive ways, a co-operative and mutual higher education system becomes visible.

Open?

Like autonomy, openness is a key cooperative value: 'open and voluntary'. Instead of the Open University (OU) competing as an autonomous establishment, *one* university among others, could there not be an open HE system for which the OU could still provide the matrix? The story of the *containment* of Harold Wilson's original thoughts about the University of the Air needs to be written. He imagined 'a new educational trust ... bringing together many institutions and organizations' rather than an independent and autonomous institution that granted its own degrees (Open University 2014). The taming by universities of Gordon Brown's University for Industry (UfI), among other examples, might reveal a similar story. It would be in the long-term interests of students and their National Union to organize 'anti-enclosure' research and development – action research perhaps (Greenwood and Levin 2001) – not only on university governance but also on the 'ownership' of degrees and other post-compulsory qualifications. The vision would be to 'make universities irrevocably part of the knowledge commons' (Boden 2012).

Openness to – and then ownership by – everyone, 'the people', was part of the idea of a university long before the Open University opened in 1971. In 1900 the Social Democratic Foundation (Shoreditch branch) used 'Oxford and Cambridge and other endowed seats of learning (as) the rightful inheritance of the people' as an argument against Ruskin as a separate 'workers' college' (Ree 1984: 191). Given the Universities of Oxford and Cambridge Act of 1571, they may have had 'civil or common law' on their side (Farrington and Palfreyman 2012: 13–14).

The new universities of the 1960s were more open than their predecessors in the UK, at least in promoting new ideas, re-thinking internal organization and generating traffic between academics and outside interests; not least in the creation of centres, institutes and 'units', on and off campus, for modern records, development studies, creative writing, science policy and business studies. But that generation of 'old-new' universities were also set in quite traditional moulds, determined to win their spurs as 'proper universities', as was the OU.

Might it be possible to develop a vision of a regional and comprehensive post-compulsory education system in which all local citizen-beneficiaries had automatic membership rights, linked to mutually-beneficial cultural institutions: libraries, theatres, galleries and sports centres, with front-room learning centres on every estate or group of streets? No more competitive admissions processes on which individual universities spend so much spirit, sifting and grading. For that matter, a mutually-constructed Open University Validation Service (OUVS) and a mutually-owned assessment/examination service working to agreed criteria they might reduce the elaborate examination and grading processes on which individual universities spend up to a whole term from a student's point of view. Instead we could encourage openly-available, voluntary membership in teaching and learning societies, federated into comprehensive, regional universities of teachers and learners all able to research and write, learn and teach, within a nationally available credit system – a co-operative and mutual Council for National Academic Awards (the CNAA, 1965–1993).

Ruskin College illustrates the problems and possibilities well. In the early 1990s, the College, under pressure from the then new FE Funding Council (FEFC), replaced its two-year diplomas with one-year courses. In response, Ruskin sought open, external, transferable validation and accreditation through the Open University Validation Service, a successor body to the CNAA. The one-year Certificate of Higher Education (Cert HE) provided 120 credits out of the 360 needed to achieve a degree, to which was added, for some subjects, a second-year Dip HE programme making 240 credits in all. Hence the College's interest in two-year, foundation or associate degree programmes. Ruskin became one of OUVS's success stories. Its Advisory Board, on which I sat, had some of the excitement, but with less of a single-institutional focus, which must have attached to the original Planning Committee for the OU which began work in 1967. By 2013, it was possible to do a full degree at Ruskin, funded from further and higher education sources, linked to different external networks and accreditation routes.

Ruskin was one beneficiary of a national credit framework. This developed from the 1980s, from a base in further education colleges such as Nelson College, and eventually became the Open College Network (OCN). It spread to polytechnics such as Preston Polytechnic, now UCLAN, reflecting Eric Robinson's (1927-2011) vision for 'People's Universities' (Robinson 1968; Pedley 1977). Robinson's 'integrated colleges scheme', starting in Lancashire, would have allowed an individual student, indeed a whole class of students, to gain degrees or other qualifications without buying into the Oxford, Sussex or any other exclusive 'brand'. Ruskin became a small part of that half-finished, potentially co-operative and mutual system. The idea remains half-finished because it lacked political backing from any government and because no university is bound to 'recognize' a student's credits. They are not legal tender, in the sense of being fully portable across a wider, open, university system (Yeo 1998).

There were moments of hope, such as when Ruskin and the other Long Term Residential Colleges for Adult Education (LTRCs) were given their unique Adult Education Bursaries in 1975. Soon after that, there was also a chance for the University of Sussex to join with the College of Education across the road and, with Brighton Polytechnic as it then was, to make moves towards regional, comprehensive arrangements for HE in Sussex. The University gave no sustained, collective thought to the matter. The result is two contiguous, autonomous universities: Brighton and Sussex – now with a joint Medical School (2002) as a symbol of the comprehensive co-operation there could have been. Regional arrangements in Sussex and elsewhere would also have made sense of LTRCs, region by region: flexible bursaries for late returners to learning, including the homeless, for whom residence and tutorial support is necessary and well-suited.

Ownership?

Whereas members of CMEs do and must own the future of their ultimately 'private' enterprises, even at the risk of democratic decisions to de-mutualize them, there is no reason why the public assets that enable universities to function should be owned in the same way. They need to be held 'in trust' for their users and beneficiaries, in a range of publicly-accountable forms such as those now being implemented within the Schools Co-operative Society. 'Ambiguity of ownership' has led to 'governance hazards' which 'include the appropriation of academic resources for managerial gain at the expense of social interests' (Boden 2012). Top managers love property development schemes whether in higher or further education, not always with manifest educational benefit.

The question then remains: should user-members, or a wider set of beneficiary-member/owners be seen mainly as entire, self-governing institutions ('the university') or could lessees also be smaller consortia of teachers, learners, researchers, writers, technicians or craftspeople who 'unite voluntarily to meet their common economic, social and cultural needs and aspirations through a jointly-owned and democratically-controlled enterprise'. In 1962, in a book which grew from teaching a WEA Class, Raymond Williams addressed the problem of ownership in relation to democratic control in the newspaper industry, another site of autonomous and powerful baronies in British culture. His approach could equally well apply to HE. In many cases it already does: public ownership (local, regional, national, community or trust) of land and other large-scale assets, with users as long-term lessees. 'It is the duty of society to hold these means [of communication] in trust for the actual contributors, who for all practical purposes will control their use' (Williams 1962: 122).

Members?

The *Statement of Co-operative Identity* mentions members and membership seventeen times. Without members co-operatives cease to be such. Hence the work led by Graham Melmoth, CEO at the Co-operative Group (previously Co-operative Wholesale Society) from 1996-2002, to make individual membership meaningful once again in consumer co-operative societies. Many of these were in danger of demutualizing themselves owing to lack of member engagement. As President of the ICA, Melmoth had started the process which resulted in the *Statement*. He then put it to work in educational programmes designed by the Co-operative College for employees and other members of Societies.

At this stage of the argument, to do equivalent – if more preliminary – work in HE is more a matter of asking questions than offering answers. Co-operative schools have multiplied rapidly, forming into clusters which have the potential to develop member-governed partnerships or co-operative education authorities. As the network develops, there is increasing scope for trade in goods and services, curriculum development and active democratic governance. But even in this dynamic movement, it would be fair to say that schools, let alone universities, as full-blown co-operatives scarcely exist in Britain yet. As in the case of full-blown co-operative banks, enabling legislation will be a necessary preliminary.

Which are the most promising units in higher education, below the level of the whole university or system within which member-ownership and member self-governance can grow? How best can we draw on surviving, if atrophied, governance models such as elected, sovereign Senates, in order to 'vest beneficial ownership and control in students and employees and help prevent excessive managerial predation'? (Boden 2012). We must also recognize that students are not perpetual and that faculty are as footloose as footballers. This means that academic-related and support staff; local authorities; professional communities of interest, global as well as local; and businesses and voluntary associations, would have to be the staid, continuing members in any stakeholder-governed model for HE.

A useable past?

As always in Britain, there is a useable past to draw on. Moving between universities and co-operatives I offer four points from the past and present of each, all of them relating to membership and to *belonging* in the sense of feeling-part-of as well as owning.

First, old-old universities like Oxford still describe staff and students as members, perhaps more frequently and with more inherited meaning than new ones. 'The University' of Oxford is something of an abstraction: tourists continue to look for it in vain. The co-operative adult educator N.F.S. Grundtvig (1783-1872) and the co-operative labour historian G.D.H. Cole (1889-1959) each identified colleges at Oxford in the 1820s and the 1920s respectively, not the university, as proto-cooperatives, presenting their members to the university (the 'Group' in Co-operative terms), preparing them for examinations or for studying at other colleges (Allchin 1997; Wright 1979). Colleges continue to be self-governing, using the language of membership and association: fellowship, election, common room, congregation, wardenship etc. Publications such as the *Oxford Magazine* continue to protest at every executive encroachment by vice chancellors who want to act as chief executives. To their members, including the students they (not the University) admit, Colleges are more meaningful than any anciently-chartered whole. Is such thinking always, and only, archaic? In a more modern register, the 2008-9 HE Funding Council and Lincoln University *Learning Landscapes* project was similarly concerned with the co-production and management of learning, defining students as well as staff as producers of their own 'arrangements' for learning at university, within carefully designed, disaggregated spaces, rather than as passive consumers of a whole-institutional offer (Neary 2009, Neary and Saunders 2010).

Secondly, to go back to the nineteenth century and the co-operative movement, mutual improvement societies were among the earliest, simplest and smallest of CMEs. The sense of belonging and often informal membership they generated was strong and remarkably productive of learning at every level (Lovett 1920: 35–6; Harrison 1961; Rose 2002: 58–91; Joint Committee 1908; Mansbridge 1914). These groups of ambitious adult learner-members combined eclectic high-level learning with basic literacy. In the digital age, their experience becomes relevant all over again. What would a hi-tech mutual improvement society look like?

It is tempting to get over-excited by the Age of Google as if *any* technology could re-make social relations, or learning, on our behalf. *An avalanche is coming: HE and the revolution ahead* (Barber et al. 2013; Murray 2010). Connectivity matters, but how? Exactly the same debates about openness, and about the commercial pressure to enclose courses to generate revenue, are raging within the massive-open-online-course movement itself: 'Will Moocs be the scourge or saviour of higher education?' (*Guardian* 2013). Discontinuous possibilities *are* opening up in this field, but on a relatively small scale apart, that is, from the millions of individuals each at their interactive terminals. Gaia University is an example of a web-enabled, global federation of small groups of learners. Scaled-down, sustainable ways of life and courses on permaculture-design are its reason for existence (www.gaiauniversity.org). Similarly, the Khan Academy has been hyped as 'free world-class education for anyone, anywhere', potentially heralding the end of campus life' (Cadwallader 2012; Khan Academy 2013).

Thirdly, co-operators are well-placed to insist, as does Gaia, on the primacy of social relations in learning, and as the OU did from its beginning, with its summer schools and tutorial support in a network of regional centres. The 'branch' of a consumer co-operative society in the North of England at any time during the late-nineteenth century was the very model of a modern learning centre (Yeo 2002). The WEA's university tutorial class system, invented by R.H. Tawney,

Albert Mansbridge and others, remains exemplary: its famous book box system would nowadays have multiple platforms to add to the printed page. Joining a tutorial class then entailed becoming a member of a local branch, part of a wider district, both federated into a national association (Mansbridge 1914).

Co-op UK's predecessor, the Co-op Union, had an elaborate Education Department which channelled co-operative societies' self-imposed education dividend through to the Co-operative College. From the mid-nineteenth to the mid-twentieth century an active member could participate in mutually-accredited lifelong learning within the movement rather than the state system, moving from qualification to qualification (Twigg 1924; Thew 1985; Attfield 1981). During the 1990s, Unison offered multi-levelled learning to its members through Unison Open College, as well as the WEA, the OCN, Northern and Ruskin colleges and other member-sanctioned FE and HE partnerships. The OCN was, in effect, a co-operative, mutual validation and accreditation network, owned and controlled by its members, its services provided from each to all and all to each.

Fourthly, back to university. Campuses sometimes look coherent. But even in a now rare single-site university they are peculiarly centrifugal, fissiparous places, full of cellular, individualistic energies, well-guarded 'academic tribes and territories' (Becher and Trowler 2001). Anyone who has worked on one knows that they are by nature more like covered markets or department stores, full of independent franchises, than airports or supermarkets, however much increasingly well-paid executives try to make them otherwise. The recent but rapidly growing literature on university management can be read as sometimes sensitive, sometimes crass attempts to corral the campus into a command organization (Clark 1998; Deem 2007; Shattock 2010). The characteristic *size* of effective units in universities has been considered in a sensitive way (Hamel 2007). But management difficulties and campus discontents perhaps indicate the potential benefits of co-operative and mutual enterprise in this setting. By nature CMEs grow federally, multiplying horizontal lines of belonging rather than vertical lines of command. I watched an early contribution to the 'science' being made at Sussex, shortly after McKinsey had been called in to cut their teeth in HE affairs (Fielden and Lockwood 1973). This was at approximately the same time as the first ever separate building for Management, 'Sussex House', was erected. And the Students' Union successfully called for action research. This took the form of an elected Committee of Inquiry into the Organisation of the University of Sussex. Its Final Report is still worth reading by democrats (*Final Report* 1973).

Human agency and the idea of a university

At the same time that E.P. Thompson identified 'The Business University' at Warwick in 1970, he was leading an exceptionally productive, co-operative and mutual Centre for Social History (Thompson 1971). The collective memory closes quickly. Human *agency* – Thompson's main historical, moral and political preoccupation – is critical to the field of co-operation and mutuality in a way that state *policy* is not. By this I mean people, would-be *members* and lifelong learners, taking action to build on residual and emergent ideas of higher education in and against dominant ideas, not necessarily on a large scale. At different times and places during my working life, academics have got further towards 'the co-operative university', cell by cell, than would now be known about by most students or seen by policymakers as contributing to Britain's competitiveness: 'jobs and growth'.

In 1970s Brighton, mutualizing developments in HE were actively underway. *The Idea of a New University: an Experiment in Sussex* (Briggs 1964) lived on until the early 1990s. Asa Briggs's 'new map of learning' was expressed through self-governing schools of study which replaced departments and fostered conscious, critical mutuality within and between disciplines. While students' programmes belonged to schools, faculty could teach across them rather than being clustered by specialism. Disciplines or 'subject groups' worked with clipped wings. The bias was towards studying problems and testing professionalisms against possible futures. School-based or critical 'contextual' courses accompanied every 'major' course. There was an arts-science programme in which every student had to participate. Academic and intellectual divisions of labour were studied as social problems rather than promoted as career opportunities. It is not surprising that research on the social history of co-operation thrived in such a setting and, in response to student demands, new courses evolved through dialogue (Yeo 1970). The sociology of knowledge – those organizational forms through which knowledge is altered, produced, distributed and exchanged, along with the disciplinary and departmental boundaries – is inseparable from its content. This is what 'knowledge is power' means: *different* knowledges from and for different arrangements of our powers of production, distribution, education and government (Benjamin 1979).

There is still space for the co-operative idea. Such has been the restlessness in education policy in England and Wales during the last 50 years that it would be odd indeed if 'the Co-op' was to remain invisible among other entrepreneurs in this field such as the militantly anti-state University of Buckingham or, more recently, the anti-populist University of Bloomsbury which relies on top-of-the-market fees (Clark 1998). Many companies, from Lloyds Bank to McDonald's, created their own less-than-universal universities. While at Ruskin, I sat on the Board of the Heart of England Training and Enterprise Council (HOETEC) with John Neil, founder of Unipart and its University. 'The U' stood for just-in-time knowledge, designed for a New Business Agenda (NBA). It had the chutzpah to challenge, in Oxford, the notion of 'warehousing knowledge'. This was seen as wasteful, like stockpiling automobile spare parts. In comparable ways, it would not be odd for large-scale consumer co-operative societies in Britain to work with the Co-operative College to form a co-operative *education* branch of their businesses alongside their farms, pharmacies, funerals, food, travel and legal services – and for that branch of Societies' work to achieve a higher return on capital employed than groceries. That could be one setting for a co-operative university: not itself a co-operative but with member ownership and governance achieved through a wider co-operative society or group.

Towards the co-operative university?

So far as I know, there are not many current examples of 'the co-operative university' in full working order. This is why ancient, non-secular examples of co-operation and mutuality in higher learning may still be useful reference points. It is also why down-to-earth work on 'co-operatives, mutuals and the idea of membership' and on 'organization for member-controlled enterprises' needs to be better known in the academy (Birchall and Simmons 2001, 2011; Parnell 2011; International Joint Project 1995). The question for today may not be how to articulate the idea of an entire university and begin to draw up constitutions, but how best to learn from the fate of anticipatory cells, including inevitable defeats, to inform future possibilities. Alongside the *universal* in 'university', the proud word 'college', or even 'school' as in schools of study, exam schools and so on, may turn out to be important, as may the co-operative word 'Society' – much used by students to organize their own interests.

In 1989 I was appointed as principal of Ruskin by a twenty-strong interview committee comprised of member-governors. This followed an open meeting of all staff who had listened to and questioned all short-listed candidates, ranking them for the committee. Is this how vice chancellors are appointed? The appointment of chief and other executives is an issue which has recently been identified as a 'morally lazy' aspect of university governance (Newman 2008). Ruskin's governing members' constituent organizations were entitled to seats on the Council according to the number of scholarships and bursaries they offered to members of their own organizations, whom they had approved to study at the College. They also commissioned and supported research and development from the College's expert units: the Trade Union Research Unit (TURU) and the Trade Union International Research and Education Group (TUIREG). Ruskin's member organizations included trade unions; the Co-operative Union; the International Co-operative Alliance and the Working Mens' Club and Institute Union – an organization with an honourable, if exclusively male, educational history including the CIU 'Club Diploma'. In this way, the College worked with *its* members to develop courses, conferences, and research opportunities for *their* members. The Co-op College still does. As happens when forms of funding change, in co-operatives as well as in educational institutions, some ideas survived and others were defeated when, as a condition of continued state funding after the Further and Higher Education Act of 1992, the College was told to transfer sovereignty from its Council to a smaller Executive. Should we have done so?

Between 2001 and 2007, with the active help of their local co-operative society, the University of Lincoln Students' Union worked as a co-operative society. In 2007, the change from a CME into a charitable company limited by guarantee, was caused by changing student cohorts, by the insurance and other costs of not conforming to more recognized models, but above all by legislative changes stipulating what student unions were and were not allowed to do. 'The State' is no more innocent than 'The Market'. Historically, for many years the Chief Registrar of Friendly

Societies fought to prevent co-operative societies allocating funds for their own, educational purposes. Examples of campus co-operatives are legion and need to be assembled. Case studies of their success as businesses but also of their containment as cherished but no more than niche institutions, need to be collected. As often happens within regional ecologies, in Lincoln in 2010 another anticipatory cell formed, a remarkable teaching and learning co-operative named 'The Social Science Centre'. This will be well able to speak for itself, offering 'free, co-operative higher education', 'organized on the basis of democratic, non-hierarchical principles, with all members having equal involvement in the life and work of SSC' (socialsciencecentre.org.uk). The Centre's name may be seen as a direct heir of the Owenite understanding – indeed invention – of *social science* as critique of the anti-social or *dismal science* of competitive political economy.

Mondragón is probably the most integrated contemporary reference point for activists as well as intellectuals in this field. Jointly owned by its academic and administrative staff, the University was founded from a group of co-operatives going back to a technical school in 1947. It now has 9,000 students. To become fully-fledged members, staff have to work in the University for at least two years and then pay euros 12,000 to buy into the university's capital. This can be withdrawn on retirement. There is a governing General Assembly, a thirty-strong representative body, made up of equal numbers of staff, students and interested outside parties. The Assembly even has the power to sack members of the senior administrative team (Matthews 2013; Molina and Walton 2011). Income differentials within the university are kept within 3 to 1, an interesting contrast to developments at the apex of British universities (Boden 2012).

The idea of a university and the idea of a co-operative and mutual are both in play in 2014 as they have not been before in my lifetime (Co-operative Free University 2013). Running through both are conflicts and struggles central to the rest of the culture (Barber et al. 2013; Ciancelli 2007; Holmwood 2011). How should production of a central social good be organized or, to put it in the active mood, how should we producers and consumers – social stakeholders every one of us – arrange our own powers?

Acknowledgements

The help of Ursula Howard, Tom Woodin, Mervyn Wilson and, most recently, Dan Cook of the University of Bristol Graduate School of Education, who is completing a consultancy project for the Co-operative College on *Realising a Co-operative University*, has been invaluable in researching and completing this essay. In just the same way that comparative courses in Labour Movements, Aristocracies and Elites, Armies and Politics and other 'General Subjects' in History were offered as part of the History degree at Sussex, a course on Co-operation, Mutuality and Higher Education in Britain and the world is now urgently needed in Brighton or elsewhere.

References

Allchin, A.M. (1997) *N.F.S. Grundtvig*, Arhus: Arhus University Press.
Anderson, R. (2006) *British Universities Past and Present*, London: Hambledon Continuum.
—— (2010) 'The "Idea of a University" today' www.historyandpolicy.org/papers/policy-paper-98 (accessed 11 June 2013).
Attfield, J. (1981) *With Light of Knowledge: One Hundred Years of Education in the Royal Arsenal Cooperative Society, 1877–1977*, London: Journeyman.
Arizmendiarrieta, J.M. (1984) *La empresa para el hombre*, Bilbao: Alkar, cited and translated in Bajo, C.S. and Roelants, B (2011) *Capital and the Debt Learning from Cooperatives in the Global Crisis*, Basingstoke: Palgrave Macmillan.
Bailey, M. and Freedman, D. (eds) (2011) *The Assault on Universities: A Manifesto for Resistance*, London: Pluto.
Bajo, C.S and Roelants, B. (2011) 'The Desjardins Cooperative Group: a financial movement for Quebec's development' and 'Ceralep Societe Nouvelle, France: David and Goliath in the global economy', in *Capital and the Debt Trap: Learning from Cooperatives in the Global Crisis*, Basingstoke: Palgrave Macmillan.
Barber, M., Donnelly, K. and Rizvi, S. (2013) *An Avalanche is Coming: Higher Education and the Revolution Ahead*, London: IPPR.
Barnett, R. (1990) 'The Idea of Higher Education', Buckingham: The Society for Research into Higher Education and Open University Press.
Becher, T. and Trowler, P. R. (2001) *Academic Tribes and Territories: Intellectual Enquiry and the Culture of Disciplines* (2nd. ed.) Buckingham: SRHE & Open Univ. Press.
Benjamin, W. (1979 edit.) 'Eduard Fuchs, collector and historian', in Benjamin, W. *One-Way Street*, London: New Left Books.
Birchall, J. (2011) *People-Centred Businesses: Co-operatives, Mutuals and the Idea of Membership*, Basingstoke: Palgrave Macmillan.
Birchall, J. and Simmons, R. (2001) 'Member participation in mutuals: a theoretical model', in Birchall, J. (ed.) *The New Mutualism in Public Policy*, London: Routledge.
Boden, R., Cinacelli, P., Wright, S. (2012) 'Trust universities? Governance for post-capitalist futures', *Journal of Co-operative Studies*, 45/2: 16–24.
Briggs, A. (1964) 'Drawing a map of learning', in Daiches, D. (ed.) *The Idea of a New University: an Experiment in Sussex*, London: Andre Deutsch.
Cadwallader, C. (2012) 'Goodbye to all this . . . Is this the end of campus life?' *The New Review, The Observer*, 11 November: 8–11.
Cholmondley, E. (1960) *The Story of Charlotte Mason 1842–1923*, London: Dent.
Ciancelli, P. (2007) '(Re)producing universities: knowledge dissemination, market power and the global knowledge commons', in Epstein, D., Boden, R., Deem, R., Rizvi, F. and Wright, S. (eds) *World Yearbook of Education 2008. Geographies of Knowledge, Geometries of Power: Framing the Future of Higher Education*, New York: Routledge.
Clark, B.R. (1998) *Creating Entrepreneurial Universities*, Oxford: Elsevier Science; IAU Press.
Collini, S. (2012) *What are Universities For?* London: Penguin.
Culloty, A.T. (1990) *Nora Herlihy: Irish Credit Union Pioneer*, Dublin: Irish League of Credit Unions.
Dale, J.A. and Dodd, L.T. (1899) 'Ruskin Hall, Oxford', *Saint George: The Journal of the Ruskin Society of Birmingham*, 2/6: 94–105.
Deem, R., Hillyard, S. and Reed, M. (2007) *Knowledge, Higher Education and the New Managerialism: The Changing Management of UK Universities*, Oxford: OUP.
Drucker, P. (1959) *The Landmarks of Tomorrow*, New York: Harper and Brothers.
Durkheim, E. (1893, 1997 edit. trans. W.D. Hall) *The Division of Labour in Society*, New York: Free Press.
Eaglesham, E (1956) *From School Board to Local Authority*, London: Routledge and Kegan Paul.
Farrington, D.J. and Palfreyman, D. (2012) *The Law of Higher Education* (2nd ed.), Oxford: Oxford University Press.
Fielden, J. and Lockwood, G. (1973) *Planning and Management in Universities*, London: Chatto and Windus for Sussex University Press.

Final Report of the Committee of Inquiry into the Organisation of the University of Sussex (1973), The University of Sussex, May 1973.
Ford, B. (1969) 'What is a University?' *New Statesman,* 24 October.
Gaia University (2013) www.gaiauniversity.org.
Goldman, L. (1995) *Dons and Workers: Oxford and Adult Education since 1850,* Oxford: Clarendon Press.
Greenwood, D. and Levin, M. (2001) 'Pragmatic action research and the struggle to transform universities into learning communities', in Reason, P. and Bradbury, H. (eds) *Handbook of Action Research,* London: Sage Publications.
Guardian (2013) 'Will Moocs be the scourge or saviour of higher education' and 'Contact time a matter of degree', *The Guardian,* letters and emails 13 May, 16 May.
Hamel, G. (2007) *The Future of Management,* Boston, MA: Harvard Business School Press.
Harrison, J.F.C. (1961) *Learning and Living 1790–1960: a Study in the History of the English Adult Education Movement,* London: Routledge and Kegan Paul.
Holmwood, J. (2011) *A Manifesto for the Public University,* London: Bloomsbury.
International Joint Project on Co-operative Democracy (1995) *Making Membership Meaningful: Participatory Democracy in Co-operatives,* Saskatchewan: University of Saskatchewan, Centre for the Study of Co-operatives.
Joint Committee (1908), *Oxford and Working Class Education,* Oxford: Clarendon.
Khan Academy (2013) www. khanacademy.org (accessed 20 January 2013).
Lovett, W. (1876)(1920) *Life and Struggles of William Lovett in his Pursuit of Bread, Knowledge and Freedom with Some Short Account of the Different Associations he Belonged to and of the Opinions he Entertained,* London: G. Bell and Sons Ltd.
Lucas, L. (2006) *The Research Game in Academic Life,* Maidenhead: Society for Research into Higher Education and Open University Press.
Maccaferri, M. (2011) '"A co-operative of intellectuals": the encounter between co-operative values and urban planning. An Italian case study', in Webster, A., Brown, A., Stewart, D., Walton, J.K. and Shaw, L. (eds), *The Hidden Alternative: Co-operative Values, Past, Present and Future,* Manchester: Manchester University Press.
Mansbridge, A. (1914) *University Tutorial Classes,* London: Longmans.
—— (1923) *Adventure in Working-class Education,* London: Longmans Green.
MacIntyre, A. (2009) *God, Philosophy, Universities: A Selective History of the Catholic Philosophical Tradition,* London: Rowman & Littlefield.
Matthews, D. (2013) 'Inside a co-operative university (Mondragón)' *Times Higher Education,* http://www.timeshighereducation.co.uk/features/inside-a-cooperative-university/2006776.fullarticle (accessed 29 September 2013)
Mauss, M. (1922) *The Gift: Forms and Functions of Exchange in Archaic Societies,* London: Routledge.
Mercier, L. (1986) *Les Universites Populairés, 1899–1914: Education Populairés et Movement Ouvrier au Debut du Siècle,* Paris: editions ouvrieres.
Merry, F. (1899) 'How to start a branch Ruskin Hall', *Young Oxford, a Monthly Magazine Devoted to the Ruskin Hall Movement,* 1/2: 9-10.
Molina, F. and Walton, J.K. (2011) 'An alternative co-operative tradition: the Basque co-operatives of Mondragón', in Webster, A. et al. *The Hidden Alternative: Co-operative Values, Past, Present and Future,* Tokyo: The United Nations University Press.
Moodie, G.C and Eustace, R. (1974) *Power and Authority in British Universities,* London: G. Allen and Unwin.
Murray, R. (2010) *Co-operation in the Age of Google,* available www.uk.coop/ageofgoogle (accessed 10 January 2010).
Neary, M. et al. (2009), *Final Report,* learninglandscapes.lincoln.ac.uk (accessed 14 May 2012).
Neary, M and Saunders, G (2010) 'Learning landscapes and leadership in higher education: the struggle for the idea of the university', *Working Paper for the Centre for Educational Research and Development,* Lincoln: University of Lincoln.

Newman, M. (2008) Use of headhunters to fill top jobs is 'morally lazy', *Times Higher*, 19 June, http://www.timeshighereducation.co.uk/news/use-of-headhunters-to-fill-top-jobs-is-morally-lazy/402440.article (accessed 12 September 2012).
Open University (2014) www.open.ac.uk/about/main/the-ou-explained/history-the-ou (accessed 10 January 2014).
Parnell, E. (2014) 'Organization for member-controlled enterprises' and 'The Member-Controlled Enterprise Model-Diagram', www.m.centerprise.org (accessed 10 January 2014).
—— (2011) *Co-operation, the Beautiful Idea*, Oxford: Plunkett.
Pedley, R. (1977) *Towards the Comprehensive University*, London: Macmillan.
Pollins, H. (1984) *The History of Ruskin College*, Oxford: Ruskin College.
Ree, J. (1984), *Proletarian Philosophers: Problems in Socialist Culture in Britain 1900–1940*, Oxford: Oxford University Press.
Robinson, E. (1968) *The New Polytechnics: the People's Universities*, Harmondsworth: Penguin.
Roff, A. (2011) *Eric Robinson 1927–2011*, www.uclan.ac.uk/news/archive/eric_robinson.php (accessed 11 December 2011).
Rose, J. (2002) *The Intellectual Life of the British Working Classes*, New Haven, CT: Yale University Press.
Rothblatt, S. (1997) *The Modern University and its Discontents: the Fate of Newman's Legacies in Britain and America*, Cambridge: CUP.
—— (2007) *Education's Abiding Moral Dilemma: Merit and Worth in the Cross-Atlantic Democracies, 1800–2006*, Oxford: Symposium.
Scott, P. (1993) 'The idea of the university in the 21st century: a British perspective', *British Journal of Educational Studies*, 41: 4–25.
Shattock, M. (2010). *Managing Successful Universities* (2nd ed.), Maidenhead: Open University Press.
—— (2012) *Making Policy in British Higher Education 1945–2011*, McGraw-Hill: Open University Press.
Swain, H. (2013) 'The free-wheeling universities' (in cafes, trailers, libraries etc.) *The Guardian, Education*, 29 January.
Taylor, R. and Steele, T. (2000) *British Labour and Higher Education 1945–2000*, Leicester: NIACE.
Thew, L.M. (1985) *The Pit Village and the Store: Portrait of a Mining Past*, London: Pluto Press.
Thompson, E.P. (1997/1968) 'Education and experience', republished in Thompson, E.P., *The Romantics: England in a Revolutionary Age*, Woodbridge: Merlin Press.
—— (1971) *Warwick University Ltd*, Harmondsworth: Penguin.
Twigg, H.J. (1924) *An Outline History of Co-operative Education*, Manchester: Co-operative Union.
University of Sussex Bulletin, 17 March 1975.
Waugh, C. (2009) *'Plebs', the lost legacy of independent working-class education*, www upstream.coop; post16 educator.org.uk (accessed 11 June 2013).
Willett, J. and Manheim, R. (1976) *Bertolt Brecht, Poems 1913–1956*. London: Eyre Methuen.
Williams, R. (1962) *Communications*, Harmondsworth: Penguin.
Wright, A.W. (1979) *G. D. H. Cole and Socialist Democracy*, Oxford: Oxford University Press.
Yeo, S. (1970) 'Social movements and political action: a preliminary view of a student initiated course', *Universities Quarterly*, 24, 4: 402–422 and in Open University School and Society Course Team (1971) London: Routledge and Kegan Paul.
—— (1998) 'The pre-history and theory of credit', *Journal of Access and Credit Studies*, 1/1: 53–69.
—— (1990) 'A college for labour: towards an academic programme for Ruskin 1990–94', ts, in Ruskin College Library.
—— (2000) *Organic Learning: Mutual Enterprise and the Learning and Skills Agenda*, Leicester: NIACE.
—— (2002) *Co-operative and mutual enterprises in Britain: ideas from a useable past for a modern future*, London: LSE Centre for Civil Society, Report no. 4.

11
Policy, principles and practice: co-operative studies in higher education

Diarmuid McDonnell and Elizabeth C. Macknight

This chapter presents the thinking behind the establishment of an innovative partnership between the Co-operative Education Trust Scotland (CETS) and the University of Aberdeen designed to embed co-operative, mutual, and employee-owned models of enterprise into tertiary curricula. It explains the strategic context for the partnership and the practical and intellectual challenges encountered in putting the co-operative principle of education, training, and information into practice within the university setting.

Knowledge Transfer Partnerships (KTP), Europe's premier funding scheme for collaboration between industry and academia, provided the framework for our project (KTP 2013). There are various ways of defining 'knowledge transfer' (or 'knowledge exchange') which, in the twenty-first century, features alongside teaching and learning and research as a core stream of activities conducted in universities internationally. The central purpose of knowledge transfer is to achieve a two-way flow and uptake of ideas between a university and a 'company' (which may be a third sector organization, including co-operatives) that is relevant and responsive to the wider context and that creates mutual benefits. In the KTP scheme, run by the UK Government's Technology Strategy Board, a KTP associate is recruited through joint agreement between the university and the company. The associate is typically a recent graduate who, under the terms of the grant, is employed by the university and works for the partner organization.

Like other not-for-profit organizations, CETS may not fit standard images of a 'company'; it holds both a Scottish company number and a registered charity number. In 2010, this posed no barrier to meeting the KTP criteria for funding eligibility. CETS is a charitable trust promoting co-operation and co-operative enterprise through a programme of education within Scottish schools. CETS is supported by the wider Scottish co-operative movement, namely, the Co-operative

Foundation, a charitable arm of the Co-operative Group; Scotmid, the largest Scottish co-operative society; and Co-operative Development Scotland (CDS). Income is also generated from continuing professional development, resource packs for classroom use, and bespoke projects.

Since its formation in 2006, CETS's activities in co-operative enterprise education had centred upon primary and secondary schools in Scotland. The KTP was designed to provide CETS with a strategic route for expanding its operations by opening up a new programme of activity at the tertiary level. By engaging with the university sector CETS hoped to facilitate support for students and graduates who wished to apply their enterprising skills to create co-operative businesses. To achieve this goal CETS required access to academic expertise for course development and programme design. The University of Aberdeen, founded in 1495, is one of Scotland's ancient universities with a rich heritage and a reputation for innovation and research excellence. One of the University of Aberdeen's major projects, commencing in 2008, was an institution-wide curriculum reform, similar to that which other leading universities of the world such as Melbourne, Harvard, and Hong Kong were undertaking at the same time (Blackmore and Kandiko 2012; Davis et al. 2008). In 2009, the Director of CETS, Hugh Donnelly, met with Elizabeth Macknight, an academic at the University of Aberdeen, and Robin Brown, Manager of the KTP North of Scotland Centre. With Robin's support and guidance, Hugh and Elizabeth applied for the KTP grant, which was sponsored by the Scottish Government and the Economic and Social Research Council. To secure the grant CETS had to demonstrate it had the ability to contribute financially to the project, in total about £20,000 per annum, over two years. This requirement represented a significant commitment for a small charity and was met by pooling the contributions of Scotmid, the Co-operative Group, and Co-operative Development Scotland.

The major outputs planned were a textbook to introduce undergraduates to the co-operative model of enterprise, a postgraduate resource to stimulate further research on co-operatives, and a guide to setting up a co-operative for students and graduates. These new educational resources, developed through the KTP, were intended to expand CETS's operations into universities, significantly raising the Trust's profile and capacity to attract further funding. CETS was obviously going to be in competition with all other enterprise offerings for space in universities' curricula. Yet because CETS was the only organization offering co-operative, mutual, and employee-owned models it had a unique product and service to bring to the education sector. In its first three years of operation the Trust had already built a strong reputation for its work among schoolteachers and pupils, so that about 40 per cent of Scottish primary and secondary schools were already engaging with CETS. There was reason to believe a similarly positive entry could be made into universities, enabling CETS to reach further across the education spectrum.

Originally the main target for the new educational resources was the 19 Scottish higher education institutions. In 2009, the co-operative model of enterprise was little known to the 12,000 or so business students and the 3,000 or so education students studying at Scotland's universities. Our objective was to ensure that the majority of these students, at least 50 per cent, had become aware of the co-operative movement on completion of their degree. Whilst the most obvious opportunities to trial the use of new materials were courses and programmes in business studies, enterprise, and entrepreneurship, there was a recognized potential to reach learners in a broad array of disciplines. International research on co-operatives, mutuals, and employee-owned business embraces a wide variety of disciplinary perspectives, from finance and management to history and sociology. In theory this means that discussion of co-operative enterprise could be integrated just as readily into a course on nineteenth-century Europe delivered by an arts faculty member, as into a course on sustainable agricultural/food communities for the future delivered by a sciences faculty member. A handful of Scottish universities – Aberdeen, Strathclyde, Stirling, and Glasgow Caledonian – had already begun to engage with CETS so there was a pool of academics potentially available to become involved in the development of the resources and thus 'buy into' the eventual product. The educational resources were to be made available on an open access basis, meaning they would be free to download from the Internet, in accordance with research council directives and international agreements in academic publishing (Read 2008).

Whilst it was not anticipated at the time of writing the KTP application, an exciting outcome of the project has been to take CETS beyond Scottish universities into the global tertiary education arena. To explain how and why that occurred, and its implications and interest for the co-operative movement, brings us first to the matter of policy.

Policy and principles

Policy contexts offer considerable potential for interventions which favour co-operative educational initiatives and this insight was not lost on the partners in this project. In Scotland, whilst universities remain formally independent and set their own agendas, they are nevertheless influenced by governmental objectives and public policy. Since we hoped to attract sponsorship from the Scottish Government for the KTP application, we were mindful of two core strategies of the Scottish Government: the skills agenda and economic growth.

The Scottish Government's Skills Strategy, first published in 2007 and subsequently updated in the wake of the global financial crisis, was presented as 'a framework to show how all of the constituent parts of our education and learning systems can contribute to giving Scotland a skills base that is world class' (Scottish Government 2010). The Skills Strategy called for many of the things that the University of Aberdeen, through its institution-wide reform of the curriculum, had discussed and referred to in its Curriculum Commission reports: encouraging people to take more ownership for their learning choices; supporting flexibility and the creation of easier transition routes between different levels of education; scope for the development of enterprise education and entrepreneurial skills; and the need to look at the development of generic and 'softer' skills.

A focus on skills for work and for life is also apparent in the Scottish Government's Curriculum for Excellence initiative implemented across Scottish schools from 2009. Curriculum for Excellence aims to enable all children to become successful learners, confident individuals, effective contributors and responsible citizens, both through skills development in literacy, communication, numeracy and IT, as well as through an informed contextual understanding of the world in the twenty-first century.

Like the Skills Strategy, the Scottish Government's Economic Strategy identifies the need for a much closer working relationship between universities and business. The Economic Strategy was introduced by the First Minister with the observation that, 'Faster sustainable economic growth is the key to unlocking Scotland's potential and strengthening our greatest asset – the people of Scotland' (Scottish Government 2011). Although the University of Aberdeen is determined to protect its role beyond economic development, and resist an overly market-driven approach to higher education, it recognizes a responsibility to contribute to the economic welfare of the country. For this reason the University is open to supporting the developments called for in the Government's Economic Strategy, for example the creation of more flexible learning opportunities, the promotion of lifelong learning, an easier transition between different levels of education, and a consideration of desired graduate attributes.

In terms of engaging policymakers in constructive discourse with the co-operative movement, CETS has had some successes during the course of the KTP project. Edinburgh City Council, following elections in May 2012, made a commitment to be the first Scottish 'co-operative council'. This descriptor is intended to encompass a broad array of possible actions and one of the Council's core manifesto promises is the promotion of co-operative education in the schools under its jurisdiction. CETS, along with stakeholders from the Scottish Co-operative Party, working closely with councillors, played an important role in drafting this commitment.

There remains enormous potential for co-operators, internationally, to tap into policy discourses in order to promote the co-operative model. Across a range of policies, for example, in fostering economic growth, food security and social care, there is scope for co-operation to offer social as well as economic benefits. Outside Scotland, a research team from Mondragón University in the Basque Country, involving academics interacting regularly with CETS, provided a powerful example of engaging policymakers. Interested in the link between co-operative ownership and health, the research team secured funding and support from one of the local Basque councils by outlining the role that research, and by extension worker co-operatives of the region, could play in improving the health of citizens. Politicians saw a method for achieving public health initiatives and duly supported the project. The Mondragón example underscores the potential for leaders in co-operative education to find effective ways of engaging with policymakers and politicians (Freundlich and Gago 2012). Aligning the co-operative education agenda with wider social and/or political issues can create significant opportunities for embedding co-operative values and principles into higher education.

However, co-operative education was not simply a flexible thing that could be adapted to any policy context. Rather, it has developed historically in relation to a clear set of values and principles. In addition to the strategic context, informed by public policy and governmental concerns, the KTP project was designed to align with two key principles of the co-operative movement: education, training and information; and co-operation among co-operatives through local, national, regional and international structures. For CETS to put these principles into practice at the tertiary level, it required materials for teaching undergraduates and postgraduates. But which kinds of materials and how should the content be chosen and organized? Multiple factors had to be taken into account: CETS's existing resources and capabilities; the state of co-operative education in Scotland's higher education institutions; global trends in higher education; prevailing pedagogies; examples of best practice in flexible delivery and e-learning; and our interpretation of what co-operative education is, and should be, at tertiary level.

The format, structure, and content of the resources were shaped by many co-operative educational concepts. Co-operative education at the university level, as we see it, consists of three key strands: learning and teaching about co-operative models of enterprise; research on topics connected with co-operative models of enterprise, for example, the Mondragón investigation into links between ownership and citizens' health; and the accumulation of the knowledge and skills needed to establish a co-operative.

One could argue that co-operative education should also offer the option of learning through co-operative pedagogies. We would agree with this assertion but felt that there were sufficient materials available on this topic for educators to be able to incorporate co-operative learning techniques into their curricula (Johnson et al. 2008; Wilkins 2011). Significantly CETS is a content producer but not involved in delivering education programmes; hence, the various mechanisms employed within universities for obtaining student feedback on teaching and learning were not available to it. Indeed, embedding new educational resources in tertiary education across the UK and abroad required intensive networking with contacts in universities.

Practice

In the initial stage of planning the project there appeared to be two main types of challenges: intellectual and operational. The intellectual challenge lay in the need to strengthen and deepen interdisciplinary collaboration in order to translate that interdisciplinary approach into the outputs of the KTP project. Much of the cutting-edge research done in universities has an interdisciplinary element. For the knowledge transfer to be successful, CETS needed to produce materials that reflected the breadth and depth of knowledge appropriate to university study, and to do this in an interdisciplinary way that is vital to much research and innovation (University of Melbourne 2006: 8). The new educational resources had to synthesize the wide-ranging information on co-operatives, mutuals and employee-ownership in such a way as to engage students from different disciplinary backgrounds. The operational dimension of the challenge appeared to be to ensure effective communication about the project, both within the co-operative movement and through relations with universities and the media, to create maximum public exposure for CETS. Communication became an especially crucial consideration owing to the United Nations International Year of Co-operatives in 2012. As a result of the promotional activities of the co-operative movement, the prominence of the co-operative model in public, political, education, and media spheres increased markedly.

Taken together, the two dimensions of the challenge were thought to create significant opportunities for the associate. These opportunities included the chance to demonstrate capabilities in desk-based research, comprehension, and synthesis; to develop practical knowledge of the pedagogic approaches and methods appropriate to university tuition, including flexible delivery; to practise professional networking and relationship building; and to hone the presentation skills necessary for progress in a variety of career paths.

Research and writing for the first of the resources, an undergraduate textbook, *Democratic Enterprise: Ethical Business for the 21st Century*, was the most intensive and longest stage of the KTP that took about 15 months to complete. The content drew variously on research from the fields of history, management, organizational behaviour and performance, economics, finance, entrepreneurship, and social policy. Although materials published on the Internet were consulted and referenced, for example, the websites of co-operative businesses and development bodies, a decision was taken very early on by the authors to prioritize peer-reviewed scholarly journals and books because these are the sources that academics value and rely upon most. We had to write a textbook that would be credible to academics so the quality of the research underpinning it was of fundamental concern. For the postgraduate resource, *The Co-operative Model in Practice: International Perspectives*, the gathering and editing of essays by 14 scholars was completed over the second year of the KTP. This occurred in tandem with the writing of the guide to setting up a co-operative, *Co-operative Entrepreneurship* (McDonnell et al. 2012a, 2012b, 2012c). For the latter resource we initially had some difficulty in balancing the academic imperative for a research-based publication for use in universities, complete with references and bibliography, and the desire of Co-operative Development Scotland for a different style of work more suited to the general public consulting its webpages. The result was a shorter book, deliberately pitched more to students and graduates than to academics.

In June 2012, the KTP project 'ended', in so far as funding from the original sponsors was concerned, and, six months later, we conducted a review of the Internet usage of our resources. The undergraduate textbook, *Democratic Enterprise: Ethical Business for the 21st Century*, had been downloaded 174 times. This resource was selected by international peer review to feature as a teaching module on Caseplace, an online library with a network of some 40,000 registered users. The postgraduate resource, *The Co-operative Model in Practice: International Perspectives*, had been downloaded 107 times. The guide to setting up a co-operative for students and graduates, *Co-operative Entrepreneurship,* had been downloaded 68 times. Importantly, the specially created virtual learning environment (VLE) for the new resources was also prospering with over 1,100 registered visitors. On the VLE, instructors and students were able to access PDF files of the resources as well as additional teaching and learning materials such as lecture slides and bibliographic aids. There were other key mechanisms by which the associate ensured the audience for CETS's work grew over the two years of the project. These included the creation of a CETS weekly blog on co-operative enterprise and education; the launch of a Twitter account for small daily doses of co-operative news; the posting of photographs from CETS's events and projects on Flickr, and the use of Vimeo for videos of CETS's events and work with schools. All of these mechanisms were crucial for boosting CETS's online presence and almost certainly contributed to the 59 per cent increase in 'new visitor' traffic to the CETS website.

Upon completion of the two-year phase of resource development, the KTP project team shifted its focus towards dissemination and promotion. This required development of a detailed strategy, for which, previously, only outlines had been considered for the grant application. In effect, having produced the new resources, the next stage was to 'take them to market' and try to ensure some of the material contained in the resources was integrated into Scottish tertiary education. This strategy entailed a number of significant challenges. First, some follow-on funding was needed to continue the work begun under the KTP; CETS was able to collaborate with stakeholders in the co-operative movement (namely CDS and Co-operatives UK) to secure the necessary finance. Second, the diversity of curricula in higher education institutions impacted upon our ability to integrate the materials. This resulted in a somewhat scattered approach to promotion, forcing us to identify a small number of receptive academics in certain universities with whom to collaborate. Finally, for those contacts who were enthusiastic about using the resources for courses or modules, significant time needed to be spent ensuring the material integrated seamlessly into the existing structure of their teaching – a task that was complicated by the administrative jungle found in universities. Such regular reviewing and updating of course content is what academics do regularly, on a personal level and in collaboration with colleagues. The resources were freely available but there was expense involved in terms of time because of the need to develop a 'lesson plan' for each course/module in which the resources were to be used. Since courses and modules tend to depend upon the individual academic who develops them, there could be no guarantee that, in the event of that academic leaving the institution, another colleague would continue to run the course/module with the CETS resources.

Despite these challenges, the dissemination and promotion project was relatively successful in integrating material into Scottish university courses/modules. Nine lectures across three universities were delivered, attended by over 150 students. A broad spectrum of courses offered at different years of study and within different degree programmes were covered. Lectures were given to first-year business studies students and to students attending MBA summer schools. With the possible exception of the MBA class, students were initially unfamiliar with co-operatives; their knowledge of the co-operative business model extended to recognizing the Co-operative Group and John Lewis uniform, but the students were unable to give a rudimentary explanation of the respective organizational structures. That said, students were receptive to the theory and practice of co-operative enterprise. Lecturers were similarly positive. Dr John Ferguson, module coordinator of Accounting Ethics at Strathclyde University, wrote in an email (21 November 2012):

> Your talk helped students appreciate that there are profitable and successful businesses out there (many of which the students had heard of, but did not know were co-ops) which do not conform to a MSW [maximizing shareholder wealth] model and the assumptions that go with it, which are formed on more democratic principles, are more equitable, and generally have a concern for the long-term interests of their employees and community.

Perhaps the most pertinent lesson arising from the series of lectures is the strength of the co-operative model as a comparator example of how to run a business. Whether the lecture was with music entrepreneurship students, or those completing degrees focused on the creative industries, co-operatives were a relevant and illuminating addition to the delivery of the course/module. In terms of impact, the University of the West of Scotland, where the majority of lectures were delivered, decided to embed co-operative education into a broad range of modules across multiple years for the academic year 2013–14. The university estimates that this will result in 650–700 students being introduced to the co-operative model each year.

Both during and after the KTP project, public engagement has been important. We launched the project with the Solutions in Enterprise conference, held at the University of Aberdeen 30 September–1 October 2010, sponsored by the Scottish Programme for Entrepreneurship. In 2012 the United Nations International Year of Co-operatives gave us further opportunities to stage events and initiate other forms of outreach. A Renewable Energy and Sustainable Business symposium, sponsored by the Grampian Area Committee of the Co-operative Membership and CETS, was held at the University of Aberdeen in May 2012. On this latter occasion we collaborated with mediaco-op for the creation of a short film 'Join the Co-op future' featuring four co-operative businesses (Edinburgh Bicycle Co-op, Tenants First Housing, Woollard & Henry, and Dulas) plus University of Aberdeen students. We also hosted or participated in additional workshops, lectures, symposia, and film screenings throughout Scotland including major events at the Scottish Parliament and New Lanark Heritage Centre in June 2012.

Co-operative education development in the UK

The next sections of this chapter build upon our practical experiences of developing learning and teaching materials about co-operatives, and attempt to connect

TABLE 11.1 Conceptualizing the development of co-operative education

Action-orientations	Creation	Transformation	Integration
Research knowledge	Co-operative research centres	Critical/applied action research	Co-op articles, books, cases, materials
Curricula & awards	New curricula and awards	Redesign curricula and assessment	Update courses and content
Learning & teaching	Develop co-operative andragogy/ transformative learning strategies		Existing pedagogies
Co-op ownership and governance	New co-operative business schools/ universities	Convert to co-op ownership/ governance	Democratize decision-making
Social inclusion	Lifelong learning Open membership	Paradigm shifting knowledge transfer projects	Existing knowledge transfer
Support networks	As context dictates		

these to co-operative education more broadly. First, a conceptual framework is presented to enable educators to think about ways in which learning about co-operatives can be embedded in higher education (Ridley-Duff 2012). This is followed by some reflections on the opportunities and barriers we feel are inherent in the process of generating a wider understanding of co-operatives. To conclude, a number of priorities for educators and co-operators are proposed.

Table 11.1 shows Rory Ridley-Duff's approach to conceptualizing the development of co-operative education. It takes in areas of action-orientation most relevant to schools and universities – such as the first three listed: research knowledge; curricula & awards; learning & teaching – but also areas of action-orientation where professional training colleges, apprenticeships, community organizations, and development bodies might play a role such as co-op ownership and governance or social inclusion. Our KTP project and follow-up work of dissemination concentrated on universities and falls mainly under the 'Integration' orientation in the right-hand column of Table 11.1. Some of the priorities for co-operative education stakeholders outlined in the next section of this paper will be more radical in perspective, shifting towards 'Creative' and 'Transformative' orientations in the centre and left-hand columns of Table 11.1.

Let us first set out some of the opportunities, available to the co-operative movement, which appear most striking and relevant for the advancement of co-operative education at tertiary level in the UK. The Quality Assurance Agency (QAA) for Higher Education issues subject benchmark statements that the co-operative movement can use as a platform to build upon in discussions with higher education stakeholders, especially academics who are involved in the approval of university courses/modules and senior managers with responsibility for institutional strategy in teaching and learning. A subject benchmark statement is understood to be 'a means for the academic community to describe the nature and characteristics of programmes in a specific subject or subject area'. A subject benchmark statement also represents 'general expectations about standards for the award of qualifications at a given level in terms of the attributes and capabilities that those possessing qualifications should have demonstrated'. Articulating principles, designed to inform practices, the QAA statement for a general business and management honours degree advocates that students should have the opportunity to learn about organizations in a broad sense: '"Organizations" should ... include a wide range of different types including, for example, public, private and not-for-profit, together with a comprehensive range of sizes and structures of organizations. Similarly, the term "business" should be interpreted generically' (Quality Assurance Agency 2007: 3). Referring to the QAA statement is one way to present the case for a course/module on co-operatives within the context of a general business and management honours degree.

The co-operative movement also needs to embrace a renewed interest in alternative enterprises, political systems and economic development, and ensure that the co-operative model is embedded in teaching on these topics. Approaches to studying finance and risk are evolving not least because of classroom discussions about contemporary events among academics and students. The corporate governance and accounting scandals of the early 2000s precipitated a rise in the interest of ethics in business schools; the mid-2000s saw renewed interest in banking studies as a result of the unsustainable performance of the global banking sector. Now, following the failures of neoliberal capitalism to achieve and sustain economic and social development, new or revived academic subjects are coming to the fore. In the UK and Western Europe, social enterprise is receiving unprecedented interest from academia and policymakers. Academic centres focusing on sustainable development, responsible business, and behavioural economics (to name but a few) are springing up within the UK.

Just as it is important to act on the opportunities that exist, co-operators need to be mindful of barriers and commit to sharing knowledge and experiences in order to find ways to overcome those barriers. One of the barriers that has been studied and written about concerns perceptions of co-operatives and the issue of student demand (Matthews 2011). University departments are increasingly conscious of the 'market value' of courses proposed by academics, although use of this term can be contentious and academics are more likely to refer to 'student demand'. At a time of increasing financial constraints, universities will seek to streamline their cost base. Unless a credible 'market' for co-operative studies can be identified and leveraged, departments and academic committees will be reluctant to approve related courses.

A second barrier, also treated in academic literature, concerns the relative lack of appropriate teaching materials. Empirical studies by Panu Kalmi for Scandinavia and Roderick Hill for the United States found that, since 1945, the study of co-operatives has gradually diminished in line with the general malaise experienced by the global co-operative movement (Hill 2000; Kalmi 2007). Co-operation and co-operative enterprise, despite experiencing a revival of late, have been more prominent in the economy and public consciousness than in academic research networks.

Perhaps this is a contributory factor to the dearth of contemporary co-operative literature. Large-scale research studies and textbooks focusing on co-operative models have not been written in significant numbers since the 1980s although that is beginning to change as our KTP project testifies. From an integration perspective, co-operatives barely warrant a mention in most economics and business management textbooks.

A third barrier is one that co-operators have the most agency to remove. It is vital that the co-operative movement overcome its natural inclination to speak in the co-operative tongue and communicate proposals in ways that can be understood by a broader range of audiences. Every co-operator knows how valuable, viable and unique the co-operative model of enterprise is; in fact, we converse about it every day. Our discourses have developed to the point where we almost have our own language. But while co-operators may be able to wrestle with terms such as 'patronage refund', 'industrial democracy' and 'social capital', members of the general public may not be able to do so. Unless the message about co-operation is conveyed in language that can be understood by a wider audience, misconceptions and misinformation will continue to abound.

A fourth barrier is that of dominant ideologies. While new business schools are flourishing, based upon their claims to legitimacy, changing them is dependent upon the crucial factor of funding (Bieger 2012). The proliferation of business schools around the globe was driven partly by capital investment from the private sector, which in turn demanded that its ideologies and teachings were given prominence in curricula. Linked to this was the primacy of the Anglo-Saxon model of enterprise that provided not only funding for business schools but also created demand amongst prospective students for qualifications that could gain them access to corporations built on that model (Khurana 2007).

Priorities for the UK co-operative education movement

In order to tackle the barriers outlined above, and capitalize on the opportunities for furthering co-operative education in universities, we propose the following four actions.

1. *Create a UK-wide Centre for Co-operative Studies* – Structured as a consortium co-operative of other research centres and organizations, such as the Cardiff Centre for Co-operative Studies and the UK Society for Co-operative Studies, the centre's overall aim would be to strengthen the academic subject of co-operative studies in the UK and internationally. The creation of a dedicated centre should help to grant co-operative studies a more prominent space in academia, particularly given the variety of academic disciplines within which research on co-operation takes place and the appeal of cultivating interdisciplinary approaches. It remains difficult for researchers in co-operative studies to make headway in an environment where scepticism and ignorance of the topic is still widespread. The centre would also act as the focal point

for experiments in curricula design and developing co-operative pedagogies. Co-operative academics would benefit from having a knowledge base of current and relevant materials, as well as having a body through which to tender for research grants.

2. *Create a Foundation for Co-operative Education (FCE)* – One of the issues affecting higher education research into co-operatives is the lack of funding opportunities, particularly for early-career researchers. Creating a fund for co-operative research in the UK, the Foundation for Co-operative Education, would help alleviate some of the difficulty of sourcing funding from bodies unfamiliar with the co-operative model. Relevant stakeholders from the co-operative movement would sit on the board of the FCE and would consult with the wider movement to identify research priorities. The FCE could have a transformative effect on co-operative research in the UK, similar to that of the Foundation for Enterprise Development (FED) in the United States. Created through an endowment from the founder of a hugely successful employee-owned enterprise, FED sponsors emerging and established academics interested in the field of employee ownership (FED 2013). Each year, some 30 scholarships are awarded, helping to strengthen and shape the relevancy of employee ownership research to issues in the US economy. The FCE would adopt a similar approach, initially on a smaller scale, to develop seed-funding grants for promising PhD and post-doctoral researchers in the UK. Funding should be sourced mainly from the co-operative movement but some of this financial burden could be shared by sourcing match-funding from related bodies, for example, the Economic and Social Research Council (ESRC), the National Lottery Fund, and the social enterprise sector. The fund could be administered by an existing body, such as the UK Society for Co-operative Studies, or by a newly created co-operative trust.

3. *Create a Professorial Chair of Co-operative Studies* – A professorial chair of co-operative studies would signal that the movement has an accomplished figurehead to represent and develop co-operative studies in higher education. One precedent for establishing this type of role is found in academic circles concerned with employee ownership in the United States. In 2011, Professor Joseph Blasi was appointed Professorial Chair of Employee Ownership at Rutgers University, New Jersey. This position was funded by the Foundation for Enterprise Development (FED). Equally many people in the co-operative education movement will be familiar with the public esteem and political capital created for the employee-ownership movement by Charlie Mayfield, Chairman of the John Lewis Partnership.

4. *Create a Co-operative Learning Space (CLS)* – Similar to the extension programmes in the United States, as well as the digital forms of public education initiatives in the UK, the CLS would be primarily a virtual platform through which members of the public could develop co-operative skills and knowledge. Co-operative expert Edgar Parnell is taking steps in this direction with his informative website, Co-op Pundit (Parnell 2013). Based on the Open

University format, the CLS would be the movement's contribution to the principles of lifelong learning, and education, training and information. CLS would contain an open access repository of co-operative studies materials (Read 2008). The cost of developing such a platform would be relatively low, relying as it would on open-source technologies and the Creative Commons License. Instigating an initiative on this scale would require an organization to lead its development, similar to the Co-operative Teach-in initiative run by the Toolbox for Social Education (TESA).

Conclusion

The Co-operative Education Trust Scotland and the University of Aberdeen have worked together successfully to address the lack of teaching of co-operative, mutual, and employee-owned models of enterprise at undergraduate and postgraduate levels in UK higher education. There is still progress to be made in marketing our new resources to the education sector but early signs of take-up, especially in the United States, are encouraging. In 2013 the resources were being used in around 70 universities worldwide as well as by development bodies and international institutions. The partnership has also supported CETS in raising its profile through academic networks, conferences, and in increasing its revenue through grant capture, which will assist in extending the reach of its future operations.

We believe that the values and principles at the core of the co-operative movement are attractive to students and graduates, but co-operators need to think creatively about how to pitch their message. Our KTP project was designed to meet students' needs and demands for opportunities to use their intellectual and creative skills to make a meaningful contribution to society when they graduate. Students understand that they will be entering a competitive job market in which employers are looking for graduates who can demonstrate flexibility, initiative, and creativity. The collaboration between CETS and the University of Aberdeen helped to expose students to innovative and alternative ways of practising business and entrepreneurship to increase their knowledge of markets and the economy and to foster an enterprising attitude. The new materials are being welcomed by academics seeking to encourage the spirit of enterprise and to incorporate into their teaching case studies of democratic ethical businesses contributing to community and economic growth.

References

Bieger, T. (2012) 'Business schools – from career training centers towards enablers of CSR', in Morsing, M. and Sauquet Rovira, A. (eds) *Business Schools and their Contribution to Society*, London: SAGE.
Blackmore, P. and Kandiko, C. B. (eds) (2012) *Strategic Curriculum Change: Global Trends in Universities*, London: Routledge.
Davis, G., O'Brien, L. and McLean, P. (2008) 'Growing in esteem: positioning the University of Melbourne in the global knowledge economy', in Katz, R. N. (ed.) *The*

Tower and the Cloud: Higher Education in the Age of Cloud Computing: 64–80. Educause. Available http://www.educause.edu/research-and-publications/books/tower-and-cloud (accessed 20 June 2013).

FED (2013) Website, http://www.fed.org/about-overview (accessed 20 June 2013).

Freundlich, F. and Gago, M. (2012) 'Cooperative employment, social capital and public health; evidence from the Basque country', paper presented at the conference 'Co-operatives and their impact on public health', Edinburgh, May.

Hill, R. (2000) 'The case of the missing organizations: co-operatives and the textbooks', *Journal of Economic Education*, 31: 281–95.

Johnson, D., Johnson, R. and Smith, K. (2008) *Active Learning: Cooperation in the College Classroom*, Edina, MN: Interaction Book Co.

Kalmi, P. (2007) 'The disappearance of cooperatives from economics textbooks', *Cambridge Journal of Economics*, 31: 625–47.

Khurana, R. (2007) *From Higher Aims to Hired Hands: The Social Transformation of American Business Schools and the Unfulfilled Promise of Management as a Profession*, Princeton, NJ: Princeton University Press.

KTP (2013) Knowledge Transfer Partnerships, http://www.ktponline.org.uk (accessed June 2013).

Matthews, N. (2011) 'Teaching about co-operatives in a UK university business school', *Journal of Co-operative Studies*, 44: 105–8.

McDonnell, D., Macknight, E. and Donnelly, H. (2012a) *Democratic Enterprise: Ethical Business for the 21st Century*, Glasgow: Co-operative Education Trust Scotland.

—— (2012b) *Co-operative Entrepreneurship: Co-operate for Growth*, Glasgow: Co-operative Education Trust Scotland.

McDonnell, D. and Macknight, E. (eds.) (2012c) *The Co-operative Model in Practice: International Perspectives*, Glasgow: Co-operative Education Trust Scotland.

Parnell, E. (2013) Co-op Pundit website, http://www.co-oppundit.org/ (accessed June 2013).

Quality Assurance Agency (2007) *Subject Benchmark Statement: General Business and Management*, Gloucester: Quality Assurance Agency.

Read, M. (2008) 'Cultural and organizational drivers of open educational content' in Katz, R. N. (ed.) *The Tower and the Cloud: Higher Education in the Age of Cloud Computing*: 140–9. Educause. Available http://www.educause.edu/research-and-publications/books/tower-and-cloud (accessed June 2013).

Ridley-Duff, R. 'Developing co-operative universities' presentation given at the conference 'Co-operation and Higher Education', New Lanark, June 2012.

Scottish Government (2010) *Skills for Scotland: Accelerating the Recovery and Increasing Sustainable Economic Growth*, Edinburgh: Scottish Government.

—— (2011) *The Government Economic Strategy*, Edinburgh: Scottish Government.

University of Melbourne (2006) *The Melbourne Model: Report of the Curriculum Commission*, Parkville: Melbourne.

Wilkins, A. (2011) 'Co-operative learning: a contextual framework', *Journal of Co-operative Studies*, 44: 5–14.

12
A turning point? Mapping co-operative education in the UK

Linda Shaw

In the UK and globally, education has long been at the heart of the co-operative movement. Education, training and information has been one of the core co-operative principles since their first international adoption in 1937, which in turn drew on those developed by the Rochdale Pioneers. Yet, until very recently, co-operative education in the UK was largely synonymous with the provision made by the movement itself and scarcely existed outside of it (Twigg 1924; Shaw 2009). Education about and for co-operatives was largely carried out, and indeed funded, by the co-operative movement.

This is not to deny the importance of education for the movement. It can be argued that education has been one of the main distinguishing features of the UK co-operative movement (Vernon 2011). Many histories of co-operatives have identified education as a key driver for commercial growth (Gurney 1996; Birchall 1997). Yet, despite this recognition, only a few studies exist, either historical or contemporary, of the practice and theory of co-operative education. I have argued elsewhere for the need for much more debate and research on co-operative education (Shaw 2009).

This chapter begins to address this gap. It reports on the findings of a survey of co-operative education in the UK, and its relation to the co-operative movement, carried out in 2011. It also draws on the contemporary experience of the Co-operative College which has played a central role in co-operative education since 1919 – originally conceived as a new form of higher education for the co-operative movement. The aim of the research was to identify the main providers and investigate the kinds of education they provided; to inform an analysis of the educational issues that arose; and to contribute to the development of related strategies for the movement. This is especially pertinent given the recent revival of co-operatives in the UK and the changes in the wider educational landscape which are opening up some new opportunities for co-operative education as evidenced by the other chapters in this book.

The historical context

No study of co-operative education starts with a clean sheet. Although this is primarily a contemporary study, it starts from a recognition of the importance of the long and complex history of co-operative education and its continuing role today. Co-operative education has been characterized by multiple meanings and a diversity of practice (Woodin 2011). Different, and often competing, visions and educational practices have emerged within the movement. They provide an important legacy which continues to resonate, bringing contemporary opportunities and challenges (Facer et al. 2012). An appreciation of the on-going importance and influence of this tradition, therefore, underpins the mapping and analysis of co-operative education today.

In the UK, in contrast to many countries, consumer co-operatives have remained the dominant co-operative form since the days of the Rochdale Pioneers who started their shop in 1844 (Birchall 1994). For most of the nineteenth and twentieth centuries, the UK co-operative movement was characterized by large numbers of autonomous consumer societies trading within their local communities. These societies guarded their independence and valued their local connections. They also assumed responsibility for providing their own educational services. This resulted in a rich ecology of educational provision. As well as formal lectures and courses, societies offered a wide range of cultural, leisure and social facilities to their members, which they viewed as part of their commitment to providing education (Facer et al. 2012). These embraced libraries and reading rooms, the co-operative press, and a range of cultural activities including support for drama and music groups. The late nineteenth century has been characterized as a 'golden age' of co-operative education (Gurney 1996; MacPherson 2002). It was a time of expansion and success for consumer co-operatives so that by 1903 there were 1,481 co-operative societies (Co-operative Union 1904).

Such large numbers reflected great variations in educational provision and there could be huge disparities between societies. Even in the 'golden age', some societies made only scant formal provision for education and only half had an education committee. It was reported that many members showed little interest in education (Robertson 2010). Co-operatives also faced the dual challenge of providing education for both their members and their staff.

As Vernon has shown elsewhere (Vernon 2013), there were several attempts made to tackle these disparities, spearheaded by the national apex body for co-operatives, the Co-operative Union. In 1882 a Central Educational Committee was set up by the Union. This was followed by the formation of local education committees, linked at a regional level and represented on the Central Educational Committee. The Central Committee promoted a series of initiatives to improve and regularize co-operative education and, by 1912/13, it was managing a programme of activities and lecture programmes (Shaw 2009). This strategy was not entirely successful as many societies continued with their own educational provision, had little engagement with the Union and continued to guard their trading and educational autonomy (Robertson 2010).

In addition, the Co-operative Union allocated resources and funding for education to other movement bodies or auxiliaries such as the Co-operative Women's Guild, the Men's Guild, the National Student Fellowship and, later on, the co-operative youth organization, the Woodcraft Folk. All these bodies also provided education and training by way of formal educational programmes. Several studies have noted their important role in nurturing informal learning. Through participation in a range of activities, members gained knowledge and experience which enabled them to progress up into the higher echelons of the movement. This was especially true for the Women's Guild. George Barnsby described it as 'a school of democratic action and empowerment for working class women' (cited in Robertson 2010: 118).

As well as the Co-operative Union, individual societies and movement auxiliaries, the Co-operative College provided education. It was set up in 1919 with support from the Union and from the wider movement to provide a 'centre for higher education in the specialized subjects required for the full equipment of the co-operator and the further development of efficiency in the Co-operative Movement'. The College managed correspondence programmes, ran residential courses (which included international students) and undertook research. In many ways, the College was a sister organization to Ruskin College at Oxford which had been established at the turn of the century with support from the trade union movement (Shaw 2009: 23).

The UK co-operative movement, therefore, has long been characterized by complex and overlapping patterns of educational provision. However, certain aspects do stand out. For the most part, education was largely resourced and provided by the movement itself rather than by the state. However, the relationships between the movement and the state in terms of education have only recently begun to be investigated. A more complex picture is emerging. At the beginning of the twentieth century, for example, following the 1902 Education Act, local education authorities were established to take responsibility for direct management and delivery of compulsory education (Vernon 2013). This resulted in the movement stepping back from delivering any services which were to be provided by the state such as school education (Todd 2013) and library services. For much of the twentieth century, adult learners formed the primary focus for co-operative education. Indeed the co-operative movement played a pivotal role in the development of adult education in the UK, especially the formation and early years of the Workers' Educational Association. Unfortunately, to date, this contribution has merited little discussion in the standard histories of adult education (Fieldhouse 1998).

As the twentieth century progressed, two differing approaches to co-operative education emerged, which at times complemented each other, and at times were a source of considerable tension. The first was essentially one of 'education for preservation' with a focus on building and strengthening co-operative institutions. The second was 'education for transformation' with a wider mission of contributing to social change and a more co-operative world, the co-operative commonwealth (Facer et al. 2012). From the 1960s, the pendulum certainly swung towards the former, as consumer co-operatives entered and endured a period of seemingly unstoppable decline. Whether education was a consequence of trading decline or was a contributory factor to it remains debatable, but the results were clear in the lack of large scale investment in education needed to resource and modernize provision against a rapidly changing educational landscape, especially the growth of higher education and the changing contours of government support.

Just after World War Two, the Co-operative College moved from Manchester to new premises in the East Midlands, Stanford Hall, with much larger residential and teaching accommodation. The move did not substantially alter the College's role in providing education for the 'able and ambitious minority' who could attend residential courses, to study via correspondence programmes or evening classes towards a certificate or diploma. Programmes for international students remained an important part of the College's work and received direct funding from the government for several decades but this had virtually disappeared by the 1990s. In addition, movement capacity and willingness to fund long term residential programmes for staff and members had also greatly diminished.

For most of the twentieth century, co-operative education remained predominantly funded by the movement with little engagement in government-supported programmes in contrast to other organizations such as trade unions and the WEA. This limited the capacity to scale up the delivery of co-operative education whereas trade union education entered a period of rapid expansion from the 1970s, supported by government funding (McIlroy 1998). The waning of co-operation also coincided with the rapid expansion of higher education from the 1960s. Unsurprisingly, the growth of business education and the new business schools in UK universities failed to engage with the co-operative business model (Ivory et al. 2006; Macpherson 2007). This trajectory is reflected in the diminishing presence of co-operatives in mainstream economic textbooks during the same period (Kalmi 2007).

However, the narrative is not simply one of decline for co-operatives. From the 1960s, new co-operative sectors, credit unions, housing co-operatives and worker co-operatives began to develop, albeit initially on a small scale. More recently, there has been a second wave of co-operative development in new sectors such as football, health, and rural services. One in five of the UK population is now a member of a co-operative and the sector as a whole has a turnover of £36.7 billion (Co-operatives UK 2013) and there has also been a revival within the contemporary consumer co-operative movement (Wilson et al. 2013).

Accompanying this renewal has been a re-focusing on the core co-operative values and a recognition of the business advantage they can offer. The 2001 Co-operative Commission's virtuous circle model reminded the movement that co-operative enterprises are in business to fulfil their co-operative purpose; by achieving commercial success they are able to invest in their co-operative and social goals, creating a co-operative advantage (Co-operative Commission 2001). Many societies began to more overtly acknowledge and put into practice the core co-operative values of equality, equity, solidarity, democracy, self-help and self-responsibility. This contemporary renewal has also led to a growing interest in education and its role in driving and sustaining co-operative development across the movement (Murray 2010).

As a result of these changes, it became clear that a more detailed picture of the contemporary provision of co-operative education was needed to help inform movement strategy in terms of educational challenges and the opportunities facing it. Effective strategies for education and development need to be based on an understanding of the current nature and provision of co-operative education especially since there was no single reference point or directory of co-operative education providers. As a result, a mapping project was carried out in 2011 by the College to identify the key providers and the main types of provision. A mixture of qualitative and quantitative methods were used with questionnaires to all main stakeholders, followed by 30 semi-structured interviews (telephone and face to face) with stakeholders from key sectors as well as consultation meetings and a literature review.

The contemporary picture

What emerged from this review? Predictably, given the history outlined above, it was a complex and fragmented landscape. There were strong continuities with the past in so far as this 'new' landscape remained characterized by overlapping areas of operation and expertise with many gaps and shortfalls in provision. There were both long established and new providers who met the specific business and governance needs of their sector but were frequently unconnected with each other. The diversity of education and training bodies was reflected in the range of provision from stand-alone, face-to-face workshops to longer accredited distance learning programmes with a strong strand of start-up support and advice.

Within this complex landscape, three main types of providers stood out: firstly, co-operative societies themselves; secondly, co-operative bodies such as Co-operatives UK (previously the Co-operative Union) and the Co-operative College together with some newer umbrella bodies from emerging co-operative sectors; and finally, completely new types of providers such as schools using a co-operative governance model.

To date, individual co-operative societies have remained the major provider of education and training. They continue to face the dual challenge of providing education for both staff and members. This is done in three main ways: firstly, the delivery of formal training programmes for staff; secondly, educational provision for members, typically those holding elected office; and thirdly, engagement strategies targeted at the broader membership of a society. This has been accompanied by a renewed emphasis on the importance of co-operatives acting in line with core co-operative values. It has been most evident in member education programmes such as those offered by the largest consumer co-operative, the Co-operative Group and in those provided by the Co-operative College.

Formal staff training programmes in the larger consumer co-operatives, typically remain the responsibility of human resources departments. Much of the provision is closely tied to job related training or to legal compliance such as food hygiene, health and safety issues and improving customer service, often with a relatively limited focus on the 'co-operative' nature of the business and its core values and philosophy. Sometimes, staff training is contracted out to local providers. Vocational qualifications will often be 'off the peg' competency based qualifications linked to national standards for various occupations and sectors. Although they will provide skills and knowledge for particular purposes, external bodies tend to provide generic business training programmes which frequently do not address the distinctiveness of the co-operative business model, in relation to membership and the ways that staff might put co-operative values into everyday practice at work.

Education and training provision for employees constitutes a real problem for many smaller co-operatives where 'on the job training' is the norm. Training needs were self-identified and, if possible, delivered in house. Taking managers or staff out of the workplace to undertake training can often appear to be too costly both in terms of money and time. Several co-operatives reported that financial and personnel constraints also acted as barriers; the challenge was to find the time and resources to provide relevant and on-going training opportunities for their staff. This is an issue common to most small and medium sized enterprises (OECD 2002).

In co-operatives, as well as other types of enterprises, gender disparities in terms of promotion and access to training were still apparent. An earlier study of the training needs of women managers in the co-operative sector in north-west England, carried out by the author, attributed this in large part to lack of time (Rawlings and Shaw 2007). Women found they could not afford to take time out of work for training and managers could not afford the time to let people go. This was particularly true for women with outside responsibilities, usually childcare, who found that the times of training programmes were often inconvenient. There was, however, support for a range of staff development options including mentoring, coaching, shadowing as well as secondments which were seen as offering more experiential learning. However, a recent survey reported that 37 per cent of directorships were held by women in co-operatives compared to 13 per cent at leading companies (Co-operatives UK 2013:11).

Member education is a second key strand of education provision made by societies. Developing better formal education programmes for elected members of consumer societies was a key recommendation of the Co-operative Commission (2001). As noted earlier, in the past, both the College and the Co-operative Union recruited directly to their own member education courses delivering residential programmes and correspondence courses and also utilized the services of visiting lecturers. More recently, Co-operatives UK has tended to focus its attention more on new co-operative development projects, as well as offering legal advice and workshops to its member co-operatives rather than the provision of direct long term educational courses and programmes. The Co-operative College has continued to recruit directly to its own member education programmes and also contracts directly with the larger consumer societies to develop and deliver a range of accredited member education programmes across the UK.

Effective member education is critical for co-operatives given the central role of members in governance and decision making. As in all co-operatives, the main boards of UK co-operatives are elected by and from their membership. Co-operative governance and decision making therefore requires members to utilize a range of skills, knowledge and expertise in finance and business management and ensure that skills gaps are addressed. Members elected to decision making positions may lack necessary skills and expertise which in turn can have a negative impact on business performance and governance standards. This has been evident in the second half of 2013 in the governance and financial crises affecting the Co-operative Group and the wider co-operative sector, leading to a series of internal and public enquiries into the failings such as the Myners Review (BBC 2013). This remains a considerable challenge, especially for some of the larger co-operatives which have continued to bear the costs of education and training programmes for individual members. Depending on the size of the programmes, it can represent a substantial financial commitment by the society.

In many ways, member education programmes fit the 'classic' model of adult education as the learners have varied educational backgrounds. There is a wide spectrum of experience, qualifications and expectations. In any group, some of the learners will hold advanced degrees while others will have little in the way of formal qualifications. Many will have had considerable experience as active members within their co-operative. Most programmes are tailored closely to the roles, responsibilities and accountabilities of elected members. They have a largely internal focus on personal skills and learning needs in relation to co-operative organization. In terms of the themes identified earlier, the emphasis has largely remained on education for the preservation of the movement rather than education for a wider transformation.

Co-operative member education programmes reflect the wider contemporary consensus in the UK on the need to improve corporate governance standards. The co-operative sector has developed its own Codes of Best Practice for co-operative governance which include recommendations on education. The Code of Best Practice for Consumer Societies in Membership of Co-operatives UK, for example, advises that preparatory training should be made available for members who intend to stand for elected positions and that society rules should incorporate a requirement for all directors to undertake training (Co-operatives UK 2005). This has helped sharpen the focus of courses on governance issues, a change which looks set to remain a central objective in light of recent failings in both corporate and co-operative governance.

The development of mandatory qualifications for directors by the largest consumer co-operative marks a significant shift within the movement. As of 2010, it is now compulsory for Co-operative Group Board members and potential members to demonstrate they have achieved a level of competency for the role. The skills and competencies needed for main Board members were jointly identified between the Co-operative College and the Co-operative Group. Training and support are available to assist candidates to reach the prescribed level.

This can raise some tensions in terms of the democratic processes within societies. Some have argued that the requirement for minimum standards of competency has limited the democratic process while others saw it as enhancing accountability. As one membership officer from a larger consumer society summarized:

> There is a real balance to be struck between training, education and skills being barriers to the democratic process, and knowing that people have the basics needed for positions.

In addition, some training has taken place on diversity issues, such as gender and ethnicity, but their impact has not been assessed in terms of changing the profile of directors and committee members. In contrast to the trade union movement, there have been no programmes, for example, designed to increase women's participation at director level.

Despite the educational emphasis on the needs of elected members, in reality, they form a very small minority of the overall membership in most societies. Ensuring the participation of members in their society is generally acknowledged to be central to ensuring good governance within co-operatives. Members need to be supported with enough information to enable their participation in democratic governance structures (Co-operative Commission 2000; Birchall and Simmons 2004a; Spear 2004). Increasing the numbers of active members is an ongoing challenge for societies and many consumer co-operatives continue to provide a wide range of activities for members. Such work with the wider membership is generally led by dedicated membership officers, one of whom commented that:

> We provide the public with information and practical demonstrations ranging from information days, to Fairtrade tastings at fairs, food and drink festivals, to working with and supporting other community groups at which we present the co-operative values and principles. We also provide talks and presentations on co-operative history, ethical trade and co-operative business.

Meeting both the challenge of education for effective democratic governance and education for members is not a new phenomenon for co-operatives. But the sheer size of the remaining consumer societies, following a protracted period of mergers, does make this a peculiarly twenty-first century challenge given that some consumer societies have millions of members (Birchall and Simmons 2004b). A hundred years ago, there were 1,400 consumer co-operative societies in the UK, by the end of 2013 there were under twenty (Bibby 2013).

For smaller co-operatives, there are additional challenges in resourcing education for their board members as these costs can appear disproportionate to the available resources. The economies of scale enjoyed by larger societies are often absent. One solution adopted by several smaller co-operatives has been to use the services of an external agency such as one of the long-established secondary co-operative bodies or a newer one grown up since the 1970s to meet the needs of emerging sectors. However, several of these long established co-operative organizations which provided training services for the wider movement failed to maintain their membership and position within the movement. One such body is the Co-operative Women's Guild, for example, which continues to operate but on a much reduced scale and with a smaller membership than in previous years, and able to offer a very reduced range of educational and other services.

As a counterbalance to this trend, newer co-operative bodies have emerged which can and do provide education services as part of a broader portfolio of activities. The provision made by these new bodies varies considerably in scope and approach. Some are sector specific and focus upon the educational needs of a specific group of co-operatives. The Association of British Credit Unions Ltd (ABCUL) is one such example. It is a secondary co-operative which represents around 70 per cent of credit unions in England, Scotland and Wales. Although the number of credit unions has fallen in recent years, largely due to mergers, membership of the remaining credit unions has been increasing. Government support for the expansion of the sector has helped to fund development of training and curriculum resources. A government scheme, Project Delta provided free training places and related curriculum resources. Learners were both elected members and employees. The end of the Delta project in 2011 meant a return for ABCUL to charging for its training and only delivering demand-driven training. A subsequent review of the training needs of the sector identified an increasing demand for bespoke courses for individual credit unions based on participatory approaches and there are currently plans to break down courses and materials into smaller units. The review also revealed a demand for more e-learning programmes and webinars as a more cost effective form of provision.

A different model is provided by the Confederation of Co-operative Housing (CCH) which was established in 1993 with membership from across the co-operative housing sector. In contrast to ABCUL, CCH have chosen not to rely on government funding for training provision, fearing that organizations can run into difficulties if government support is withdrawn. CCH argued that it should deliver its own programmes in order to ensure that appropriate training and support were available because many freelance trainers knew little about the co-operative model, and about housing co-operatives in particular. For CCH there are three main avenues for training and education: firstly the annual conference which is attended by both members and non-members and offers expert speakers alongside workshop sessions. Secondly, bespoke training programmes provided in response to member and non-member requests and run on a commercial basis using curriculum materials developed by CCH. Finally, there are a number of accredited programmes on offer such as *In the Driving Seat*, a course to develop board skills and leadership and which is accredited by the Chartered Institute of Housing (CIH). These programmes were developed in partnership with external agencies such as local authorities and the Tenant Service Authority. Programmes covered all aspects of housing co-operatives including values and principles, governance, financial control, and practical services.

By contrast, the work of co-operative development agencies (CDAs) is not normally confined to a single sector. They focus on both start-up assistance and the provision of a range of business development services. During the 1980s, a first wave of CDAs emerged, including those with a local brief, such as the ones located in Greenwich, Cambridge and Hackney. Scotland and Wales both have CDAs with a national remit, also called co-operative development bodies (CDBs). They can vary in size from single person operations to large scale organizations such as the Wales Co-operative Centre with over 50 staff. During the last ten years, a second wave of CDBs started, often as part of a wider focus on social enterprise development. They include individual consultants, small consultancies as well as larger co-operative consortia. They offer a range of services often with a focus on start-up support such as business plan development, funding advice, and project management skills. Some also provide short training programmes to meet the needs of individual co-operatives. Others run seminar series and other professional development events. Many specialize in different aspects of co-operative development such as governance, impact assessment and employee buyouts.

Patterns of funding and support for CDBs also vary considerably. Co-operative Development Scotland, for example, receives financial support from the Scottish government. It works to support the growth of co-operative enterprise in Scotland from developing consortia to employee buyouts. They act as a knowledge centre, provide business advice and work with a range of stakeholders to develop more collaboration in tourism, renewable energy, forestry and other areas. It works closely with the Scottish Agricultural Organisation Society which is itself the lead agency supporting agricultural co-operatives in Scotland. In comparison, the Co-operative Enterprise Hub is run by the Co-operative Group which allows co-operatives up to four days free support from a business adviser on business planning, financial, staffing, legal and governance advice and other related issues. Most of the beneficiaries, but certainly not all, are new ventures. The support package is delivered locally by CDBs and individual consultants, usually in the form of one-to-one sessions.

It is a major challenge to ensure quality and consistency across this diverse range of co-operative development services, especially as some providers do not have in-depth co-operative knowledge and experience. The Co-operative Enterprise Hub is currently working with a partner to develop a bespoke national training and development programme based on draft standards designed for sector professionals. It is anticipated that ultimately these standards will be converted into units that can be accredited by an external awarding body.

Several respondents to the survey highlighted the challenge of capacity and scaling-up to meet increasing demand. For example, at the time of the survey, there had been a recent emphasis on building capacity and skills to support SME development. Meeting the support needs of a large scale conversion to mutual or co-operative ownership of a public sector body would present a major problem in training and supporting new staff. Further obstacles to co-operative development related to the lack of research findings and evidence on good practice. For some, the current development practices were not effective and there have been calls for a radical re-assessment (Co-operative Futures 2012). Indeed, a focus group on the research needs of the co-operative movement, held in May 2013, argued that there is an urgent need for further research to inform and shape strategies for co-operative development.

Many CDBs are members of Co-operatives UK which provides a regular newsletter and a directory of their business development members. Co-operatives UK also provides a range of information and guidance on setting up new co-operatives and acts as a partner in the Mutuals Information Service. The members of Co-operatives UK consist of individual co-operatives and federal members including Regional Co-operative Councils and the Worker Co-operative Council. They benefit from the provision of legal and financial advice and occasional workshops for Co-operative Company Secretaries and others. There are a number of guides to legal and governance processes for co-operatives available online (Co-operatives UK 2012a). Some training and development support is linked to specific projects such as the Making Local Food Work project which offered free training workshops on governance and legal issues.

By comparison to its earlier role, Co-operatives UK now has a much smaller part to play in co-ordinating a formal co-operative education scheme and programmes. The Institute of Co-operative Directors, established in 1987 by the former Co-operative Union to improve the knowledge and skills of elected members by offering information and guidance and by running training programmes through the College, is no longer in operation. With the focus on advice, advocacy and start-up programmes, the role of Co-operatives UK has clearly shifted significantly from its earlier emphasis on more formal educational provision. For example, promoting co-operation has become a central concern through initiatives such as the annual Co-operatives Fortnight, started in 2010, which is Co-operatives UK's national campaign. In 2011, across the UK over 290 events, activities and promotions were held and there was a highly effective social and digital media campaign which reached more than 1.7 million people. The overall reach of the campaign is difficult to quantify given the limitations of the data. Nonetheless, the campaign has undoubtedly been a success in raising public awareness of co-operatives in the UK (Co-operatives UK 2012b).

Moreover, the Co-operative Union/Co-operatives UK's oversight of co-operative education is much diminished. It is no longer a home for the Central Education Committee which was in turn linked to a network of regional educational committees. Today, the Co-operative College is the main provider of such programmes. The College's move back to Manchester in 2001 provided an opportunity for the College to reshape its educational role and take over the residual educational functions of the former Co-operative Education Department of the Union. In line with the recommendations of the Co-operative Commission, membership programmes were revised and externally accredited. The new programmes were put into modular form with workshops delivered locally. The curriculum was based on the knowledge and skills needed for effective participation in the governance of a co-operative including co-operative identity, financial knowledge, soft skills such as team working and chairing, encouraging member participation and governance issues. To date, the College is the only provider across Europe of accredited programmes that sit within a national qualifications framework and which aim to improve both skills and knowledge of the learners (European Co-op Campus 2013).

Education at the Co-operative College is increasingly characterized by flexible approaches that embrace both skills and knowledge through a range of pedagogical innovations. Professional discussions, widely used within learning and assessment practice in the UK, are increasingly used by the College as it is felt that they hold a particular value for co-operatives by enabling participants to present evidence on the relationship of (co-operative) values to their behaviour. They also provide a way of formally recognizing a candidate's existing experience and skills. A growing number of distance and e-learning programmes have also been developed by the College. In recognition of the often large disparities between the skills, experience and knowledge of elected members, audits of board skills can identify gaps and inform the development of personalized learning programmes. Materials from the National Co-operative Archive are increasingly being used across all of the College educational provision. As the movement has grown more successful and confidence has returned after years of prolonged decline, there has also been an interest in re-engaging with its history. The archive collections have provided a rich resource to revisit the past. They have helped to underpin the development of a range of learning resources and publications including *Making Connections* (a Fairtrade Towns pack), online resources, and the revival of the College academic paper series.

Outside the movement, it became clear that co-operatives had only a weak presence in teaching and research in the UK higher education sector. To date, there are only a small number of university programmes and short courses on co-operatives despite rising interest in social enterprise and the third sector. Academics with expertise in co-operatives remain thinly spread across a number of UK universities and located in different disciplines. There are very few universities with more than one or two staff members with an interest in co-operatives. Research and teaching generally occurs across a wide range of different academic departments rather than in a multi-disciplinary centre with a clear co-operative focus. The danger is that staff may move to other universities taking their co-operative expertise and interests with them and leaving behind no institutional memory or capacity to develop co-operative approaches. The exception to this is the Co-operatives Research Unit at the Open University with over 30 years of continuous research activity and consultancy. However, it is also evident that there are a growing number of academics interested in the co-operative sector in a number of disciplines. This trend is especially marked among early career researchers including those on doctoral programmes.

Overall, the findings from the research revealed that the nature of educational provision continued to be characterized by a considerable diversity of providers and of the programmes they offered. The landscape reflects the differentiated layering of organizations over a long period with long term formal accredited programmes, standalone 'one-off' workshops as well as formal and informal mentoring and support schemes. Online and distance learning is still in its infancy within the movement though a start had been made in some areas. The pedagogical approaches adopted varied considerably from provider to provider with no clear or well defined 'co-operative' approach emerging. It is also indicative of the limited resources that have been available for the development of programmes that are long term or large scale. Nonetheless, to date, the nature of co-operative education remains ill-defined and little discussed within the movement and has proved of greater interest to academic commentaries, as this volume attests, rather than internal movement debate.

A turning point?

There are, however, signs that the provision and nature of co-operative education may be reaching a turning point. This is happening in several ways. While an expanding number of providers has encouraged fragmentation through both duplication and the creation of gaps in provision, it also reflects a growing and diverse co-operative sector. The recent focus on business start-up support and enterprise development can be viewed as marking an important shift away from an emphasis on movement preservation towards a wider and more growth oriented, if not transformatory, agenda.

Co-operative education is also ceasing to be delivered solely within and by the movement. The pace of change is beginning to speed up in both the schools sector and in higher education. By January 2014, for example, there were over 700 co-operative schools formally established with more in the pipeline. The bulk of these were co-operative trusts and converter academies. A co-operative trust model was developed following the 2006 Education and Inspection Act, which accelerated the transformation of the role of the local authority in the provision of education services. Schools within a trust become foundation schools with the trust as the foundation. The land and assets are transferred from the authority to the trust which also becomes the employer and admissions authority. A co-operative trust is essentially a multi stakeholder co-operative with membership drawn from parents and carers, students, staff and the local community together with external institutional partner organizations who also appoint trustees. Institutional partners are drawn from a wide range of local organizations such as further and higher education institutions as well as enterprises. A similar multi-stakeholder co-operative model for converter academies received Department for Education approval in 2011. In both cooperative trusts and converter academies the schools adopt an ethos based on the globally defined co-operative values, with a view to ensuring they become embedded in the curriculum and pedagogy as well as the governance of schools. The Co-operative College and the Co-operative Group worked together to facilitate this transition. Well over 250,000 students now attend co-operative schools. Indeed, this may well represent a phase where co-operative models for education offer a real challenge to the principles and practice of state education especially in relation to primary and secondary provision.

These developments have helped to break the insularity that previously characterized much co-operative education. They are supported by a number of other initiatives. Alongside schools, in higher education, serious consideration is being given to developing a co-operative university through a variety of networks. In addition, there has been a renewal of both practitioner and academic interest in the development and use of specifically co-operative pedagogical approaches – the notion of 'co-operative learning'. A recent edition of the UK *Journal of Co-operative Studies* focused on co-operative education with an emphasis on collaborative and co-operative pedagogies which could be used in a number of educational settings.

At the same time, apart from reaching out to new sectors, education needs to continue to play a crucial role in sustaining and retaining co-operative identity within the existing movement. On the one hand, there is a need to support new co-operatives which are grounded in the core co-operative values and, on the other, to sustain existing co-operatives. It is now recognized that the issue of funding and resourcing for education is undoubtedly one of the most critical challenges the movement faces (Murray 2010). There is no shortage of examples internationally of the benefits to co-operative movements of taking education seriously. The success of the Mondragón co-operative model, for example, indicates how much can be achieved with a core commitment to education and research (Bajo and Roelants 2011). In the UK, the changing landscape of state and public education, raises opportunities to re-assert the relevance of co-operative models. However, the movement needs to be in a position to respond effectively to the educational challenges this brings. Co-operative education itself has the potential to move from the margins into the mainstream of education provision building on, but not constricted by, its rich movement legacy. If this is to be a turning point for co-operative education, there is a need for the movement itself to revisit, reflect on and develop its own practices and theoretical understandings of education. There is much to do.

References

Bajo, C. S. and Roelants, B. (2011) *Capital and the Debt Trap Learning from Co-operatives in the Global Crisis*, Basingstoke: Palgrave Macmillan.

BBC (2013) Myners to earn £1 a year for Co-op Group review, online at http://www.bbc.co.uk/news/business-25345253 (accessed 20 December 2013).
Bibby, A. (2013) 'Why are co-operative societies on the decline?' *Guardian*, Co-operatives and Mutuals Hub, 14 November, http://www.theguardian.com/social-enterprise-network/2013/nov/14/cooperatives-declining-company-mergers-retail (accessed 20 November 2013).
Birchall, J. (1994) *Co-op: The People's Business*, Manchester: Manchester University Press.
—— (1997) *The International Co-operative Movement*, Manchester: Manchester University Press.
Birchall, J. and Simmons, R. (2004a) 'What motivates members to participate in co-operative and mutual businesses', *Annals of Public and Cooperative Economics*, 75/3: 465–495.
—— (2004b) *What motivates members to participate in the governance of consumer co-operatives? A study of the Co-operative Group*, Research Report No 2. Stirling: University of Stirling, http://www.uwcc.wisc.edu/info/consumer/rr2.pdf (accessed 20 September 2009).
Co-operative Commission (2001) *The Co-operative Advantage, Creating a Successful Family of Co-operative Businesses*, Manchester: Co-operative Union.
Co-operative Futures (2012) *2012 Conference Report*, http://www.futures.coop/wp-content/uploads/2010/11/Future-Co-operatives-2012.pdf (accessed 31 July 2013).
Co-operative Union (1904) *Statistics of Societies, Trade etc. for 1903*, Manchester: Co-operative Union.
Co-operatives UK (2005) *Corporate Governance: the Code of Best Practice for Consumer Societies in Membership of Co-operatives UK*, Manchester: Co-operatives UK.
—— (2012a) Simply legal, http://www.uk.coop/simplylegal (accessed 20 March 2013).
—— (2012b) *Our Impact in 2012*, Manchester: Co-operatives UK.
—— (2013) *The Co-operative Economy*, Manchester: Co-operatives UK.
European Co-op Campus (2013) www.coopcampus.eu (accessed 20 December 2013).
Facer, K., Thorpe, J. and Shaw, L. (2012) 'Co-operative education and schools: an old idea for new times?', *Power and Education*, 4/3: 327-341.
Fairbairn, B. (2003) *Three Strategic Concepts for the Guidance of Co-operatives*, Saskatoon: Centre for the Study of Co-operatives, University of Saskatchewan.
Fieldhouse, R. (1998) *A History of Modern British Education*, Leicester: NIACE.
Gurney, P. (1996) *Co-operative Culture and the Politics of Consumption*, Manchester: Manchester University Press.
Ivory, C., Miskell, P., Shipton, H., White, A., Moeslein, K. and Neely, A. (2006) *UK Business Schools: Historical Contexts and Future Scenarios*, London: Advanced Institute of Management Research, 303.
Kalmi, P. (2007) 'The disappearance of co-operatives from economics textbooks,' *Cambridge Journal of Economics*, 31/4: 625–647.
MacPherson, I. (2002) 'Encouraging associative intelligence', in *Co-operative Learning and Responsible Citizenship in the 21st Century*, Manchester: Co-operative College.
McIlroy, J. (1998) 'Education for the labour movement: UK experience' in Fieldhouse, R. (ed.) *A History of Modern British Adult Education*, Leicester: NIACE.
—— (2007) *One Path to Co-operative Studies*, Victoria: New Rochdale Press.
Murray, R. (2010) *Co-operation in the Age of Google*, Manchester: Co-operatives UK.
OECD (2002) *Management Training in Small SMEs*, Paris: OECD.
Rawlings, B. and Shaw, L. (2007) *Third Sector Women in Management Project: Final Research Report*, Inside Track and Co-operative College: Manchester.
Robertson, N. (2010) *The Co-operative Movement and Communities in Britain*, Farnham: Ashgate.
Shaw, L. (2009) *Making Connections, Education for Co-operatives*, Manchester: Co-operative College.
—— (2011) 'International Perspectives on Co-operative Education' in Webster, A., Brown, A., Stewart, D., Walton, J.K. and Shaw, L. (eds), *The Hidden Alternative: Co-operative Values, Past, Present and Future*, Manchester: Manchester University Press.
Spear, R. (2004) 'Governance in democratic member-based organisations', *Annals of Public and Cooperative Economics*, 75/3: 33–60.

Todd, N. (2013) 'The Wallsend Owenites', *Forum*, 55/2: 279–291.

Twigg, H. (1924) *An Outline History of Co-operative Education*, Manchester: Co-operative Union.

Vernon, K. (2013) 'Co-operative education and the state, c1895–1935,' *Forum*, 55/2: 293–307.

——(2011) 'Values and vocationalism: educating the co-operative workforce in Britain, 1918–1939', in Webster, A., Brown, A., Stewart, D., Walton, J.K. and Shaw, L. *The Hidden Alternative: Co-operative Values, Past, Present and Future,* Manchester: Manchester University Press.

Wilson, J., Webster, A. and Vorberg-Rugh, R. (2013) *Building Co-operation*, Oxford: Oxford University Press.

Woodin, T. (2011) 'Co-operative education in Britain during the nineteenth and early twentieth centuries: context, identity and learning' in Webster, A., Brown, A., Stewart, D., Walton, J.K. and Shaw, L. (eds), *The Hidden Alternative: Co-operative Values, Past, Present and Future,* Manchester: Manchester University Press, 78–95.

Woodin, T. and Fielding, M. (2013) 'Co-operative education for a new age?' *Forum* 55/2: 179–184.

13

Mainstreaming some lacunae: developing co-operative studies as an interdisciplinary, international field of enquiry

Ian MacPherson

The co-operative movement, co-operatives and the thought associated with them are, with few exceptions, ignored or patronized in the academy. Academics with an interest in co-operatives usually have difficulty establishing their careers, unless they are in one of the very few research and teaching institutions concerned with co-operatives and co-operative thought. Even then, they usually have to struggle to gain acceptance and support from other colleagues. Typically, too, they have to divide their time between the normal demands of academic life and the often-complex ways in which they have to engage co-operatives in pursuing their work. It is not an easy path through the groves of academe.

Curricula in virtually all disciplines are generally silent on the co-operative movement – or, even worse, misrepresent it. Consequently, only a minuscule percentage of university students can study the co-operative movement in a serious and sustained way (Lans 2005). The movement generally is overlooked in sociology, anthropology, history, political science and economics, with the exception of agricultural economics and institutional economics in mid-twentieth century America. Regional studies programmes, such as those examining Latin America, Asia and Africa, ignore co-operation, despite its historic and contemporary importance. Most law faculties pay scant attention to it. Business schools, almost without exception, disregard it and, when they do consider it, commonly apply an inappropriate framework based upon capitalist businesses. Education faculties, which often consider 'content' as well as methods, neglect the movement, thereby helping to ensure that students will not be encouraged to learn about an alternative form of business and an avenue for youth entrepreneurship.

This lacuna is all the more surprising given the size and significance of the movement. The co-operatives affiliated with the International Co-operative Alliance, the main international co-operative organization, are owned by some 1,000,000,000 members (ICA 2013a). Many of those memberships are really family memberships including several people: for example, in co-op stores or co-operative financial institutions in India or Australia; agricultural co-ops in Sweden or Canada; and housing co-ops in Denmark or the United States. At the same time, it is also true that many people belong to more than one co-operative. It is not possible to enumerate precisely how many individuals are actually involved in the international movement, but the number is doubtlessly substantial – it is arguably the world's largest social movement.

There are other ways to measure the statistical importance of co-operatives. The annual sales of the 300 largest co-operatives in the world today are about the same as Canada's Gross Annual Product (GAP), the tenth largest national economy in the world today (World Bank 2007); although they employ 20 per cent more people. There are another estimated 100,000 smaller co-ops distributed widely in virtually every country around the globe. The Canadian co-operative leader, Alexander Laidlaw estimated that co-operatives meet over 300 needs; in fact nearly all those felt from birth to death. The United Nations, appreciating the movement's breadth of services, estimates that three billion people – about half of the world's population – use co-operatives for one reason or another (ICA 2013b).

This chapter argues for co-operative studies as a joint community/academic pursuit, one that has the potential to engage the interest of more researchers, teachers, and students in the academy. It calls for greater support from the movement, proposing a strong community/university partnership developed in a creative, reciprocal, and genuinely respectful way. It envisions a field of enquiry whose practitioners consider systematically how best to undertake their research, individually and collectively. The countries selected for the following brief discussion are those that tended to become the most prominent in the generally Eurocentric development of the movement between 1850 and 1950. They are briefly discussed to demonstrate the complexities and richness of the sources for co-operative development and co-operative thought. It considers only briefly, because of space limitations other countries in Central, Eastern, and Southern Europe in which co-operatives were significant. It leaves for later discussion the growth of co-operatives in other parts of the world.

Arguments from European history

The movement's history stretches back at least some 160 years though some would push it back even further by another 100, 500, or more years to the Enlightenment or the emergence of the guild system, Germanic tribes and the catacombs of Rome. Even taking the 160 years 'birth date', it is not difficult to demonstrate how broad and deep its impact has been, both historically and in the contemporary world. Most registered forms of co-operatives began in Europe. They did not develop in isolation but were embedded in many of the main trends of modern history, including key intellectual debates, economic developments, social innovation and various research activities. They created organizations that came to play significant roles economically and socially, especially on the local level, but often on national levels as well. They were not minor developments on the margins of what was really important – a point the following is intended to demonstrate.

In the United Kingdom, Robert Owen and the Owenites played a major role in co-operative developments during the early nineteenth century. They have been credited, in the United Kingdom at least, with coining the term 'social science', a form of enquiry they thought would help ordinary people to better understand the world around them and develop institutions like trade unions and co-operatives to improve their lot (Claeys 1989: 16; Chushichi 1992). Owen's emphasis on early childhood and lifelong education significantly influenced educational theory generally and the co-operative movement specifically, arguably down to the present day (Bonner 1961: 116–36). From the beginning, the British movement provided a broad education for its members, operating lending libraries, offering classes on numerous topics, preparing a wide array of educational materials, pioneering in adult education, and helping to establish the Workers' Educational Association. It enlisted the support of many important thinkers and educators, including Beatrice and Sydney Webb, George Jacob Holyoake, G.D.H. Cole, A.M. Car-Saunders, C.R. Fay, and T.W. Mercer. The movement played a major role in the empowerment of the working and agricultural classes during the later nineteenth and early twentieth centuries. Educational and research activities were carried on by the Co-operative College, established in 1919. From the interwar period, it became a major international centre for co-operative learning and publications, print and film. Currently, it is enjoying a renaissance as it embraces new technologies and reaches out around the world. In addition, in recent years the UK Society for Co-operative Studies has produced important studies of mutual and co-operative enterprise. Yet, despite the size, impact and promise of the movement, the UK remains deficient in recognizing and teaching about the movement (see Shaw in this book).

'Co-operation' in the United Kingdom became arguably the most successful of the world's nineteenth century movements. It embraced a remarkable entrepreneurial vision calling for the transformation of the economy and society generally through intelligent, fair, and responsible consumerism, an idea which retains increasing cogency in the early twenty-first century. The power of this idea – and the remarkable entrepreneurial spirit that gave it life – was reflected in the innovative institutions it created: co-operative wholesales in England and Scotland (1863 and 1868), the Co-operative Insurance Society (1867) and the Co-operative Bank (1876), both of them established as subsidiaries of the English wholesale, and the creation of the Co-operative Union (1869-70). Subsequently, the movement added farms in the UK and overseas, operated factories and travel agencies, funded various publication activities, and developed funeral services. By the early twentieth century, the movement was serving over 25 per cent of the British population. Co-operatives became central to a wide range of issues including class relationships, workplace management, consumption patterns, the reformulation of gender relations, shifting community patterns, political change and the transformation of the countryside.

In France, the co-operative movement also has deep intellectual roots, most obviously reflected in the impact, during the nineteenth century, of Charles Fourier and Henri Saint-Simon. Fourier's search for alternative social forms fostered numerous intentional communities in Europe and especially North America (Spahn 1989; Guarneri 1991). Saint-Simon studied social organizations 'scientifically', searching for ways to overcome what he perceived as an ethical crisis in European society (Taylor 1975). He sought institutions that could combat the evils of industrialism and provide ethical guidelines for people losing their moral compass in an increasingly secular world. Along with his one-time mentor, Auguste Comte, he profoundly influenced French co-operativism throughout much of the nineteenth and early twentieth centuries.

The French co-operative tradition is rich in theory and reflection, and it has long been on the cutting edge of many theoretical debates, both within and without the movement, especially those concerning worker and consumer co-operatives (Birchall 1997; Draperi 2008). One of its intellectuals, Charles Gide, was perhaps the most important co-operative theorist of the early twentieth century. The School of Nîmes, with which he was prominently associated, became a key international centre for co-operative thought and theoretical investigation.

Following the Second World War, intellectuals and activists associated with the French movement were arguably the main leaders in the development of the social economy tradition. They sought to establish commonalities in structure and purpose, values and policies among non-capitalist organizations, such as co-operatives, mutuals, associations, and government institutions. They envisioned creating an efficiently functioning economy able to respond effectively and fairly to all social and economic needs, one in which co-operative enterprise would play a central role. It is a perspective that recently has attracted renewed attention. It has also been noted how co-operatives in other countries, such as Spain, Portugal and Greece, have tended to be grouped in the social economy rubric.

The German, Italian, and Nordic traditions contributed significantly to co-operative thought and activism from the late nineteenth century. In Germany, the movement emerged in rural areas in the wake of failed harvests in 1846-1847. In 1847, Friedrich Wilhelm Raiffeisen organized the first aid association in Weyerbusch (Westerwald) to help poverty-stricken rural people; some 17 years later, he created the 'Heddesdorfer Darlehnskassenverein' (Heddesdorf Loan Society), the first co-operative in what became the Raiffeisen tradition. That tradition, concerned with rural poverty and instability, has consistently addressed many of the intellectual and cultural issues of rural life, a perspective that has resonated well internationally.

The movement in the German towns and cities started at about the same time, chiefly through the efforts of Hermann Schulze-Delitzsch. He was concerned primarily with financially-struggling artisans and small business people. Basing his organizations on principles of self-help, self-administration, and self-responsibility, he founded the first 'raw materials association' for carpenters and shoemakers in 1847, followed by the first 'thrift and loan association' in 1850. In contrast to the moral conservatism of the Raiffeisen approach, the Schulze-Delitzsch system, despite sharing similar values, was more 'liberal' and individualistic, more preoccupied with personal economic advancement than with community engagement. It developed a sophisticated legislative and regulatory framework that significantly affected co-operative development around the world.

As the nineteenth century ended, the German consumer movement emerged, largely among the working classes in industrializing areas. It formed a wholesale in 1889 and a national organization in 1903. In the 1890s, residents in larger German cities started organizing housing co-operatives in significant numbers; they too quickly became an important part of the German movement. Overall, Germany possessed a vibrant, distinctive movement by the early twentieth century. Much of it survived the dislocations of the Great War of 1914-1918. With its strong and diverse intellectual currents, its growing support by the working and agrarian classes, its essential pragmatism, and effective legislative frameworks, it became one of the most important forces within co-operative circles. After the Second World War, the German movement became involved with one of the world's strongest and most persistent efforts to create academic analyses of the movement. It helped establish ten university centres, most of them essentially concerned with the German experience, though the centre at Marburg, under the leadership of Hans Muenkner, became prominent in overseas work; its graduates are easily found in co-operatives and within public service in many Asian and African countries. Although the German centres have contributed significantly to co-operative science, especially in law and economics faculties, their work is little understood or considered outside of the Germanic parts of the world.

The Italian movement emerged during the last half of the nineteenth century, its beginnings associated with the creation of a consumer co-operative in Turin in 1854 and a worker co-op in Savona shortly afterwards. In the 1880s, farmers influenced by Leone Wollemborg and urban workers led by Luigi Luzzatti started the financial co-operative movement. In the same decade, farmers' co-operatives began to appear. The Italian movement was rooted deeply in the national experience, institutions, and social systems. It became noteworthy for its wide range of co-operatives, based on specific ideological and religious configurations. Many Italian socialists embraced co-operatives as a key element in their programmes, and co-operatives were important for their first national organizations formed in the 1890s. In the first half of the twentieth century, the socialist perspective was reconfigured by the powerful writings of Antonio Gramsci who argued for the left to recognize the full scope of working class organizations. In the same time frame, many Roman Catholics, encouraged by Leo XII's papal encyclical *Rerum Novarum*, released in 1891, embraced a wide range of co-operative activity, ultimately supporting many of the same kinds of co-operative endeavours as their left-wing contemporaries.

These two broad divisions, complicated by further divides within the Italian Left after the Second World War, provide fertile ground for research and intellectual controversy. They particularly demonstrate the complex relationships between co-operatives and the state, municipal governments and political parties. They developed innovative ways to fund co-operative enterprise and to build legislative frameworks that support strong co-operative development. They ultimately fashioned one of the most important models for flexible and innovative co-operative development, especially in the field of social co-operatives.

In recent years, research into, and education about, the Italian movement has been pursued vigorously at both the University of Trento and the University of Bologna. Under the current leadership of Professors Carlo Borzaga and Stefano Zemagni respectively, organizations based on democratic practice and the distribution of surpluses on participation have been placed at the heart of contemporary economic theory. Their work, through games and firm theory, contest the assumption that successful co-operatives will ultimately become investor-owned firms. They argue for a more sustainable basis for co-operative endeavour by stressing the importance of reciprocity and an appreciation for how pluralistic motivation can create sustainable economic institutions. It is a perspective of profound importance for the modern world (Earle 1986; Ocampo et al 2000; Borzaga and Defourney 2001; Borzaga and Spear 2004; Screpanti and Zamagni 2005).

The Nordic movements have also been prominent within European co-operative development. The Swedish movement, especially the consumer movement, had its roots among liberal groups concerned about the Social Question – how, amid so much prosperity, is poverty possible? It spread through worker societies and educational movements during the later nineteenth century, despite being initially opposed by Marxists who saw it as a diversion from the class struggle. However, in the twentieth century, with the support of Social Democrats, strong central organizations were established, notably a wholesale and an insurance company. The Swedish movement prospered, becoming known for its business efficiency, architecture, consumer education, and innovative styles. It created a strong housing movement and, after the Second World War, became significantly engaged in overseas development, particularly in Africa (Hedberg 1949; Mulani 1966; Schediwy 1989; Pestoff 1991). It also expanded to include virtually all the nation's farmers served by a maze of co-operative institutions reflecting geographic and commodity priorities. Numerous cultural and social activities were organized and governments were lobbied on rural issues. The movement became a major economic force in the country, not only for the marketing of farm produce but also for the harvesting of forests, the development of rural banking services, the creation of research and advisory services, and the training of co-operative personnel. Over the last 50 years, rural co-operatives were able to respond to increased competition, changing government policies, growing capital needs, and institutional integration.

The Swedish movement was closely tied into the main currents of Swedish history. It has also achieved a contemporary resonance by sustaining member involvement at a time when urbanization seemingly undermined the communitarianism of past times. It has wrestled with the great challenges of finding the best relationships between local, regional, and national associations within an increasingly difficult and competitive situation. It readily demonstrates many of the most complex issues that co-operatives everywhere face within 'modern' circumstances.

Further examples could be developed based on Finland and Norway where issues of industrialization and the role of co-operation in political divisions, often connected to farmers, workers, feminist and educational movements, have been paramount. Successful examples of consumer, housing, fishing and forestry co-ops were paralleled in Norway. The movement has also served as a microcosm of wider industrial and urban developments (Ilmonen 1986, 1992; Schediwy 1989b; Skurnik and Vihriälä 1999).

In addition, Eastern Europe also carries rich potential for co-operative studies, not least in the multiple cultural, ethnic, political and ideological influences which have affected these movements since the nineteenth century. While they borrowed much from western and northern Europe, they were also outgrowths of specific needs within the Austrian and Russian empires, particularly in rural areas. As with many co-operatives, they reflected the diverse cultural identities – including Ukrainian, Russian, Polish, Austrian and Bulgarian – of those remarkably diverse regions. Their history was much buffeted by the rise of Marxism and then Nazism, particularly the former. Their current revitalization, especially in health, social, and worker co-ops, suggest how deeply embedded co-operative approaches are among the peoples of those regions.

The field of co-operative studies quickly becomes complex – and rewarding – when one considers the European experience. It opens up new avenues for research and learning, to compare and contrast co-operatives themselves, a counterpoise to the more common comparisons made with private enterprise organizations; but it becomes even more interesting when viewed globally.

Arguments for developing international perspectives

However muted or restrained it might sometimes appear to be, the co-operative movement has always had international dimensions. The movement's earliest leaders shared, albeit less systematically, the international perspectives of such nineteenth century ideologues as Marx, Mill, Bakunin, and Kropotkin. They too sought universal truths and global influence. Many among the rank and file agreed with them. British consumer co-operators followed reports of new co-ops overseas, especially in the Empire/Commonwealth, through the pages of *The Co-operative News*. An international network of co-operative banking enthusiasts emerged to promote financial co-ops throughout much of the world (MacPherson 1999: 5-76). Some trade unions and political parties promoted consumer and worker co-operatives. The remarkably widespread agrarian press sought to improve rural life through agricultural co-operatives. These international ambitions found a voice within the work of the International Co-operative Alliance and ultimately the International Labour Organisation and the United Nations.

There are no simple answers to such questions. Despite the growth of co-operation internationally, actual co-operatives have remained located in specific places and cultures. It is not right to assume uniformity and easy transfers from one movement or organization to another, from one culture to another. Co-operative studies need to explore contextual differences much more intensively than has been done in the past. The common attempt to put a gloss of consistency over the diversity of the international movement by appealing to the 'Rochdale tradition' has achieved only limited success. There is a need to think more seriously about the movement's diverse intellectual and cultural roots in dramatically-different places.

Co-operatives cannot be isolated in history. They have been, for example, important dimensions in the rise of empires, an uncomfortable issue for some co-operative enthusiasts to acknowledge. Imperial officials responsible for co-operative development could exhibit a mixture of racist, humanitarian and even idealistic motivations (Rhodes 2013). Imperial powers organized co-operatives primarily to expand marketable agricultural production or to mobilize funds for market-based economies. Each northern empire had its own approaches to developing co-ops, creating variations in objectives and the distribution of authority between imperial, colonial, and local administrators (Develtere 1994). They have been variously affected by the activities of non-government enthusiasts, typically people bringing strong co-operative backgrounds from the North. Most importantly, there is a need to acknowledge indigenous influences. In much of the literature, credit for establishing 'colonial' co-operatives goes to immigrants within governments, co-operative institutions, churches, and development agencies. Rarely, however, is the emphasis on 'outsiders' a sufficient explanation. Many successful co-operatives in the South have relied heavily upon indigenous traditions of collaboration, kinship, and mutuality, a debt that needs to be more frequently acknowledged. The mixed imperial record in developing co-operatives raises fundamental questions about the relationships between spontaneous co-operation (what human beings automatically do), traditional co-operation (what they inherit from their cultures and kin associations), and what they are required to do by governments (forced or encouraged co-operation) (Craig 1976). The varied ways in which human beings learn about and practise co-operative behaviour is a central issue for co-operative studies.

There have been at least two other major waves of international co-operative endeavour over the last seventy years. Almost all the independence movements that emerged after the Second World War supported co-operative development. Independence leaders, like Nehru, Gandhi, Sukarno, Nyerere, Nkrumah, and Williams, generally allowed 'old order' co-ops from the colonial period to adjust after independence. They saw them as ways to sustain economic vitality, to train local leaders, and, in some instances, to provide for patronage appointments (Birchall 1997). They also promoted several kinds of co-ops, though differing considerably in how much help they provided. Exploring these differences more systematically should offer considerable insight into how to promote co-operative development today.

The co-operatives of Central and South America also deserve special attention, particularly by those living outside the regions. From the 1950s, many Latin

American governments, and their opposition movements, promoted co-operatives to help build local communities. The history of co-operatives in Brazil and its Spanish-speaking neighbours, therefore, is particularly interesting and complicated. In Central America, Colombia, and Peru there were bitter struggles over co-operatives between left and right wing groups, struggles that still reverberate decades later.

In more recent years, as elsewhere, there has been a remarkable surge in co-operative development within Latin America. It includes small-scale co-operatives to create work, build financial resources, provide housing, and meet health needs. Worker co-ops have been developed to take over failing firms, notably in Argentina. Other new co-ops help people scavenging reusable goods from the garbage of the major cities, engage in Fairtrade, develop tourism opportunities, create youth employment, and organize housing co-ops. Health co-ops, a form of co-operative enterprise in which South America has a remarkable record, have expanded. The list is long and impressive. The research possibilities are rich.

A further feature of the international co-operative process is the way that co-ops have emerged from all the great migration movements of the last 150 years. People 'on the move', to urban as well as rural settings, have readily embraced co-operative strategies. They band together in kin groups or simply as people sharing experiences, creating support institutions of various kinds, including co-operatives. The settler co-ops, from the agrarian movements of the later nineteenth century to the Kibbutz movement of the twentieth century, provided social as well as economic benefits, particularly for women and youth. They reflected changes in rural life in how they were operated and in how they represented rural societies to governments and urban consumers. Much can be revealed as we learn about what happened to them during the settlement era, as they became institutionalized, adapted to the market place and struggled to sustain rural voices in countries where urban concerns were becoming dominant.

State relationships

The role of the state in developing co-operatives is another major issue which affects all co-operatives and is particularly pertinent in the Global South and within centrally-planned economies. Co-operative studies can offer fascinating insights into the state with significance for both historical and contemporary understanding. For example, many co-operatives in much of the Global South were developed by imperial authorities or by independence movements that tended to rely heavily on state assistance and direction. Governments saw co-operatives as tools for economic development and found it difficult to remain aloof given the potential to raise significant amounts of economic and human power. Some leaders, trained in the centrally-planned economies of Central and Eastern Europe and China (Birchall 1997), replicated what they had seen and learned.

Most importantly, though, co-operatives are playing important roles in the emergence of the 'new Africa' and co-operatives are being formed to respond to the

HIV/AIDS pandemic, to create employment, to provide housing, to participate in Fairtrade, and to meet the special needs of youth (Rollwagen 2008; MacPherson et al. 2006). New cadres of leaders are emerging, while better informed public servants appear to be providing assistance and leadership. If Africa was the 'graveyard' of co-operatives for much of the twentieth century, it might prove to be the nursery for many new developments in the twenty-first.

The co-operatives within the former centrally planned economies of Central and Eastern Europe generally suffered greatly in the wake of *Perestroika* as they were, in part fairly – in part not fairly – accused of being puppets of the old regimes. In recent years, the co-operative model, based on more creative state relationships, has begun to reappear and the future looks much better for co-operative development. In the remaining centrally-planned economies, notably China, there are gradual promising reforms in government policies concerning co-operatives.

The issue of state relationships, though much muted, is no less important in countries where market forces are given greater opportunities to function. The unique nature of co-operatives also helps us to re-think the nature of the state in market societies. Because co-operatives serve so many needs and vary in their stages of development, they require sensitive and often complex relationships with the state. Agricultural, insurance, consumer and social co-ops may all have different needs as will new and well-established co-ops. The state cannot respond uniformly to these differences, a difficulty compounded by the fact that the variety of co-operatives will not easily fit within the purview of any one Ministry. Thus, a study of the state is an urgent necessity for co-operative studies.

The importance of inequality

The state is closely bound up with unequal power relations. An important but under-examined dimension of the development of co-operative movements has been the role of women. Addressing it requires some rethinking of the movement's roles and contributions. Many co-operatives had their beginnings – and continue to operate – primarily serving the needs of women. Consumer co-operatives, for example, have been and are patronized more by women than by men. It is not surprising, therefore, that the first strong manifestation of feminist interest in the movement was associated with consumer co-operatives – the International Co-operative Women's Guild. From its beginnings in the 1880s, the Guild – along with its national organizations – became the conscience of the movement, and so fulfilled a role traditionally assigned to women (Co-operative Women's Guild 1915; Davies 1977; Gaffin and Thoms 1993). It sponsored remarkable research into the challenges confronting women and their families in industrializing areas of the United Kingdom. It argued for intelligent consumerism as a defining force in modern life, insisting that all producers and workers be fairly paid and that only healthy food be sold. As war clouds swept over Europe, many Guildswomen became resolutely pacifist, a perspective that arguably had considerable cogency before and during World War One, but became harder to accept amid the atrocities perpetuated by the Nazis, Stalin, and other repressive regimes in the twentieth century (Scott 2007). Yet, in some contexts, women have gained power through co-operative associations, for example by supporting franchise movements and campaigns for dower and other rights when doing so was controversial.

Women, however, have not commonly been elected to co-operative boards. Some exceptions exist such as craft, poultry, housing, health, and childcare co-ops, that is, in co-operatives that are very obviously extensions to household concerns. Today, the roles of women in financial institutions in Muslim communities, in Fairtrade, and in social co-operatives generally, suggest that women's efforts are becoming more important. On the other hand, women are still not prominent in the governance of larger cooperatives, especially financial, agricultural, and consumer co-ops. In addition, as employees, women can be found in consumer and financial co-operatives, often on the 'front line', as cashiers and member service representatives, or in human resources; they are much less numerous in the higher echelons of management and this is only changing slowly. More needs to be learned. The contradiction between public pronouncements and the lived experience throws up important issues which need to be clarified and addressed through research.

In addition, co-operatives in many countries have often been closely associated with working class and agrarian movements, which partly explains why they developed such deep community bonds and responded to social and economic challenges, for example in North America from the mid-nineteenth century and, later, in countries such as Singapore. In Africa and South America such co-operatives have clustered in urban centres such as Nairobi and Buenos Aires. To see co-operatives as merely by-products of other movements, however, is misleading, though that perspective is often advocated. Many of the movement's chroniclers have come from labour and/or left wing circles, and naturally emphasize the importance of these relationships. They have tended to downplay the co-op movement's own inner strengths, ideological perspectives, and institutional dynamics. The fact that, today, co-operative studies can take a more independent perspective, is indicative of its significance in contemporary society and politics.

The challenges of association – the social economy

Parallel developments can be identified in relation to the social economy, an approach which spans a range of community-based activities, including charities, associations, foundations, and government enterprises. Analysing such organizations can be a very useful exercise for co-operators who can place their contribution within a broader social purpose. The concept of the social economy helps to illustrate the historical provenance of these arguments which were rooted in the first half of the nineteenth century. Deep-seated concerns emerged about simplistic notions of market efficiency that disrupted social relationships and impoverished some communities as they privileged others. The idea grew slowly but steadily in France and Belgium, somewhat belatedly in Italy, Spain, Portugal and Greece, particularly gathering strength as the Roman Catholic Church gradually withdrew from social programmes.

Social economy and co-operative traditions were closely connected in France and other countries. These ideas influenced the International Co-operative Alliance in the early twentieth century involving exchanges at conferences, collaboration in publishing information, and support for research activities and shared leaders, most particularly Charles Gide and Albert Thomas. In the 1930s, the two movements drifted apart as social economy circles became increasingly attracted to academic, 'scientific' discourses that, for many co-operators, were not particularly relevant to their contemporary priorities. More recently, those divisions have subsided somewhat and the social economy concept, though in many countries often queried by new formulations, such as the solidarity economy, has been gaining favour in countries where previously it had little support – such as Sweden, the United Kingdom, and English-speaking Canada (there have long been strong associations with Québec). The challenge in developing the co-operative/social economy relationship is essentially a matter of respect for diversity. For those relationships to develop and deepen it must be within a spirit of tolerance. The co-operative option has its own identity, processes, and purposes that should not be ignored or glibly passed over, as sometimes occurs. It is an important issue for co-operative studies.

Understanding co-operative effectiveness

The success of the co-operative movement, of course, has always depended upon the effectiveness of its institutions and their management. Co-operative studies, therefore, must research into, teach about, and contribute to, the effective management of co-operative organizations. Currently, basis for doing this is limited with a sprinkling of researchers in this field within business schools and schools of commerce in North America, Europe and Asia as well as in the co-op colleges.

In the final analysis, co-operatives should be examined through the lens of their achievements. In the late nineteenth and early twentieth centuries the co-operative world provided many original entrepreneurial structures and innovations that were achieved through new alliances and federations. They found new ways to raise capital through mass organization drives, innovative contractual relationships with members, and revolving member accounts. They mingled volunteers with paid employees, raising 'social capital' in creative ways that dwarfs what most consider possible today. Some of the early institutional structures, for example, the major co-operative wholesales, some of the farm co-operatives, many of the financial co-operatives, were among the more inventive business organizations of their times. They were not boxed in by restrictive mantras about 'what business are we in' … they were in the member and community enhancement business. They found ways to make enterprises out of social and economic needs and they used the surpluses to enhance the lives of the people they served. The challenge for co-operatives is to restore that creative capacity in order to empower the remarkable wave of new co-operative energies evident today.

In the last 70 or 80 years, however, co-operatives have tended to replicate practices developed within the private sector. The ideas associated with 'Management by Objective', Tom Peters, re-engineering, and 'values-based management' have all echoed along the corridors of many co-operative organizations. While this 'borrowing' has often been helpful, it has also created some problems. Capitalist firms typically have different fundamental purposes and structures; imitating them can unwittingly transform co-operatives. Members become customers, the common good gets lost in the struggle for individual advantage, conventional rather than innovative ways are pursued to raise and reward capital, the great co-operative advantage of long-term perspectives gives way to short-term advantage, the value of collaborating with co-operatives in different fields fades, and the relationships between employed leaders and elected leaders become confused.

For co-operative studies, the bedrock for understanding how co-operatives could be most effective must be the movement's values and principles and the institutional dynamics that flow from them. It is a challenging task because it must even-handedly address at least five interconnected spheres of concern: the engagement of members; involvement in communities, however defined; associations with other co-operatives and not just their own kind; relations with the state; and, keeping these four spheres in mind, the ways in which resources are managed. Developing co-operatives by paying attention to all these spheres, can be thought of as 'co-operative stewardship' (Fig.13.1), the special roles that leaders (elected and employed), members, and staff undertake in carrying out their responsibilities.

It is not easy. The concept of membership varies with types of co-ops and the rewards of membership must be more than just dividends. Responding to communities can be complicated, particularly as co-ops grow larger. Ensuring that co-ops relate effectively with each other – through federations, alliances, and informal collaboration – always requires rethinking and adaptation, not just quick fixes through amalgamations and mergers. The issues of conventional management – marketing approaches, accounting systems, human resource development, long term planning, maintenance of physical plants, succession planning – are as pressing

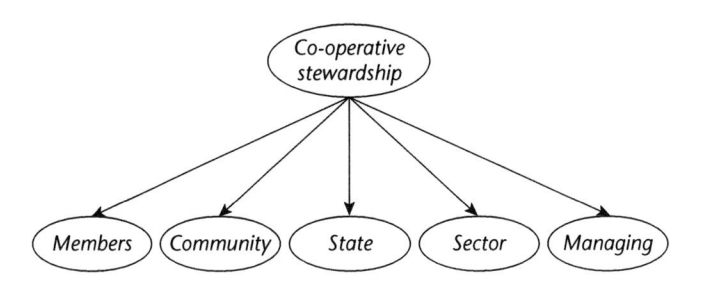

FIGURE 13.1 Co-operative stewardship

Formative → Stabilizing → Building → (Re-examining → Reformulating)

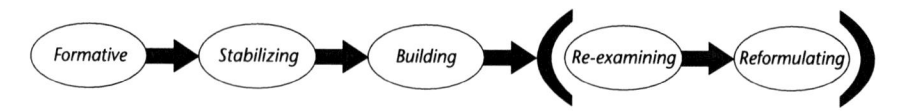

FIGURE 13.2 Stages of co-operative development

as in other forms of enterprise, but they can become more complicated because of the impact of the other spheres of concern. In this way, the economic sphere is connected to wider social and community interests.

Co-operatives also change as they go through stages of development: formative, stabilizing, and building, followed by repeated stages in which co-operatives re-examine and re-formulate their vision and practices (Fig. 13.2). Understanding these phases – what they typically involve, how the spheres of concern can be kept in concert, how they affect different kinds of co-ops – are fundamental questions for co-operative studies.

Beneath all of this rests the fundamental question of democracy. Co-operatives embody the belief that democratic processes can be as useful in developing economic and social institutions, as they should be in providing good governments. 'Democracy', however, extends beyond the requirements of elections and board responsibilities. Understanding the state and meaning of democracy across the diversity of co-operatives remains a major challenge for co-operative studies. Indeed, efforts to understand the distinctive management, governance, and democratic requirements of co-operative enterprise raise a range of questions rarely asked in the study of capitalist firms or government organizations. They create a rich terrain for co-operative studies.

The ideological challenges

Although the co-operative movement has engaged with fundamental economic and social issues of the last 160 years, the lack of serious consideration is striking. A number of reasons might be suggested. At the heart of this explanation is the fact that the movement's fundamental ideology has never been easily grasped. Co-operativism did not flourish amid the ideological warfare of the twentieth century: the struggles for hegemony from such aggressive ideological 'camps' as laissez-faire capitalism, Marxism, various forms of socialism, and anarchism. Those struggles shaped much recent history, resulting in what many see as the triumph of laissez-faire liberalism, still others as the 'end of history' (Fukuyama 1992).

For many reasons, co-operativism did not fare well among these struggles. First, it had its own internal weaknesses. Consumer co-operation and its theoretical perspectives came to dominate international co-operative circles by the early twentieth century but it was not the only strong perspective. Many worker, financial, and agricultural co-operative movements also had powerful intellectual roots as well. The international movement, therefore, could not present a common and compelling alternative, a deadly weakness when compared to the other more easily grasped, reified, and assertive ideological perspectives. From a position of intellectual and research vigour in the later nineteenth and earlier twentieth centuries, the movement declined – despite periods of popularity and demonstrable success – as a commonly recognized alternative way to address the main issues of the day.

Secondly, co-operative ideas, or even ideology, are invariably rooted in practice. People form co-ops because of pressing needs. They develop their co-ops pragmatically, meaning that relatively few members grasp the movement's full potential. They seldom aspire to the creation of Iron Laws, grand theories or have pretensions to universality. They are rarely concerned with developing strong and pervasive theoretical bases. One of the tasks for co-operative studies is to help conceptualize such bases.

Thirdly, the more powerful ideological systems have shaped research agendas in the academy and outside for decades, and they have not been kind to co-operativism. For instance, most Marxist traditions were particularly critical, seeing co-operatives as creating 'false consciousness' far removed from the vanguard of revolutionary change. That is partly why Marxist or neo-Marxist regimes so easily assume too much control over their co-operatives. There were, of course, significant exceptions, notably in Italy, France, and parts of Latin America, where less doctrinaire and flexible forms of Marxism emerged and supported the effective development of co-operatives generally independent of the state. The role of co-operatives within the centrally-planned economies of Central and Eastern Europe, as well as in China, North Korea and southern countries that emulated the Communist world needs to be considered more carefully. In the ideological swings of the 1980s and 1990s, co-operatives in the Communist countries were assumed to be akin to state agencies. It is easily ignored that co-operatives forced Lenin to accept their survival and that co-operatives may well have been centres of resistance to central state policies as well as agencies for local empowerment. They are possibilities that need to be explored seriously by researchers.

The attitudes emanating from the liberal world dominated by capitalist ideologies have not been fundamentally different. They often perceived co-operatives as useful institutions when the market 'failed' to provide fair or adequate value or to meet the needs of small-scale capitalist production, notably in rural areas. They could also be useful in helping organize economic and social responses to cultural needs, a kind of 'social entrepreneurship' that individual initiative or stock market enthusiasm could not readily address. The result was that the movement has frequently been ignored and marginalized, something you might do until you could enter 'real' business. These complex relationships with the most powerful ideological movements of the last 150 years – and the 'quieting' of much of the movement in recent decades – raises significant challenges for co-operative studies in clarifying the essential features of 'co-operativism' as well as the features that distinguish it from other ideological systems.

Conclusions

Co-operative studies should invariably involve ongoing relationships between those who conduct research and those who are actively engaged in co-operatives. These are not necessarily separate groupings: many people who research into co-operatives are also involved as participants; many who hold key positions in co-operatives also undertake research. The essential point, though, is that most research should involve collaboration between the observers and the observed, with both sides having the right if not the duty to validate – or disagree – with the work of the other.

Co-operative studies, therefore, is partly a kind of community based research, requiring researchers within the academy to make adjustments, the inclusion of 'outside' researchers, an association with co-operative activists, and involvement with co-operatives. It is about creating a knowledge base that informs teaching, learning, and reflection about the movement; one that can contribute to greater co-operative effectiveness, and that is accessible to policymakers.

The current knowledge base is extensive but it is also generally inaccessible, even in many universities and co-op institutions, let alone in the public arena where most people gain their understandings. Public media ignore co-operatives and politicians rarely refer to them. They are not conspicuous in public debates, even as much as they were a century ago.

People engaged in co-operative studies should collaborate in developing systematic, extensive accessible resources reflecting the diversities of co-operative studies. They must overcome the information gap that is one of the main reasons for the slow development of the field. The communication revolution that is one of the hallmarks of our era should make this all easily possible – the missing element is the will to do so.

The objective must be to develop courses examining all kinds and sizes of co-operatives, courses readily available through a mixture of online and in-person teaching environments. A few concentrations of interested researchers/teachers and a scattering of researchers, no matter how dedicated and enthusiastic, is not enough to fully establish co-operative studies as a recognized field of study. It should be considered from a wide movement perspective, and not just from the point-of-view of a specific co-op or sector, a given university or co-op college. Ultimately, it is the links beyond the local that are the important ones, the limitations and narrow interests of individuals and organizations that are the barriers.

People in the field should also create more clearly identifiable publication outlets for the work that is being done. That means reaching across institutional homes – universities, co-ops, government departments, development organizations – and overcoming narrow personal interests. It means helping young researchers find meaningful careers in the field. It means seeking ways to compensate researchers outside the academy so they can contribute. It means thinking strategically about organizing research agendas, communicating results, and affecting practice.

Though much is starting to be done, for example through the International Co-operative Research Committee of the International Co-operative Alliance, one should not underestimate these challenges. Bringing academic and non-academic researchers, co-operative activists, and co-operative organizations together is not easy. Each group has its own research interests and needs, each its own criteria for measuring the value of completed research. Each has to strive to understand the needs of the others, to evaluate research in the context within which it is produced, and to understand the need for developing research for the common good. Research, particularly as it tends to develop in the academy is conspicuous for its competitive nature – the 'war of ideas' – a way of thought that may well ultimately not be ideally suited for practitioners of co-operative studies.

What then are the parameters of co-operative studies? They start with the recognition, seldom evident in public discourse, even less frequently in the academy and not always in co-operative circles, that the movement, given its size, diversity, history, and current revitalization is worthy of serious and distinct attention; that it has created a force that has accomplished much; that it deserves to be better understood and, where it proves useful, to be more widely applied.

References

Birchall, J. (1997) *The International Co-operative Movement,* Manchester: University of Manchester Press.
Bonner, A. (1961) *British Co-operation,* Manchester: Co-operative Union.
Borzaga, C, and Defourney, J. (eds) (2001) *The Emergence of Social Enterprise,* New York: Routledge.
Borzaga, C. and Spear, R. (2004) *Trends and Challenges for Co-operatives and Social Enterprises in Developed and Transitional Countries,* Trento: Edizioni 31.
Chushichi, T. (1992) 'Robert Owen and social science', in Chushichi, T. (ed.) *Robert Owen and the World of Co-operation,* Tokyo: The Robert Owen Foundation: 31–48.
Claeys, G. (1989) *Citizens and Saints,* Cambridge: Cambridge University Press.
Co-operative Women's Guild (1915) *Maternity: Letters from Working Women,* London: G. Bell.
Craig, J.G. (1976) *Multi-National Co-operatives: an Alternative for World Development,* Saskatoon: Western Producer Books.
Davies, M.L. (1977) *Life as We Have Known It,* London: Virago.
Develtere, P. (1994) *Co-operation and Development with Special Reference to the Experience of the Commonwealth Caribbean,* The Hague: Acco.
Draperi, J.-F. (2008) 'The ethical foundations and epistemological position of co-operative research' in MacPherson, I. and McDougall-Jenkins, E., *Integrating Diversities within a Complex Heritage,* Victoria: British Columbia Institute for Co-operative Studies: 323–344.
Earle, J. (1986) *The Italian Cooperative Movement: A Portrait of the Lega Nazionale delle Cooperative e Mutue,* London: Allen & Unwin.
Fukuyama, F. (1992) *The End of History and the Last Man,* Toronto: Maxwell Macmillan Canada.
Gaffin, J. and Thoms, D. (1993) *Caring and Sharing: The Centenary History of the Co-operative Women's Guild,* Manchester: Holyoake Books.
Guarneri, C.J. (1991) *The Utopian Alternative: Fourierism in Nineteenth Century America,* Ithaca: Cornell University Press.
Hedberg, A. (1949) *Consumers Co-operation in Sweden,* Stockholm: Kooperativa Föbundets Bokfrlag.
ICA (2013a) http://ica.coop/ica/index.html
ICA (2013b) Statistics, http://www.ica.coop/coop/statistics.html

Ilmonen, K. (1986) *The Enigma of Membership*, Helsinki: Central Union of Consumer Co-operation.
Ilmonen, K. (1992) *The End of the Cooperative Movement? Sociological Essays on Cooperative Affiliation and Morality*, Helsinki: Labour Institute for Economic Research.
Lans, C. (2005) *University Teaching of Co-operative Business and Philosophy in Canadian Universities*, Victoria: British Columbia Institute for Co-operative Studies.
MacPherson, I. (1999) *Hands Around the Globe: The World Council of Credit Unions and the International Credit Union Movement to 1996*, Madison: Horsdal and Schubart.
MacPherson, I., Puga, R. and Smith, J. (2006) *Youth Reinventing Co-operatives*, Victoria: BCICS.
Mulani, J.M. (1966) *Report on the Study of the Swedish and British Co-operative Movement*, Ahmedabad: Gujarat State Co-operative Union.
Ocampo, J.A., Zamagni, S., French-Davis, R. and Pietrobelli, A. (2000) (eds) *The Globalization of Financial Markets and the Emerging Economies*, Santiago: ECLAC and the International Jacques Maritain Institute.
Pestoff, V.A. (1991) *Between Markets and Politics: Co-operatives in Sweden*, Frankfurt am Main: European Centre for Social Welfare Policy and Research.
Rhodes, R. (2013) *Empire and Co-operation: How the British Empire Used Co-operatives in its Development Strategies*, Edinburgh: John Donald.
Rollwagen, K (2008) *A Choice for the Living*, Victoria: BCICS.
Schediwy, R. (1989a) 'The Consumer co-operatives in Sweden', in Brazda, J. and Schediwy, R. (eds) *Consumer Co-operatives in a Changing World, Volume One*, Geneva: International Co-operative Alliance: 232–339.
Schediwy, R. (1989b) 'The consumer co-operatives in Finland', in Brazda, J. and Schediwy, R. (eds) *Consumer Co-operatives in a Changing World, Volume Two*, Geneva: International Co-operative Alliance: 575–668.
Scott, G. (2007) 'Darkness at the end of the tunnel: pacifism, democracy, and the Women's Co-operative Guild in England in the 1930s', in Emmanuel, J. and MacPherson, I. (eds), *Co-operatives and the Pursuit of Peace*, Victoria: BCICS: 73–84.
Screpanti, E. and Zamagni, S. (2005) *An Outline of the History of Economic Thought*, 2nd ed., Oxford: Oxford University Press.
Skurnik, S. and Vihriälä, V. (eds) (1999) *The Role of Cooperative Entrepreneurship in the Modern Market Environment*, Helsinki: Pallervo.
Spahn, E.K. (1989) *Brotherly Tomorrows: Movements for a Cooperative Society in America, 1820–1920*, New York: Columbia University Press.
Sveriges Lantbruksförbund (n.d.) *Swedish Farmers' Organisations*, Stockholm: Sveriges Lantbruksförbund.
Swedish Co-operative Centre (n.d.) *Farmers' Co-operation in Sweden*, Stockholm: LTs Förlag.
Taylor, K. (ed.) (1975) *Henri Saint-Simon: Selected Writings on Science, Industry and Social Organization*, London: Croom Helm.
World Bank (2007) World Development Indicators Database, 1 July, http://siteresources.worldbank.org/DATASTATISTICS/Resources/GDP.pdf

Co-operation and competition – a commentary

Tim Brighouse

Before embarking on a focused set of personal reflections on three experiences where I grappled with the sometimes conflicting pressures of competition and co-operation or collaboration, it is worth taking stock of the chapters here. They act as a corrective to my self-justifying accounts of pragmatism and of being caught up as an actor within the system which, as Richard Pring points out, was changing beyond recognition during the course of those events. Indeed his chapter acts as a salutary reminder of how much has changed since the 1944 Education Act. A world of post-war trust and co-operative idealism where each – central and local politician, teacher, parent and administrator – played their part, has disintegrated into a largely atomized system where national politicians have put their faith in a 'market' of schooling.

So it is timely to be reminded of the barriers created for true co-operation. Both Michael Fielding's chapter and that of Gail Davidge, John Schostak and Keri Facer provide philosophical and theoretical educational underpinning of the case for co-operation and the dangers of competition. The fascinating contributions on co-operative schools and the co-operative movement (Philip Woods, Tom Woodin and Linda Shaw) illustrate the recent growth of co-operative education and school trusts which are so immediately appealing to educators, parents and school leaders with their strong moral purpose and determination to create a better society. Moreover, Ashley Simpson's vivid account of being a student at Reddish Vale reminds us how difficult it is to sustain co-operative values in practice and that the core purpose needs to be renewed with each generation of staff and students. This is similarly qualified from a different perspective in the account of teacher development at Lipson Co-operative Academy in Plymouth (Sarah Jones).

In my own career within the changing education system, I sought to harness both competition and co-operation. In this contribution, I shall focus on three practical examples where it was possible to reconcile the tensions between competition and collaboration, at least so far as inter-school activity is concerned. The first, in Oxfordshire is from a different era – the 1980s – prior to the torrent of educational legislation which changed the educational landscape. The second and third, which took place in Birmingham and London in the 15 years which straddled the millennium, are firmly rooted in a world where schools were encouraged to treasure autonomy and when governments saw no advantage, which they now do, in partnerships and collaborative arrangements among schools.

First however a word about context: the direction of education policy and practice changed in the late 1970s. It ceased to be a largely unchallenged part of the public service as it became entangled with economic theory. So White Papers, preceding what become an incontinent torrent of educational legislation, bristled with a mantra of words such as 'Choice (for parents and for HE students)' 'Diversity (of types of school or university)' and 'Autonomy (of institution whether school or university)'. Of course 'equity' and 'equality' got a mention: well, how could they not when 'treating pupils as they might become rather than as they annoyingly are' has always been the unstated moral underpinning of good schools and of the very vocational aspect of teaching as a profession? The other three words, however, soon ceased to be strange newcomers to educational discourse. In the acclaimed academic productions of *'Educational theory, policy and practice'*, philosophers and psychologists exited stage left, while economists entered right and took centre stage. Just in case practitioners failed to get the message politicians included one more word in their new educational lexicon – 'accountability'.

I confess, as an actor, I rather enjoyed it. For me, competition and co-operation have never been strange or incompatible bedfellows. I have enjoyed them both, especially in teams. Even as an individual I wanted to do better in tests and, as a teacher, certainly wanted all my pupils to excel in what I knew to be normatively referenced external exams. I even 'question spotted' and taught exam techniques! More recently I have discovered the impact of 'contextual dependent memory' from cognitive scientists and made sure that revision classes in schools I know, take place in the exam hall bedecked with artefacts as clues linked to the memorizing of 'expected to be vital' ingredients in exam success. In short, even now in a highly competitive schooling system, I cannot resist the temptation to compete. But I also collaborate.

It has been like that for me since taking on the role of chief education officer in Oxfordshire in 1978. Conservative councillors there had just decided to publish examination results at 16 'in order that parents could make a better choice of school'. This was 15 years before there was a national decision to publish league tables. Secondary school headteachers in Oxfordshire begged me to get the County Council to reverse their decision but, given the Conservatives had a majority of 61 to 8, that request seemed unlikely to be met. Clearly we needed both to get Oxfordshire secondary schools to improve faster than elsewhere on the five or more higher grade measure in the then GCE/CSE metric, and to take the sting out of the Council's decision. In short I needed to find a mechanism which discharged the Council's imperative but did not lead to unhealthy and protective inter-school rivalry. It was an unpromising climate in which to promote inter-school co-operation and collaboration: after all, we were in a period of declining school rolls with the consequential need to close some schools.

The first requirement – to minimize the impact of publishing exam results – was easily solved. We simply published lots of analyses which we made available to interested parents and the press who, in those days, were not able to reduce what we published to a simple league table.

The second issue, not just to avoid a dogfight between schools but proactively encourage co-operation in order to learn from each other, was potentially more challenging. In practice we used something called the 'uncapped pool' of inter-authority expenditure to send teachers, in considerable numbers, on term or year courses at what was then the Oxford Polytechnic (now Oxford Brookes University) and the Oxford University Department of Education. Both of these local HE institutions were happy to co-operate in making sure the courses included or were focused on pieces of action research on a self-chosen common curriculum theme and each theme involved more than one teacher – sometimes half a dozen drawn from two or more schools so they could learn from each other's environment. Teachers themselves proposed topics to research. Headteachers liked this arrangement since it bought time, as secondary school rolls declined, to reduce teacher numbers while simultaneously helping the morale, intellectual curiosity and quality of teachers. Most importantly, it brought groups of teachers from different schools together in carefully designed joint curricular and pedagogical exercises as part of the academic requirements expected by the two universities.

The outcome was that, during the decade of the 1980s, Oxfordshire secondary schools, comparatively, raced ahead of other authorities on the five or more, higher grade measure in GCE/CSE1 metric. Now it may be argued that they were exceptional and favourable times; exceptional in that there was neither publication nationally of exam results, nor of HMI (now Ofsted) reports on schools. Some circumstances were favourable, others less so. The device of the 'uncapped pool' for teachers' professional development was invaluable but eventually this was closed down by the government as they reigned in public expenditure. But acute and chronically-falling school rolls is the worst climate in which to promote inter-school collaboration and learning.

The other two examples are taken from the period 1993-2007 in Birmingham and then London, when, as we have noted, times were very different. By then the vital metric had changed to five or more higher grades in GCSE (formed from a merger of GCE and CSE) or its 'equivalences' and primary schools joined the game with SAT results and their own league tables of test results for each cohort at age 11. The media enjoyed their publication and each year has devoted pages to the outcomes in comparative form. School inspection results are published with sometimes dire consequences for key personnel, particularly the headteacher, should the school be found to be seriously deficient. Personally, I had moved on by then. Over a four year period at Keele University I taught and established a research centre into successful schooling and was able to underpin what had gone on in Oxfordshire with theory and research. From there I went to Birmingham, then 97th out of 103 local education authorities in GCSE league tables – not an enviable position. Moreover, it was unlikely to improve unless we could get schools to co-operate and learn from each other using a common language of 'school improvement' to do so. What is more, if we could identify best practice, beyond Birmingham, and learn from it, we would add the knowledge to our shared 'best practice' arising from inter-school co-operation within the city.

There were two ways in which our approach was different from elsewhere at that time. First we focused on encouraging teacher development and schools learning from each other. Second we brought into play our (then) unrivalled knowledge of school improvement with a series of workshops, and countless follow-up activities, at school level. As a part of this, we shared a very strong database with schools, called the 'Family of Schools data set', which at primary level had schools in groups of about 25 according to our best estimate of their socio-economic background with SAT performances in a graph where the vertical axis was the rate of school improvement and the horizontal was absolute points per pupil. At secondary school level we had just 78 secondary schools so we contented ourselves with a similar axis but supplemented it by setting out results by subjects in GCSE. The 'Family of Schools data set' was not shared with the press. The emphasis was on a document for professionals committed to 'learning from each other'.

Various devices were used to encourage co-operation. A newly formed University of the First Age for youngsters in school holidays was supported by a large grant from the Paul Hamlyn Foundation with a focus on teacher development to help extend styles of teaching and learning. Subscribing schools joined. We also gained another large grant from the Gatsby Foundation which tried to make 'collegiates' or partnerships of schools more firmly rooted. There was a clear focus on continuing professional development (CPD) and finding 'low/effort high/impact' interventions in the classroom or the school as a whole. Some of these 'collegiates' survive more than ten years later. In Birmingham the expressed aim, widely shared by the heads and staff in schools, was to make it the best city for schooling in England and, in terms of five or more higher grade GCSE or equivalents (later five or more including maths and English), it has moved from the bottom to above half-way in the league tables.

London schooling, especially the secondary sector, in 2002 was a 'basket case' or so supposed the combined opinion of press and politicians. Hence the London Challenge, a focused programme of school collaboration and improvement. Twelve years later, it is regarded as having been an unqualified success (Cook 2013). In London and Birmingham there were contextual differences both between the cities and, on a day-to-day basis, among schools. But there were many common ingredients, such as using a 'Family of School data set' to learn from each other, CPD opportunities, sharing a map of school improvement to establish a common language and, for the first time through the National College for School Leadership, developing leaders by learning from each other. But at the heart of both was a collective common purpose that, through partnership and collaboration, the cities were going to be regarded as the best places to be for schooling. Certainly the outcome for Birmingham was transformational improvement. Independent research suggests that London's school improvement is even more pronounced and its schools now outperform other regions of the UK in almost every respect. However you cut the statistics, London now has the most successful schools anywhere in England.

In all three places, Oxfordshire, Birmingham and London, our pride in those communities, 'being the best place to be for teaching and learning', was not simply based or measured by exam and later test results. We did not simply focus on exams but were energetic in promoting the arts, music, outdoor and residential education and a whole range of worthwhile 'experiences' in which every child should have to find their talent, taste success, think for themselves and act for others. It was underpinned by a moral purpose which sees education as a key ingredient to a civilized society and, in the end, fundamental to social justice, political freedom and, for the individual, the capacity to argue a just case. This moral purpose was not heavily underscored or preached about. It was rather a rudder to which we – heads, teachers and advisers – returned when facing some new imperative or possibility for change. That being the case, we never focused narrowly on the government imposed measurable targets.

What I have sought to do is make a case for the use of both 'competitive' and 'collaborative' impetuses to improvement at the level of the school, the local and regional community and more widely. Clearly they can each be overdone: belonging to too many ill-defined or poorly organized partnerships brings exhaustion and no profit, while unbridled local competition can bring a false sense of despair or induce complacency. On a daily basis, individual teachers judge how far to spur on the learner by comparisons with others, but they always use the learner's own previous best to prompt improvement. And the best teachers promote a feeling of 'we' – i.e. the class being a co-operative effort – through group work and collective tasks. It is perhaps best to see 'competition' and 'collaboration' not as warring opposites but as in twin harness requiring of the educator the skill and judgement to get the best out of each.

Clearly I was a more or less willing actor in these events which were largely shaped by national forces. Some of those forces could be changed to make co-operative activity less of an uphill battle. The nature of examinations could be much less individualistic as David Brockington's account of ASDAN reveals. Ofsted inspections could be based on partnerships of schools and the financing of schools could reward inter-school co-operation and co-operative trusts. Universities – and there are fascinating accounts here (Stephen Yeo; Diarmuid McDonnell and Elizabeth MacKnight; and Ian MacPherson) of just how competitive universities have become and how even so the flame of co-operation is still alive – could be linked to schools to remove some of the competitive scramble for places. Admissions to schools could be less a matter of choice.

All these changes are desirable, as would be a debate about the role of the private sector and the market in the provision of public education. But to believe we can remove competition from education entirely seems to fly in the face of reason. All we can do is seek to moderate its undue influence, and there's plenty in this book to arm those who would seek to do that.

Reference

Cook, C. (2013) 'London schoolchildren outperform the best', Financial Times, 13 January, available from http://www.ft.com/cms/s/0/8f65f1ce-5be7-11e2-bef7-00144feab49a.html#ixzz32Rtggyi3 (accessed 20 May 2014)

Conclusion

Tom Woodin

Co-operative models of education and learning are opening up new possibilities and new perspectives on contemporary changes in education. Educators have started to redress historical silences about co-operatives as educational organizations and their role in the curriculum. The chapters in this book reveal multiple understandings of co-operation; they assess existing practices in relation to values, institutions and histories; they reflect upon specific examples of co-operative education; and they also provide more visionary analyses of what might be. Central contradictions in education are highlighted and new areas of scholarship, where research and practice can come together in productive ways, are delineated.

Restrictive definitions of co-operative education have been avoided. Despite having a long historical pedigree, it is a nascent area that is drawing upon diverse elements of educational and social thought. Key stakeholders in education, including teachers, learners, parents and communities, long denied an effective voice, have begun to take on more active roles in defining the future. Co-operative activity is also encouraging systematic thinking about education in a way that returns to basic principles. It highlights the growing contradictions between rising costs and ever-tighter regulation of learning on the one hand and the scope for mutuality, social action and common understanding on the other. Moreover, co-operative schools and networks have provided important insights into the transformation of post-war educational structures at the same time as beginning to develop alternatives based on a vision of democracy and common ownership.

In the long run, if co-operative education is to strengthen its identity and expand, it will need to consciously engage in policy arenas while continuing to nurture and articulate the voices of its own constituents. Most visibly, the emergence of co-operative schools represents a major innovation which has taken place away from the central direction of policymakers and politicians who have had to respond to a development not of their own making. Until now, it has proved difficult for commentators to pigeonhole co-operative education. As a movement, it navigates both public and private spheres and has attracted supporters from all major political parties, a fact which recently became clear at Westminster. Shortly after the Labour MP for Sheffield Heeley, Meg Munn, put forward a 10 Minute Bill supporting co-operative schools, Steve Baker, the Conservative MP for Wycombe, organized an adjournment debate on co-operative schools and noted that erstwhile political opponents were in danger of falling into 'fierce agreement' on the topic (Co-operative Party 2013; Hansard 2013). Of course, if such sympathies were to find their way into the heart of policymaking, being closely associated with any particular government would carry a further danger when subsequent policymakers attempt to overthrow the old order. Were the schools movement to continue its current rate of growth, it will no doubt begin to attract greater public attention. At this point, a simmering wariness about co-operative schools, which can be identified at present, may well coalesce into open hostility. How far co-operative education as a whole can continue down a road of equality and democracy within the current restrictive setting remains to be seen. Issues such as standards, competitiveness and choice will continue to infuse every aspect of education and broad popular support will be needed to redefine them in an equitable way.

The fact that we continue to conceptualize co-operative education as an alternative betrays its subordinate status. The ex-Prime Minister Gordon Brown was keen to capture the legacy of Adam Smith for the left and delighted in saying that Smith's ideas depended not only on dynamic competitive markets and a division of labour but also moral sentiments and social obligations which helped to bond society together. But the balance of forces was clear in his account. Even taking into consideration all the practical achievements of schools, co-operative education has found itself in a similarly subordinate position – as a potential prop for competitive tendencies. To move further out of this cocoon will take a sustained effort and involve wider social changes. This provides an agenda for both research and practice. Identifying the sources of, and potential for, co-operation is certainly a challenge that lies ahead.

Co-operative education has developed a core of dedicated enthusiasts and a much broader number of followers who may view co-operative values as just one potential resource, among other options, which can be grafted onto existing practice. Indeed, the success of co-operative education may weaken its distinctiveness as educationists rework co-operative values and principles as their own in order to handle the fast manoeuvrings of education policy. Yet, by recognizing the myriad forms of actually existing co-operation and collaborative communities, new connections may be made in both theory and practice. This involves surveying educational institutions in the past and present as well as more informal modes of learning and communication. Understanding the complexity of these forces and drawing them together in a creative dialogue promises to reap rewards for both academics and practitioners.

Bridging contradictory elements of education policy will throw up more conundrums. Indeed, education does not exist in a world of its own, and there are underlying social forces which determine the major disparities that afflict us all. Foremost among these are the levels of social and economic inequality that continue to exert a dominant influence upon education in spite of all the important work, for example, of the school improvement movement. Deepening national and global inequalities are coming to be seen as a threat to social and economic stability (Piketty 2014). For decades now, long traditions of scholarship and practice have identified overlapping and debilitating forms of inequality based on social differences including class, race, disability, sexuality and gender that have proved to be so entrenched. Responding to these challenges in a policy environment which only partly recognizes their significance, will certainly pose additional problems.

But such obstacles provide the reasons why co-operation remains so important. Democratic and co-operative organizations, that articulate the voices of learners and educators, present us with the potential to reshape education and learning for all. It is hoped this book makes a contribution to understanding these trends and shaping a new agenda.

References

Co-operative Party (2013) Co-operative schools bill brief, March. http://party.coop/files/2013/04/Co_operative_School_Bill_Brief.pdf?1030c5 (accessed 29 March 2013).

Hansard (2013) Co-operatives in education. Adjournment debate, Westminster Hall, col 109WH-132WH, 23 October. http://www.publications.parliament.uk/pa/cm201314/cmhansrd/cm131023/halltext/131023h0001.htm (accessed 30 October 2013).

Piketty, T (2014) *Capital in the Twenty First Century*, Cambridge: Belknap.

APPENDIX

Statement of Cooperative Identity

In 1995, the Statement on the Co-operative Identity was adopted by the General Assembly of the International Co-operative Alliance held in Manchester.

Definition

A co-operative is an autonomous association of persons united voluntarily to meet their common economic, social and cultural needs and aspirations through a jointly owned and democratically controlled enterprise.

Values

Co-operatives are based on the values of self-help, self-responsibility, democracy, equality, equity and solidarity. In the tradition of their founders, co-operative members believe in the ethical values of honesty, openness, social responsibility and caring for others.

Principles

The co-operative principles are guidelines by which co-operatives put their values into practice.

1. *Voluntary and open membership*

Co-operatives are voluntary organizations, open to all persons able to use their services and willing to accept the responsibilities of membership, without gender, social, racial, political or religious discrimination.

2. Democratic member control

Co-operatives are democratic organizations controlled by their members, who actively participate in setting their policies and making decisions. Men and women serving as elected representatives are accountable to the membership. In primary co-operatives, members have equal voting rights (one member, one vote), and co-operatives at other levels are also organized in a democratic manner.

3. Member economic participation

Members contribute equitably to, and democratically control, the capital of their co-operative. At least part of that capital is usually the common property of the co-operative. Members usually receive limited compensation, if any, on capital subscribed as a condition of membership. Members allocate surpluses for any or all of the following purposes: developing their co-operative, possibly by setting up reserves, part of which at least would be indivisible; benefiting members in proportion to their transactions with the co-operative; and supporting other activities approved by the membership.

4. Autonomy and independence

Co-operatives are autonomous, self-help organizations controlled by their members. If they enter into agreements with other organizations, including governments, or raise capital from external sources, they do so on terms that ensure democratic control by their members and maintain their co-operative identity.

5. Education, training and information

Co-operatives provide education and training for their members, elected representatives, managers and employees so that they can contribute effectively to the development of their co-operatives. They inform the general public – particularly young people and opinion leaders – about the nature and benefits of co-operation.

6. Co-operation among co-operatives

Co-operatives serve their members most effectively and strengthen the co-operative movement by working together through local, national, regional and international structures.

7. Concern for community

Co-operatives work for the sustainable development of their communities through policies approved by their members.

Index

Abingdon 38
academic freedom 132
academy schools 1, 5, 10, 11fn1, 34, 35, 36, 37, 75, 113, 121, 174
accountability 3, 22, 31, 38, 40, 45, 47, 78, 113, 115, 196
action research 29, 64, 80, 140, 192
Adonis, A. 125
adult education 7, 60. 133, 167, 179
Africa 3, 177, 181, 182, 185, 186, 187
age groups, mixed 28, 66
agrarian movements 181, 183, 185, 187
agriculture 7, 177, 179, 184, 186, 187, 190
Ainscow, M. 125
A Level 37, 38
alternatives 42–7
alumni 5, 117
anarchism 190
Andalusia 2
Anderson, R. 132
andragogy 154
Anti-Academies Alliance 4
apathy 89, 94, 117
Apple, M. 62
Apollinaire 106
apprenticeships 34, 37, 38, 99, 154
Arab Spring 59
Arendt, H. 88
Argentina 185
Arizmendiarrieta, J.M. 133
Arnold, P. 61, 116
Arrighi, G. 58
arts 93, 117, 141, 199

ASDAN 10, 99–110, 199
Ashman, R.F. 3
Asia 3, 177, 181, 188
assessment 32, 36, 66, 69, 101, 109
assessment for learning 109
assimilation 46–7, 49, 51
association 7, 59, 180, 187–8
Association of British Credit Unions (ABCUL) 169
attainment 101
attainment gap 101–2
Attfield, J. 140
Audsley, J. 113
Australia 3, 178
Austria 183
autonomy 2, 4, 9, 43, 69, 76, 77, 79, 93, 104, 122, 132, 134, 196
Axelrod, R.M. 2

Bailey, M. 132
Baines, S. 69
Baiocchi, G. 64
Bajo, C.S. 2, 133, 174
Baker, S. 115
Baker, S., MP 202
Bakunin, M. 183
Balibar, E. 57, 59, 63
Ball, S.J. 4, 51, 62, 63, 120
Balls, E. 33
banking 7, 156, 182
banking crisis *see* financial crisis
Barber, M. 139, 143
Barnett, R. 132

Barnsby, G. 163
base groups 79, 80
Basis for Choice, a 33
Basque Country 2, 150
Battle, M. 110
Beattie, N. 3
Becher, T. 140
behavioural economics 156
Belgium 187
Benefiel, M. 51
Benjamin, W. 141
Benn, M. 4
Benn, T. 105
Berg, L. 23
Berlin 23
Berliner, D. 36
Bernstein, B. 99
Bibby, A. 169
Bieger, T. 157
Biesta, G. 88, 89, 93
Birchall, J. 142, 161, 162, 168, 180, 184
Birley, Sir R. 23
Birmingham 196, 198, 199
Bishcoff, Sir W. 38–9
black and minority ethnic groups 102
Blackmore, P. 148
Blair, T. 58, 62
Blase, J. 77, 82, 85
Blatchford, R. 19
Blitz, the 29
Bloom, A. 9, 22, 23–9
Bloom, B.S. 99
Boden, R. 114, 135, 137, 138, 143
Bolden, R. 44
Bonner, A. 179
Borger, J. 59
Borzaga, C. 182
branding 67–8
Brazil 3, 185
Brecht, B. 132
Breeze, M. 114
Bridgeland 29
Briggs, A. 132, 141
Brighouse, T. 11
Brighton 141
Brighton Polytechnic 137
Brigshaw Co-operative Trust 95, 122
Briscoe, R. 2
Bristol 33, 117
Britain 4, 134, 137, 138, 141
British Aerospace 134
British Empire/Commonwealth 183
British Humanist Association 27
Brockington, D. 10, 99, 109, 199

Brown, G. 58, 135, 202
Brown, R. 148
Budmouth College 38
Buenos Aires 187
Bulgaria 183
Burgess, K. 59
business 2, 3, 4, 5, 6, 7, 8, 31, 33, 34, 35–6, 38, 43, 49, 57, 122, 143, 148, 149, 177
business and enterprise (subject) 5, 94, 156
business and enterprise colleges 5
business schools 156, 164
business studies 154

Cable Street 23
Cambridge 170
Cameron, D. 58
Cameron, D.H. 49
Campbell's Law 35–6
Canada 2, 3, 10, 48, 178, 188
Canovan, M. 88
capabilities 120
capitalism 10, 18, 20, 44, 57, 58, 63, 133, 156, 177, 189, 190
Cardiff Centre for Co-operative Studies 157
Careers Academy UK 39
Carr-Saunders, A.M. 179
Caseplace 152
catacombs 178
Catalonia 2
celebrity culture 20
Central America 184, 185
centralization 4, 34, 35, 43, 45, 104, 113
Centre for Co-operative and Community Based Economy 3
Centre for Co-operative Studies 157–8
Centre for Engineering and Manufacturing Excellence (CEME) 34
Centre for Excellence in Industry Links (CEIL) 38
Centre for Social History 140
Centre for the Study of Co-operatives 3
Certificate of Higher Education 136
Certificate of Personal Effectiveness (CoPE) 102, 108
Certificate of Pre-Vocational Education 33
Certificate of Secondary Education (CSE) 196, 197
character 7, 60
charitable trust 92, 114, 147
charity 52, 99, 142, 187
charter schools 36
Chartered Institute of Housing (CIH) 170
cheating 20, 21, 22

Index

Chesbrough, H. 49
Chief Registrar of Friendly Societies 143
childcare 1, 166, 187
child-centred education 58
childhood 62, 179
children 7, 23, 24, 26, 28
children's books 24
children's centres 95
China 58, 185, 186, 191
Chitty, C. 4, 113
choice 1, 4, 10, 31, 35, 46, 113, 196, 202
choirs 7
Chomsky, N. 91, 92, 97
churches 32
Church of England 99
church schools 115
Chushichi, T. 179
Ciancelli, P. 143
citizenship 7, 69, 88, 91, 96, 97, 113, 117
City and Guilds 33
civil society 8, 88, 93, 114, 119
Claeys, G. 179
Clark, B.R. 140, 141
Clark, J.B. 18
Clark, K. 62
Clause 4 (Labour Party) 8
Clegg, N. 58
clusters 2
Coalition Government (2010–) 4, 38, 86, 100, 109, 113, 122, 124
co-construction 78, 80, 81, 82, 83, 85, 105
Code of Best Practice for Consumer Societies in Membership of Co-operatives UK 167
Cohen, G.A. 22
Cole, G.D.H. 139, 179
collegiality 74–86
Collini, S. 132
Colombia 185
colonies 184
Committee of Inquiry into the Organisation of the University of Sussex 140
common ownership 8
commons, the 8, 114, 135, 159
communism 191
communitarian 57
community 1, 2, 5, 6, 8, 18, 23, 27, 31, 32, 36, 40, 44, 45, 50, 59, 60, 67, 68, 69, 70, 83, 84, 87, 90, 91, 92, 95, 105, 112, 115, 116, 120, 125, 154, 173, 178, 181, 187, 188, 192, 199, 201
community activism 93
community education 8, 113, 118

competition 11, 17, 18–29, 31, 35, 40, 42, 43, 44, 57, 61, 63, 66, 68, 75, 77, 92, 97, 105, 159, 195–200
competitiveness 113, 141, 202
complexity theory 44
comprehensive schools/education 8, 19, 37, 38
Compte, A. 180
Concept of Mind 107–8
Confederation of Co-operative Housing (CCH) 169
conflict 19
Connor, B.T. 64
Conservative Party 58, 196, 202
consumer co-operatives 7, 114, 117, 125fn1, 139, 141, 143, 162, 164, 165, 169, 182, 183, 186, 187, 190 *see also* co-operative movement
consumerism 179, 186
continuing professional development 10, 35, 39, 74, 75, 105, 148, 198
co-operative and mutual enterprises 2; history of 2, 6–9, 124, 132, 133, 140, 142
Co-operative Bank 179
Co-operative College (UK) 5, 44, 45, 49, 50, 61, 65, 99, 114, 120, 121, 132, 133, 138, 140, 141, 161, 163, 164, 165, 16, 167, 168, 172, 174, 179; Stanford Hall 164
co-operative colleges 3, 188
Co-operative Commission (2001) 164–5, 166, 172
co-operative commonwealth 164
Co-operative Company Secretaries 171
co-operative council 150
co-operative development agencies (CDAs) 170
co-operative development bodies (CDBs)
Co-operative Development Scotland 148, 152, 170
Co-operative Education Trust Scotland (CETS) 10, 147–9, 150, 151, 152, 153, 154, 159
Co-operative Entrepreneurship 152–3
Co-operative Enterprise Hub 170
Co-operative Foundation 147–8
Co-operative Free University 143
Co-operative Futures 171
Co-operative Group 5, 7, 8, 44, 61, 121, 122, 124, 138, 148, 154, 166, 167, 168, 170, 174
Co-operative Heritage Trust 132
Co-operative Identity Mark (CIM) 6, 65–6
Co-operative Insurance Society 179

co-operative learning 3, 6, 10, 27, 33, 79, 82, 93, 94, 99, 101, 102, 104
Co-operative Learning Space 158
Co-operative Men's Guild 163
Co-operative Model in Practice: International Perspectives 152
co-operative movement 3, 5, 6–9, 17, 18, 19, 20, 28, 60–1, 114, 147, 161, 177–93
Co-operative News 183
Co-operative Party 6, 88, 150, 202
co-operative schools 1, 5, 7, 10, 18, 20, 22, 31, 35, 40, 44, 45, 49, 51, 60, 61, 64–70, 74–86, 87–98, 99, 104, 112–125, 138, 165, 173–4, 201
Co-operatives Fortnight 171
Co-operatives Research Unit 3, 173
co-operative studies 10–11, 99–100, 158, 177–93
Co-operatives UK 6, 153, 164, 165, 166, 167, 171
Co-operative Teach-In 159
co-operative trust schools 1, 10, 45, 61, 67, 68, 87, 99, 121, 173
Co-operative Union 140, 142, 162, 163, 166, 171, 179
Co-operative Union Central Education Committee 162, 171
co-operative university 10, 131–48
co-operative values and principles 1, 5, 6, 10, 40, 44, 45, 49, 50, 61, 69, 75, 76, 77, 82, 87, 89, 95, 100, 109–10, 112–25, 150, 159, 161, 164, 166, 170, 174, 195, 202, 204–5
Co-operative Wholesale Society 138
Co-operative Women's Guild 7, 163, 169
Co-op Pundit 158
Corelli College 119
Cornwall 35, 68, 122
corporal punishment 23, 28 *see* punishment
Cotham Co-operative Academy 117–18
Council for National Academic Awards (CNAA) 134, 136
Court, M, 45
Craig, J.G. 184
Crane, W. 19, 20
creative arts 93
Creative Commons License 159
creativity 17, 159
credit unions 2, 133, 164
Crehan, E. 74, 78, 84
Cronin, K. 119
Cronin, R. 84
Cuban, L. 9, 36
Culloty, A.T. 133

cultural capital 49
culture 6, 7, 9, 20, 26, 27, 28, 42, 46, 49, 51, 57, 59, 65, 68, 77, 78, 79, 81, 84, 86, 114, 137, 143, 162, 180, 182, 183, 184; counter culture 26, 28
curriculum 1, 4, 5, 6, 10, 28, 32, 34, 35, 36, 39, 40, 58, 84, 95, 99, 101, 104, 105, 115, 119, 141, 147–59, 174, 177, 197
Curriculum Commission 149
Curriculum for Excellence 150
customer service 166

Dagenham 34
Daily Mirror 23
Dale, J. A. 133
Dale, R. 33
dance 93, 117
Davidge, G. 10, 125, 195
Davies, M.L. 186
Davis (USA) 2
Davis, G. 148
Day, C. 49
Dearden, R. 19
Deem, R. 140
Defourney, J. 182
Delgado, A. 3
democracy 1, 2, 3, 5, 6, 9, 10, 18, 20, 23, 26, 28, 29, 31, 32, 42, 44, 48, 49, 50, 51, 58, 59, 63, 66, 68, 69, 74, 75, 77, 80, 81, 82, 83, 84, 87–98, 112, 115, 122, 124, 133, 143, 145, 168, 201, 202, 203; deliberative democracy 119; democratic association 59; democratic deficit 117
Democratic Enterprise: Ethical Business for the 21st Century 152
demutualization 8, 137, 138
Denmark 178
Department for Children, Schools and Families (DCSF) 33
Department for Education (DfE) 5, 102, 109, 113, 123, 124, 174
Department of Education and Science (DES) 33
Department of Trade and Industry (DTI) 33
Desjardins Credit Unions 2
Develtere, P. 184
Devon 35, 122
Dewey, J. 50, 58, 102–3
Dip HE 136
Diplomas, 14–19, 33, 38, 136
disability 38
disciplines 19, 115, 141, 149, 157, 172, 173, 177
discourse 51, 68, 150, 157

distance learning 173
Donnelly, H. 148
drama 7, 93, 162
Draperi, J.-F. 180
Dulas 154
Durkheim, E. 133
Dweck, C. 76, 99

Eaglesham, E. 132
Earle, J. 182
early years education 1, 6
East End 23
East London Advertiser 27
Economic and Social Research Council (ESRC) 148, 158
Economic Strategy (Scotland) 150
economy 4, 17, 43, 48, 49, 57, 59, 60, 61, 62, 63, 70, 88, 89, 90, 94, 100, 150, 158–9, 177, 178, 179, 180, 181, 182, 184, 185
Edinburgh Bicycle Co-operative 154
Edinburgh City Council 150
Edison Learning 36
edu-business 31, 37
Education Act (1902) 7, 32, 132, 163
Education Act (1944) 31, 32, 195
Education and Employers Taskforce 102
Education and Inspections Act (2006) 5, 92, 173
Education Committee on School Partnerships and Education 6, 45
education markets 4, 35, 124
education policy 1, 4–5, 8–9, 38, 40, 42–4, 45, 46, 51, 100, 113, 124, 141, 149–51, 196, 202
Education Reform Act (1988) 4
égaliberté 59, 63
Egypt 59
e-learning 151, 169
elections 32, 94
Elementary Education Act (1870) 7, 31
elementary schools 32
Elites/elitism 57, 62, 64, 70, 97
Elliot, L. 59
empire 184
employee ownership 147, 148, 149, 152, 158, 159, 170
employers 31, 33, 34, 37, 38–9, 40, 101
employment 101
emulation 9, 18–22, 29, 74, 77, 79
engineering 33–4, 38
England 3, 4, 17, 18, 21, 28, 31, 36, 43, 45, 48, 49, 75, 88, 97, 100, 107, 108, 141, 166, 169, 198, 199
English (subject) 5, 94, 102, 198
Enlightenment 178

enrichment days 115
enterprise 2, 3, 5, 7, 10, 17, 45, 100, 108, 132, 134, 137, 140, 141, 142, 147, 148, 149, 150, 151, 156, 157, 159
entrepreneurialism/entrepreneurship 17, 42, 44, 49, 152, 154, 159, 177, 179, 188
equality 10, 20, 22, 58, 59, 65, 66, 92, 100, 112, 115, 116, 118, 196, 202
Equality Trust 100
equity 2, 44, 63, 77, 100, 112, 124, 196
Erbmann, R. 3
ethics 103, 104, 115, 156, 180
ethos 6, 9, 26, 40, 75, 93, 115
Eton school 23
Eun, B. 76, 78
Europe 3, 57, 58, 156, 172, 178, 180, 182, 183; East Europe 183, 185, 186, 188, 191
European Research Institute on Co-operative and Social Enterprise (EURISCE) 3
Eustace, R. 132
Evening News 23
evolution 18
Eymeri-Douzans, J.M. 43
examinations 24, 84; 11-plus 106, 118, 196, 199
experience 23, 26, 101, 199
extended services 123

Facer, K. 5, 10, 63, 66, 114, 162, 164, 195
failure 106–7
fairness 51
Fairtrade 3, 93, 100, 115, 118, 168, 185, 187
Fairtrade Towns 172
faith organizations 52
faith schools 75
family breakdown 39
Family of Schools dataset 198
Fay, C.R. 179
Federation of Worker Writers and Community Publishers 133
fellowship 9, 20, 22, 64
feminism 183, 186
Ferguson, J. 154
Fieldhouse, R. 163
Fielding, M. 4, 5, 8, 9, 19, 28, 29, 58, 63, 87, 88, 112, 114, 195
financial co-operatives 188
financial crisis/crash 58, 96, 100, 149
Finland 3, 86, 183
firm theory 182
First Minister (Scotland) 150
First Nations 48
Fisher, M. 69
Flickr 153

Flinders, M. 42
football supporters' trusts 88, 164
Ford 34
Ford, B. 131
Fordism 104
foundation degrees 34
Foundation for Co-operative Education 158
Foundation for Enterprise Development 158
foundation hospitals 9
Fourier, C. 180
France 3, 180, 187, 188, 191
Franji, D. 62
Fraser, N. 57
freedom 10, 20, 22, 57, 59, 199
freedom with equality 57, 64, 66, 68, 69, 70
free schools 1, 5, 11fn1, 34, 38, 75, 113
Freinet, C.
Freire, P. 58
Freunlich, F. 150
Friedman, M. 57
Frost, D. 49
Fukuyama, F. 57, 190
funeral services 179
Further and Higher Education Act (1992) 142
further education 1, 6, 9, 10, 32, 33, 34, 37, 38, 40, 99, 101
Further Education Funding Council (FEFC) 136
Further Education Unit 33

Gaffin, J. 186
gagging orders 36
Gago, M. 150
Gaia University 139
Gamble, A. 114
game theory 182
gaming 35, 109, 113
Gandhi, M. 184
Gardner, H. 108
Gatsby Foundation 198
General Certificate of Education (GCE) 196, 197
General Certificate of Secondary Education (GCSE) 37, 94, 102, 109, 197, 198
general election 61
Geography for the Young School Leaver 32
Germanic tribes 178
Germany 3, 23, 180
Gibton, D. 51
Gide, C. 180, 188
Gillies, R.M. 3
Glatter, R. 5, 37, 113

Godwin, W. 57
Gold, A. 117
Goldman, L. 133
Goodson, I. 57, 63
Google 139
Gove, M. 4, 62, 101
governance 5, 6, 31, 36, 43, 61, 64, 92, 94, 95, 101, 103, 104, 113, 114, 116, 117, 121, 154, 156, 166–73, 190
grammar schools 29fn1, 75
Gramsci, A. 181
Gratton, L. 49
Greece 59, 180, 187
Greenwich 170
Grimmett, P. 74, 78, 84
growth mindset 76, 77, 81, 99
Grundtvig, N.F.S. 139
Guardian 139
Guarneri, C.J. 180
Guilford, J.P. 108
Gunter, H. 116
Gurney, P. 6, 162
Gvirtz, S. 48

Habermas, J. 89
Hackney 170
Haig-Brown, C. 48
Hamel, G. 140
Hargreaves, A. 76, 77, 78, 82, 85, 103
Hargreaves, D. 121
Harrison, D. 102
Harrison, J.F.C. 139
Harrow 38
Harvey, D. 57
Hatcher, R. 123
Hayek, F.A. 57
health and safety 166
health co-operatives 164, 185, 187
health service 9
Healthy Schools 65
Heart of England Training and Enterprise Council 141
Hedberg, A. 182
Heddesdorf Loan Society 180
Hemming, J. 27
hidden curriculum 102–4
hierarchy 5, 51, 61, 62, 63, 65, 66, 81–2, 85, 95, 116
Higgins, S. 101–2
Highbury 32
higher education 1, 2, 4, 6, 9, 10, 40, 101, 131–43, 147–59, 161, 172, 174, 196, 197
Higher Education Funding Council 139
higher grade education 132
high stakes testing 35

Hill, R. 3, 156
historical perspectives 6–9, 18–19, 23–9, 31–5, 44, 60, 112, 138–42, 162–5, 178–93
history (subject) 5, 32
History 13–16, 32
HIV/AIDS 186
Hodson, J. 48
Holden, G. 49
Holmwood, J. 132, 143
Holyoake, G.J. 44, 179
housing co-operatives 164, 169–70, 178, 181, 182, 183, 187
Howerth, I.W. 18
human capital 62
Humanities Curriculum Project 32
human resources 166
Human Utopia 93
Humboldt, A. von 132
Hume, D. 103
Huntington, S.P. 58
Hyde, M. 59

ICT (subject) 5
identity 83, 115, 122
Ilmonen, K. 183
Inclusion Quality Mark 65
India 58, 178
Indignados 59
Individual/individualism 3, 7, 25–7, 42, 43, 45, 49, 68, 69, 77, 85, 181, 199
industrial and provident society legislation 6
industrial history (classes) 7
industrialization 60, 104, 180, 181, 183,
inequality 5, 20, 43, 58, 100, 113, 124, 186–7, 202
Information, Advice and Guidance (IAG) 37, 40
innovation 2, 8, 17, 32, 40, 44, 49, 51, 125, 188
inspection 4, 37, 43, 58, 65, 84
INSTEAD 105
Institute of Co-operative Directors 171
Institute of Education, London 67, 114, 119
insurance 7, 143, 179, 182, 186
intellectual property 36, 37, 39
intelligence 107–10
International Association for the Study of Co-operation in Education (IASCE) 3
International Co-operative Alliance (ICA) 75, 76, 100, 132, 138, 142, 177–8, 183, 188, 192
International Co-operative Research Committee 192

International Co-operative Women's Guild 186
International Co-operator's Day 7
International Labour Organisation 183
International Year of Co-operatives 2, 152, 154
internships 39
Investors in People Award 65
Ireland 59
Islamic schools 48
Israel 3
Italy 3, 124, 180, 181–2, 187, 191

Jackson, M. 110
Jaffe, T. 119
James, D. 102
Joas, H. 50
John Lewis Partnership 154, 158
Johnson, D. 151
Johnson, D.W. 80
Johnson, R.T. 80
Joliffe, W. 3
Jolly, W. 19
Jones, S. 10, 115, 121, 195
Journal of Co-operative Studies 174
Julian, C. 2

Kagan, S. 3, 80
Kaletsky, A. 58
Kalmi, P. 3, 156, 164
Kandiko, C.D. 148
Kant, I. 103
Keele University 197
Khan Academy 139
Khurana, R. 157
Kibbutz movement 185
Kingswood Partnership 33, 38
Klein, M. 57, 58
Kleinig, J. 19
Knowledge 3, 7, 10, 24, 37, 40, 43, 62, 64, 78, 79, 82, 86, 88, 89, 101, 105, 107, 108, 125, 131–4, 135, 141, 147, 151, 152, 154, 155, 156, 158, 159, 163, 166, 167, 170, 171, 172, 192, 198
knowledge economy 62, 133
Knowledge transfer 10, 147–59
Kohlberg, L. 102
Kolb, D.A. 107
Kropotkin, P. 2, 18, 57, 183

Labour Government 33, 34, 38, 101
labour movement 8, 122
Labour MP 96, 202

Labour Party 4, 8, 90, 113
Laclau, E. 59
Laidlaw, A. 178
Laird, A. 5
laissez-faire 44, 190
Lampl, P. 101
Lancashire 137
Lao Tse 104
Latin America 58, 177, 184–5, 191
Laurence, P. 122
Layward, G. 28
Leaders/leadership 43–4, 50, 66, 74, 77, 78, 79, 81–2, 84, 85, 91, 92, 95, 96, 105, 116; distributed leadership 43, 50, 51, 116, 119, 195, 197
league tables 26, 34, 35, 37, 58, 105, 112, 115, 134, 197, 198
learners 1, 33, 34, 36, 37, 39, 103, 104, 141, 149
learning community 48
learning organization 133
Learning School Improvement Group (LSIG) 79
learning styles 105, 106–10, 198
learning to learn 101, 102, 105, 108
Leeds 5, 95, 121, 122
legislation 51, 115
Lenin, V. 191
Leo XII 181
Lewis, S.C. 58
Liberal Democrats 58, 89
liberal education 33
liberal market democracy 57
liberty 97
libraries 7, 60, 162
Lincoln 143
Lipson Co-operative Academy 10, 74–86
listening 102–4
Lloyd, M. 84
Lloyds Banking Group 38, 141
local authorities 34, 35, 39, 40, 42, 67, 75, 91, 121–2, 124
Local education and training boards 40
local education authorities 4, 32, 39, 40, 113, 163, 198
local management of schools 33
Logue, C. 106
London 9, 23, 27, 29, 196, 197, 198, 199
London Challenge 198
London County Council (LCC) 27
London Head Teachers' Association Bulletin 29
London Thames Gateway Regeneration Scheme 34
Long Term Residential Colleges for Adult Education 137

Lovett, W. 133, 139
Lowe, R. 113
Luzzati, L. 181

MA (Master of Arts) 80, 87
MBA 154
McCormick, J.P. 64
McCrum 59
McDonalds 141
McDonnell, D. 10, 199
Macedo, D. 91, 92, 97
McGovern, P. 122
Machado, A. 109
Machiavelli, N. 64
Machiavellian 70
McIlroy, J. 164
MacIntyre, A. 132
McKinsey 140
Macknight, E. 10, 199
MacPherson, I. 2, 10–11, 125, 162, 183, 186, 199
magistrates 7
mainstreaming 9, 49, 51
Making Connections 172
management 7, 8, 32, 33, 34, 35–6, 39, 40, 65, 66, 80, 86, 91, 95, 96, 101, 105, 135, 140, 156, 166, 170, 187, 188
managerialism 42, 43, 65
Manchester 5, 9, 49, 89, 121
Manpower Services Commission 33
Mansbridge, A. 139, 140
Mansell, W. 36
Māori 45–7
marketization 58, 62, 86, 94, 113
markets 4, 17, 22, 31, 36, 42, 43, 44, 57, 63, 65, 68, 69, 75, 88, 104, 133, 142, 150, 156, 186, 187, 191, 195, 202 *see also* education markets
Marx, K. 183
Marxism 4, 57, 182, 183, 190, 191
massive open online course (MOOC) 135, 139
mass schooling 58
mathematics 38, 94, 100, 102, 198
Matthews, D. 3
Matthews, N. 156
Mauss, M. 133
May Day 19
Mayfield, C. 158
Melmoth, G. 138
member education 266–73
membership 7, 10, 35, 44, 66, 67, 68, 75, 77, 79, 82, 84, 95, 104, 117–21, 124, 138, 141, 142, 154, 165; voluntary membership 119–20, 132, 133, 166, 177–8, 182–3, 189

Mercer, T.W. 179
Mercier, L. 133
Merry, F. 133
Mexico 3
Miettinen, R. 51
migration 185
Mill, J.S. 103, 183
Miller, M. 59
Minvielle, L. 48
modern languages 37
Mode 3 CSE 105
Molina, F. 143
Mondragón 2, 143, 150, 174
Moodie, G.C. 132
More Knowledgeable Other 79, 81
Morris, W. 19
Moss, P. 5, 28, 29, 58, 63, 87
Mouffe, C. 69, 89, 97
Muenkner, H. 181
Mulani, J.M. 182
municipal government 8, 181
Munn, M., MP 6, 202
Murray, C. 62
Murray, R. 139, 164, 174
music 93, 118, 154, 162
Muslim communities 187
mutual/mutuality 2, 7, 8, 17, 18, 47, 48, 50, 51, 59, 60, 61, 63, 64, 66, 77, 79, 83, 92, 95, 96, 108, 110, 116, 121, 124, 131–42, 147, 148, 149, 151, 159, 171, 179, 180, 201 *see also* demutualization
mutual aid 18
Mutuals Information Service 171
Myners Review 167

Nairobi 187
Nash, R. 23
NASUWT 52
National Archives 58
National Association of Head Teachers 27, 105
National College for School Leadership 198
National Co-operative Archive 172
National Council for Vocational Qualifications (NCVQ) 108
national curriculum 4, 32, 33
National Curriculum Review 109
National Health Service 58
nationalisation 8, 113
National Lottery 159
National Student Fellowship 163
National Union of Students (NUS) 135
National Youth Agency 39

Nazism 183
Neary, M. 139
NEET (not in education, employment or training) 39
Negri, A. 59
Nehru, J. 184
Neil, J. 141
Neill, A.S. 27
Nelson College 136
Nemerowicz, G. 116
neoliberalism 4–6, 9, 17, 29, 51, 57, 59, 62, 63, 64, 66, 68, 69, 70, 77, 89, 94, 156
Netherlands 3
networks 2, 3, 6, 10, 35, 40, 44, 49, 63, 94, 95, 97, 99, 113, 121–4, 134–8, 174, 201
New Business Agenda 141
New Era 23, 26
New Labour 4, 58
New Lanark 60
Newman, J.H. 132
New Map of Learning 132, 141
new public governance 43
new public service 43
News Chronicle 23
Newsom, J. 109
Newsom Report (Half Our Future) 109
Nichols, S. 36
Nîmes 180
NISAI Learning 38
Nkrumah, K. 184
No Child Left Behind 36
Noddings, N. 22
Norden/Nordic 180, 182
North America 3, 4, 103, 177, 180, 187, 188
North East Music Co-operative 135
Northern College 140
North Korea 191
Norton, A. 57
Norway 182
Not-for-profit 147, 156
Nuffield Review of 14–19: Education and Training 100
nursery schools 6
Nyerere, J. 184

Oates, T. 108
Obama, B. 59
Observer, the 8
Ocampo, J.A. 182
Occupy Movement 59
OECD (Organisation for Economic Co-operation and Development) 112, 166
Ofsted 4, 37, 65, 75, 78, 80, 89, 93, 105, 120, 197, 199

O'Hair, M.J. 48
online learning 38
Open College Network 136, 140
Open University Validation Service (OUVS) 136
Osborne, S.P. 43
Ostrom, E 8
Outhwaite, W. 89
Owen, R. 6, 60, 179
Owenites 6, 179
Ownership 4, 8, 44, 58, 59, 88, 92, 93, 96, 117, 118, 119, 132, 135, 137–8, 150, 151, 155, 171, 201 *see* employee ownership
Oxford 38, 141, 163
Oxford Magazine 139
Oxford Polytechnic (now Oxford Brookes University) 197
Oxfordshire 35, 37, 196, 197, 199
Oxford University Department of Education 197

Pageants 7
Panzer, G. 23
parents 4, 5, 11fn1, 67, 70, 87, 90, 92, 103, 112, 116, 117, 119, 120, 173, 195, 196, 197, 201
Parents National Education Union 132
Parliament 6
Parnell, E. 142, 158
partnership 4, 31–40, 42, 49, 68, 113, 121, 123, 138, 178, 196, 198, 199
Paul Hamlyn Foundation 198
payment by results 36
PDSA (Plan; Do; Study; Act) 80
pedagogy 3, 4, 6, 9, 27, 28, 39, 64, 74, 75, 79, 84, 88, 93, 94–5, 96, 151, 152, 158, 172, 173, 174, 197
Pedley, R. 136
people's universities 136
Perestroika 186
performativity 42–3, 44, 49, 120
performing arts 117
personalization 80
Peru 185
Pestoff, V. A. 182
Peters, T. 189
Philippines 3
philosophy of education 19, 103
physics (subject) 37, 38
Piaget, J. 102
Pickett, K. 100
Pierre, J. 43
Piketty, T. 202

PISA (Programme for International Student Assessment) 101, 112
Plan, Do, Review 107
Planned Programme Budgeting 133
pluralism 89, 97
Plutarch 99
Plymouth 74, 195
Poland 3, 183
policy 1, 4–6, 8, 9, 38, 40, 42–4, 45, 46, 51, 86, 96, 100, 103, 121, 192, 201
political economy 6
Pollard, A. 43
Pollins, H. 133
Poole, E. 51
Poor Man's Guardian 131
Portugal 59, 180, 187
post-14 education 34, 100; Working Group on 14–19; Reform 104–5
post-16 education 38, 99
post-war (second world war) 4, 7, 8, 9, 23, 113, 201
Power, S. 62
presentism 77, 78, 83, 85
Preston Polytechnic 136
primary education 3, 9, 32, 174
primary schools 3
Pring, R. 5, 10, 37, 43, 100, 103, 104, 121, 195
private schools 101
private sector 4, 5, 8, 49, 156, 201
privatisation 4, 5, 35, 37, 42, 58, 89, 92, 94, 113
Privy Council 134
prizes 20, 25, 26, 27–8
profession/professionalism 25, 32, 37, 39, 40, 43, 77, 78, 104, 105, 116, 154
professional and managerial class 133
professional development 74–86, 197
profit making 5, 35–6, 57
progress 18
progressive education 19, 58
Project Delta 169
psychology 105, 106
public education/sector 4, 5, 28, 34, 36, 42, 49, 69, 113, 114, 122, 137, 171, 174, 199, 201
public services 8, 31, 35, 43, 58, 89, 100, 156
punishment 28 *see* corporal punishment
pupils 5, 8, 10, 34, 69, 70, 87, 112, 115, 117 *see also* students *and* learners

Qualifications 10, 33, 37, 38, 80, 101, 102, 103, 106, 108–9, 136–7, 154, 156, 157, 196, 197, 198

Quality Assurance Agency for Higher Education (QAA) 155–6
Québec 188

racism 184
Raffeisen, W.H. 180
raising of the school leaving age 32, 99, 112
Rancière, J. 64, 70
Rawlings, B. 166
Raymond, E. 24
Raynor, M. 69
Read, M. 149, 159
reading rooms 7, 162
reciprocity 182
Reddish ROC (Redeeming Our Communities) 96
Reddish Vale 87–98, 195
Ree, J. 133
Reese, S.D. 58
Reggio Emilia 64
Regional Co-operative Councils 171
regional structures 121–4
religion 32, 50
religious schools 116
Rerum Novarum 181
research assessment exercise (RAE) 132
research centres 3
residential education 27, 29fn1, 199
Restakis, J. 2
results 10, 22, 36, 43, 94, 115, 196, 199
revolution 59
Rhodes, R. 184
Ridley-Duff, R. 154
Roach, P. 113
Roberts, A. 43, 49
Roberts, D. 59
Roberts, L. 59
Robertson, N. 162, 163
Robinson, E. 131, 136
Rochdale 9
Rochdale Pioneers 6, 161, 162
Rochdale tradition 184
Roelants, B. 2, 133, 174
Rogers, C. 104
Rogers, S. 120
Rollwagen, K. 186
Roman Catholic faith schools 99
Roman Catholic Church 181, 188
Rome 178
Rose, J. 7
Rose, N. 62
Rosi, E. 116
Rousseau, J.J. 29
RSA 108
RSA Manifesto 108

rural areas 122, 180, 182, 183, 185, 191
rural co-operatives 164, 180
Ruskin, J. 19
Ruskin College 132, 133, 136, 137, 140, 141, 142, 163
Russell Group 33, 134
Russia 183
Ryle, G. 107–8

St George in-the-East (school) 9, 23–9
Saint-Simon, H. 180
Sandell, M.J. 57
Saskatchewan, University of 3
SAT (standard assessment test) 197, 198
Savona 181
Scandinavia 156
Scargill, V. 119
Schediwy, R. 182, 183
Schmitt, C. 57
school boards 7, 9, 31, 40
school chains 4, 5, 31, 36, 37
school collaboration 10
school council 27, 28, 90
school forum 5, 91, 93, 95, 104, 117, 119–20
school improvement 66, 74–86, 118, 123, 198, 202
school leavers 33
Schools Co-operative Society (SCS) 6, 44, 52, 100, 114, 121, 122, 123, 137
Schools Council 32
Schostak, J.F. 10, 57, 58, 59, 62, 63, 70, 195
Schostak, J.R. 59, 63, 70
Schulze-Delitzsch, H. 180
science (subject) 38
Scotland 60, 147–59, 169, 170
Scotmid 148
Scott, G. 187
Scottish Agricultural Organisation Society 170
Scottish Co-operative Party 150
Scottish Government 148, 149
Scottish Parliament 154
Scottish Programme for Entrepreneurship 154
Screpanti, E. 182
secondary education 9, 32, 37, 57–70, 74–86, 174
secondary school 34, 37, 38, 99, 196, 198
secondary modern school 23, 25, 29fn1
Secretary of State for Education 4, 31, 62, 101
self-evaluation 78

Index

self-help 2, 44, 74, 77, 84, 92, 93, 112, 123, 180
self-responsibility 2, 5, 44, 77, 81, 84, 112, 123, 180
Sen, A. 120
Sennett, R. 2
Shakespeare, W. 109
Shattock, M. 132, 140
Shaw, L. 3, 10, 63, 66, 161, 163, 166, 179, 195
Sheffield 202
Simkins, T. 43, 49
Simmons, R. 168
Simon, B. 32, 61
Simpson, A. 10, 116, 195
Singapore 187
sixth-form 37, 38
Skidelsky, R. 59
skills 3, 20, 21, 25, 33, 34, 99, 105, 108, 149–50, 158, 166–7, 171, 172
Skills Strategy 149
Skurnik, S. 182
slates 27
Slavin, R. 3, 49, 80
Sloan-Wilson, D. 2007
small and medium sized enterprises 166, 171
Smith, A. 202
social capital 49, 68, 157, 188
social co-operatives 182
social Darwinism 18
Social Democratic Federation 135
Social Democrats 182
social economy 180, 187 social enterprise 74, 93, 156, 158, 191
socialism 19, 57, 60, 181, 190
socialization 25
social justice 43, 49, 50, 58, 67, 70, 97, 103, 106, 199
social mobility 100
social psychology 3
social question 182
social science 143, 179
Social Science Centre 143
Society for Co-operative Studies (UK) 157, 179
Society for Educational Studies 114
sociology 141
solidarity 2, 40, 44, 59, 63, 67, 74, 77, 84, 112, 115, 188
South (Global) 184, 185
South Africa 110
South America 184, 187
South West 68
Soviet Union 57

Spahn, E.K. 180
Spain 2, 59, 124, 180, 187
Spear, R. 182
special educational needs 102, 123
special measures 67
Spencer, H. 18
Spinoza, B. 59
spirituality 50
sport 7, 25, 26–7
Stacey, R. 44, 51
Stakeholders 5, 44, 91, 92, 95, 104, 114, 116, 117, 120, 138, 143, 154, 173, 201
Stalin, J. 187
standards 1, 17, 20, 25, 35, 105, 112, 113, 124, 202
standardization 78
Stanfield, J.B. 5
state 2, 4, 5, 7, 8, 9, 23, 47, 49, 59, 60, 62, 100, 103, 134, 141, 142, 163, 185–6, 189
Statement of Co-operative Identity 2, 8, 100, 115, 117, 131, 138, 204–5
Steele, T. 133
Steiner schools 48
Stenhouse, L. 39
Stepney 23
Stevenage 34
Stevenson, H. 113
stewardship 189
Stewart, W. 101
Stockport 61, 87, 88, 89
Stockport County Supporters' Co-operative 88
Stoke on Trent 5, 121
Stoll, L. 84, 116
Strauss, L. 57
students 26, 28, 38, 40, 45, 47, 92, 95, 119, 135, 142, 173, 178, 201 *see also* learners *and* pupils
Sukharno 184
Summerhill School 27
surveillance 63, 65, 67, 69, 76, 78, 79, 84
sustainability 43
Sutton Trust 101
Sutton Trust Education Endowment Foundation 101
Swain, H. 132
Sweden 178, 182–3, 188
synthetic phonics 86
Syria 59

Tao TeChing 104
targets 35, 36, 39, 43, 65
Tawney, R.H. 7, 140
Taylor, K. 180
Taylor, R. 133

teachers 5, 11fn1, 22, 23, 24, 25, 28, 31, 32, 34, 36, 39, 40, 74–86, 89, 90, 92, 94, 96, 103, 104, 117, 118, 119, 135, 178, 195, 197
teachers' centres 32, 34, 36, 37, 40
Teachers' Standards 84
teaching assistants 66, 80
teamwork 33, 36
technical schools 29fn1
Technical and Vocational Education Initiative (TVEI) 33
technical school 143
technology 65, 66, 93, 97, 139, 179
Technology Strategy Board 147
Tenants First Housing 154
Tenant Services Authority 170
textbooks 148, 152, 157, 164
Thatcher, M. 58
Thew, L.M. 140
third sector 114, 147
Thomas, A. 188
Thompson, E.P. 140
Thoms, D. 186
Thorpe, J. 63, 66
thrift 180
Times, The 23, 27
Times Educational Supplement 24, 26, 27
Todd, N. 7, 163
Tomlinson, M. 104–5
Toolbox for Social Education (ESA) 15964
trade union education
Trade Union International Research and Education Group (TUIREG) 142
Trade Union Research Unit (TURU) 142
trade unions 6, 52, 142, 163, 164, 179, 183
training 7, 10, 33, 34, 40, 99, 154, 159, 161, 165–73, 182
travel agencies 179
Trentino 2
Trento University 3
Trowler, P.R. 140
trust schools 11fn1, 67, 92
TUC 6
Turin 181
tutoring 38
Tutu, D. 110
Twitter 153
Twigg, H.J. 140, 161
Tyack, D. 9

Ubuntu 110
UCAS 108
underclass 62
unemployment 33
university technical college (UTC) 75

Ukraine 183
UK Uncut 59
Unger, R. 29
Unipart 141
Unison 140
Unison Open College 140
United Kingdom (UK) 8, 42, 68, 100, 151, 154, 156, 158, 159, 161, 162, 164, 167, 172, 174, 179, 186, 188, 199
United Nations 2, 152, 154, 178, 183
United States of America (USA) 3, 36, 48, 59, 100, 102, 156, 158, 159, 178
universities 3, 10, 33, 34, 37, 38, 66, 106, 131–43, 147–59, 164, 172, 174, 177, 199; Harvard 148; Glasgow Caledonian 149; Mondragón 143, 150, 151; Open University 3, 135, 136, 158–9, 173; Rutgers 158; Suffolk University campus 134
university extension 7
University for Industry (UfI) 135
University of Aberdeen 147–51, 154
University of Bloomsbury 141
University of Bologna 182
University of Buckingham 141
University of Durham 101
University of East Anglia 135
University of Essex 134
University of Exeter 134
University of Hertford 34
University of Hong Kong 148
University of Leeds 88
University of Lincoln 139, 142
University of Lincoln Students' Union 142
University of London 134
University of Manchester 88
University of Melbourne 148, 151
University of Oxford 134, 137, 138–9, 197
University of Oxford and Cambridge Act (1571) 136
University of Reading 134
University of Southampton 134
University of Stirling 149
University of Strathclyde 149, 154
University of Sussex 132, 137, 140
University of the Air 135
University of the First Age 198
University of Trento 182
University of Warwick 140
University of West of England 101, 102
utopianism 60

values 1, 5, 6, 17, 22, 25, 35, 36, 40, 42, 43, 44, 45, 49, 50, 51, 61, 69, 76, 77, 82, 87, 92, 100, 103, 114, 115, 132, 189

see also co-operative values and principles
Vernon, K. 7, 161, 162
Victoria, University of 3
Vihriälä, V. 183
village college 119
Vimeo 153
virtual learning environment (VLE) 153
vocational education 33, 34, 38, 40, 101, 108, 166; Review of Vocational Education (Wolf Review) 109
voice 28, 59, 69, 70, 76, 90, 96
voluntary bodies 31, 32
voluntary sector 114, 122
Vygotsky, L. 74, 79

Waitere, H. 45
Wales 141, 169, 170
Wales Co-operative Centre 170
Waller, W. 61, 69
Wallerstein, I. 58
Wallsend 7
Wall Street 59
Walton, J.K. 7, 143
Waltzer, M. 57
Ward, M. 2
Watkins, C. 99
Waugh, C. 133
Webb, B. 179
Webb, S. 8, 179
Webster, A. 9
welfare 3, 8, 58, 62, 122–3
Weyersbusch (Westerwald) 180
Weymouth 38
White, R. 99
wholesale business 86, 138, 179, 181, 182, 188
Wilkins, A. 151
Williams, R. 137–8
Williams, R.C. 2
Willis, P. 62
Wilkinson, R. 100

Wills, D. 28
Wilson, H. 135
Wilson, J. 5
Wilson, M. 67, 121, 122, 164
Winter's Tale 109
Wise, G 3
Wolf, A. 109
Wollemborg, L. 181
women 32, 166, 168, 186–7
Woodcraft Folk 7, 163
Woodin, T. 2, 4, 5, 6, 8, 10, 60, 112, 114, 162, 195
Woods, G.J. 44, 45, 47, 48, 51
Woods, P. 10, 42, 43, 45, 47, 48, 50, 51, 116, 195
Woollard and Henry 154
work-based education 4
Worker Co-operative Council 171
worker co-operatives 164, 185, 190
Workers' Educational Association (WEA) 7, 137, 140, 163, 164, 179
working class(es) 7, 179, 181, 187
Working Men's Club and Institute Union (CIU) 142
World Bank 178
World War One 23, 181, 186–7
World War Two 23, 164, 180, 181, 182, 184
Wright, T. 114
Wycombe 202

Yeats, W. B. 99
Yeo, S. 6, 44, 132, 137, 140, 141, 199
Yorkshire 123
Young Co-operatives 3, 61, 118
Young people/youth 88, 89, 90, 94, 95, 96, 116, 119, 177, 185, 186
Youth Parliament 119
Youth Service 31, 39
Youth Space 93

Zemagni, S. 182
zone of proximal development 74, 79

eBooks
from Taylor & Francis
Helping you to choose the right eBooks for your Library

Add to your library's digital collection today with Taylor & Francis eBooks. We have over 45,000 eBooks in the Humanities, Social Sciences, Behavioural Sciences, Built Environment and Law, from leading imprints, including Routledge, Focal Press and Psychology Press.

Choose from a range of subject packages or create your own!

Benefits for you
- Free MARC records
- COUNTER-compliant usage statistics
- Flexible purchase and pricing options
- 70% approx of our eBooks are now DRM-free.

Benefits for your user
- Off-site, anytime access via Athens or referring URL
- Print or copy pages or chapters
- Full content search
- Bookmark, highlight and annotate text
- Access to thousands of pages of quality research at the click of a button.

ORDER YOUR FREE INSTITUTIONAL TRIAL TODAY

Free Trials Available

We offer free trials to qualifying academic, corporate and government customers.

eCollections
Choose from 20 different subject eCollections, including:
- Asian Studies
- Economics
- Health Studies
- Law
- Middle East Studies

eFocus
We have 16 cutting-edge interdisciplinary collections, including:
- Development Studies
- The Environment
- Islam
- Korea
- Urban Studies

For more information, pricing enquiries or to order a free trial, please contact your local sales team:

UK/Rest of World: **online.sales@tandf.co.uk**
USA/Canada/Latin America: **e-reference@taylorandfrancis.com**
East/Southeast Asia: **martin.jack@tandf.com.sg**
India: **journalsales@tandfindia.com**

www.tandfebooks.com